PHILOSOPHY OF MODERN MUSIC

PHILOSOPHY OF MODERN MUSIC

Theodor W. Adorno

translated by Anne G. Mitchell
and Wesley V. Bloomster

Sheed & Ward - London

CONTENTS

CONTENTS

TRANSLATORS' INTRODUCTION
AND
PREFACE

TRANSLATORS' INTRODUCTION

This book, published for the first time in 1948 in Germany, is a product of the years of exile which Theodor Adorno spent in the United States while National Socialism triumphed and fell in his European homeland. It is an irony of the modern historical process that this book, written in America, only now becomes accessible to the English-speaking reader.

The *Philosophy of Modern Music* is a pioneer effort in a unique direction. Adorno is among the first to work upon the design of a sociology of music. Even that designation, however, is too narrow to categorize accurately the text which here follows. The book is of most direct concern to the reader with a thorough understanding of music, but it is of equally valid importance to the philosopher, the sociologist, and the man of literature.

The significance of the book—and this particularly for the American reader—can perhaps be indicated by viewing it as somewhat of a companion piece to another German work created in the United States: the novel *Doctor Faustus* by Thomas Mann, completed in California in 1947. Both Mann and Adorno resided in the Los Angeles vicinity at this time. Mann had already undertaken his composition when Adorno brought him the manuscript of the *Philosophy,* thinking it might well be of interest to the novelist. In his diary Mann recalled: "Here indeed was something important. The manuscript dealt with modern music both on an artistic and on a sociological plane. Its spirit was remarkably forward-looking, subtle, and deep, and the whole thing had the strangest affinity to the idea of my book, to the 'composition' in which I lived and moved and had my being. The decision was made of itself: this was my man."[1]

Adorno was to remain "his man" through the years spent on the novel, serving the author as a regular consultant. Mann made record of evenings during which he read his work to Adorno, repeatedly expressing his gratitude to him and his realm of thought. This is perhaps as broad a testimony to the importance of the *Philosophy of Modern Music* as is to be found.

Mann offered a brief biographical sketch of Adorno, emphasizing those qualities and characteristics in the man which are most obviously present in the following text:

Theodor Wiesengrund-Adorno was born in 1903 in Frankfurt-am-Main. His father was a German Jew; his mother, herself a singer, was the daughter of a French army officer of Corsican—originally Genoese—descent and of a German singer. He is a cousin of Walter Benjamin. . . . Adorno—he has taken his mother's maiden name—is a person of similar mental cast, uncompromising, tragically brilliant, operating on the highest level. Having grown up in an atmosphere entirely dominated by theory (political theory as well) and artistic, primarily musical interests, he studied philosophy and music. In 1931 he assumed the post of lecturer at Frankfurt University and taught philosophy there until he was expelled by the Nazis. Since 1941 he has been living in Los Angeles, so close to us as to be almost a neighbor.

All his life this man of remarkable intellect has refused to choose between the professions of philosophy and music. He felt that he was actually pursuing the same thing in both divergent realms. His dialectic turn of mind and bent towards social history is interlinked with a passion for music. The phenomenon is no longer unique nowadays and is doubtless connected with the whole complex of problems of our time. In pursuit of this passion, he studied composition and piano, at first with music instructors in Frankfurt, then with Alban Berg and Eduard Steuermann in Vienna. From 1928 to 1931 he was editor of the Vienna *Anbruch,* and was active in promoting radical modern music.[2]

1. Thomas Mann, *The Story of a Novel*, New York, 1961, 43.
2. Mann, 43–44.

In the *Philosophy of Modern Music* Adorno has singled out two composers who, for him, represent the two mainstreams in Western musical composition dominant thus far in the twentieth century. The composers are Arnold Schoenberg and Igor Stravinsky. The study on Schoenberg was written in 1941; the essay on Stravinsky in 1948. The introduction, intended to relate the two studies, was actually written following the completion of the Stravinsky study.

The mainstreams which Schoenberg and Stravinsky represent are inextricably bound up with the social forces which produced them and are intrinsically in dialectical opposition to one another. In essence, Schoenberg represents the more progressive forces; Stravinsky the more reactionary.

Adorno's point of departure is the socio-historical context within which all human endeavors—in this case, particularly art, and specifically music—are to be viewed. He states that forms of art reflect the history of man even more truthfully than do documents.

Music, therefore, does not manifest the machinations of natural laws. Adorno's Hegelian outlook is evident in his assumption that there are only historical tendencies present within the musical subject matter itself. It is Schoenberg who has most uncompromisingly developed the logical consequences of these tendencies in this century. According to Adorno, Stravinsky's failure is that he does not develop but, rather, acquiesces to collective tendencies of the times. He clings to outmoded sounds and to the obsolete shells of forms. It is important to realize at the outset, however, that the directions taken by Schoenberg and Stravinsky do not represent totally unrelated and hostile camps. For Adorno they manifest two extremes within a single context.

It can also easily be anticipated that Adorno views the twelve-tone system as a product of historical necessity, as it was seen by its founder, Schoenberg. Its origin was the next logical step following late nineteenth-century chromaticism. This perspective gives Schoenberg his unique socio-historical position.

Adorno expounds at length on the basic principles of twelve-tone technique: the basic presentations of the row and its various possible permutations and derivations. He believes that Schoenberg's uncompromising consistency is illustrated by two important aspects of his technique: that none of the twelve tones may dominate another and that, essentially, none of the tones is to be repeated before the other eleven have been heard.

The difficulty of Adorno's German is a matter of legend to those familiar with his works in the original language. The intensity of his thought results in a hard-wrought syntax, often of esoteric vocabulary, which at times defies comprehension upon first sight and makes translation seem impossible. A negative view of this particular type of idiom might well employ a term used by Adorno to characterize the language of others: jargon. Adorno is often guilty of falling into a jargon which is detrimental to whatever he would hope to express. In so doing, he takes a place in a long, though not necessarily enviable or admirable, German tradition.

Adorno, however, is to be praised for the honesty with which he admitted to this tendency in the *Philosophy of Modern Music*. In 1964 he wrote a particularly well-defined attack upon the language of the German philosopher Martin Heidegger. In a footnote to that work Adorno pointed out that he was totally unaware of his own inclination towards jargon at the time of the *Philosophy* and came to realize it only when a German critic pointed it out to him. He concluded: "Even he who despises jargon is by no means secure from infection by it—consequently all the more reason to be afraid of it."[3]

ANNE G. MITCHELL
WESLEY V. BLOMSTER

Boulder, Colorado

---

3. Theodor W. Adorno, *Jargon der Eigentlichkeit*, Frankfurt, 1964, 68.

PREFACE

This book attempts, with the help of an Introduction, to combine two studies originally separated by a period of seven years. The structure and character of the entire book warrant a note of explanation.

In 1938 the author published an essay "On the Fetish Character in Music and the Regression of Hearing" in the *Zeitschrift für Sozialforschung*.[1] The intention at that time was to portray the change in function of music in today's world, to point out the inner fluctuations suffered by musical phenomena through their integration into commercialized mass production, and to illustrate, at the same time, how certain anthropological shiftings in standardized society extend deeply into the structure of musical hearing. At that time, the author was already making plans to include in his dialectical treatment the state of composition itself, which is at all times the decisive factor influencing the state of music. He clearly perceived the force of the sociological totality even in apparently derivative fields such as music. He could not deceive himself into thinking that this art—in which he had been schooled—was even in its pure and uncompromising form excluded from such an all-dominating materialization. For precisely in its endeavor to defend its integrity, music produces from within itself traits of that very nature against which it struggles. It was his concern, therefore, to recognize the objective antinomies in which art, truly remaining faithful to its own demands, without regard for effect, is unavoidably caught up in the midst of heteronomous reality. The antinomies can be over-

1. "Über den Fetischcharakter in der Musik und die Regression des Hörens," in *Zeitschrift für Sozialforschung*, later published in the collection of essays *Dissonanzen*, Göttingen, 1956.

come only if they are pursued without illusion to their final conclusion.

These ideas gave rise to the study on Schoenberg, which was not written down until 1940–41. It was not published at that time, however, and, except for a very small circle at the New School for Social Research in New York, was accessible only to a few people. It now appears in its original form with several additional comments on works by Schoenberg composed after 1941.

After the war, when the author decided upon publication in German, it seemed necessary to accompany the essay on Schoenberg with a study on Stravinsky. For if the book were really to make a statement regarding modern music as a whole, then its method, unreceptive to all generalization and classification, would have to extend beyond the treatment of one particular school. This would be necessary even if this were the only school which does justice to the present objective possibilities of the elements of music and stands up to the difficulties involved without compromise. The diametrically opposed procedure practiced by Stravinsky offered a contrasting viewpoint, not only because of its wide popular recognition and its compositional niveau—for the concept of niveau cannot be assumed dogmatically and is always open to discussion as a matter of "taste" —but, above all, it underscores the need to prevent the comfortable evasion that, if the consequent progress of music leads to antinomies, then anything is to be hoped for from the restoration of the past, or from the self-conscious revocation of musical logic. There is no legitimate criticism of progress save that which designates the reactionary moment in the prevailing absence of freedom, and thereby inexorably excludes every misuse in the service of the status quo. The seemingly positive return to the outmoded reveals itself as a more fundamental conspiracy with the destructive tendencies of the age than that which is branded outrightly as destructive. Any order which is self-proclaimed is nothing but a disguise for chaos. A critical investigation of Schoenberg, a radical composer inspired by a drive for expression, can be conducted on the plane of musical objectivity. Any treatment of Stravinsky, the anti-psychologist, on the other hand, raises the question of damage to the subject which forms the basis of his composition. Here again a dialectical motive asserts itself.

The author would not wish to gloss over the provocative features of his study. In view of what has happened in Europe and what further threatens the world, it will appear cynical to squander time and creative energy on the solution to esoteric questions of modern compositional techniques. Furthermore, obstinate artistic arguments appear often enough in the text; they would seem to be immediately concerned with a pragmatic reality which has long since lost interest in them. From an eccentric beginning, however, some light is shed upon a condition whose familiar manifestations are now only fit to disguise it. The protest inherent in this condition finds expression only when the public suspects departure from the beaten track. This discussion concerns itself, rather, exclusively with music. How is a total world to be structured in which mere questions of counterpoint give rise to unresolvable conflicts? How disordered is life today at its very roots if its shuddering and rigidity are reflected even in a field no longer affected by empirical necessity, a field in which human beings hope to find a sanctuary from the pressure of horrifying norms, but which fulfills its promise to them only by denying to them what they expect of it.

The introduction presents considerations upon which both parts of the book are based. Although it attempts to emphasize the unity of the entire work, the differences between the older and the newer sections—particularly those which are matters of language and style—remain evident.

In the time separating the two parts, a common philosophy has evolved out of the author's work with Max Horkheimer, which extends over a period of more than twenty years. The author is, to be sure, solely responsible for matters pertaining concretely to music. However, it would be impossible to distinguish whose property this or that theoretical insight is. More properly, this book should be regarded as an extended appendix to Horkheimer's *Dialektik der Aufklärung* (*Dialectic of the En-*

lightenment).[2] I would like to express my gratitude to Hork-heimer for his intellectual and human integrity, and for everything in this study which exhibits steadfastness and faith in the helping strength of concrete negation.

2. Max Horkheimer and Theodor Adorno, *Dialektik der Aufklärung,* Amsterdam, 1947; English translation, New York, 1972.

PHILOSOPHY OF MODERN MUSIC

INTRODUCTION

> For in human Art we are not
> merely dealing with playthings,
> however pleasant or useful they
> may be, but . . . with a revelation
> of truth.[1]

CHOICE OF SUBJECT MATTER

"The history of philosophy viewed as the science of origins is
that process which, from opposing extremes, and from the
apparent excesses of development, permits the emergence of
the configuration of an idea as a totality characterized by the
possibility of a meaningful juxtaposition of such antitheses inherent in these opposing extremes." This principle, adhered to
by Walter Benjamin as the basis of cognitive criticism in his
treatise on the German tragedy, can also serve as the basis for
a philosophically oriented consideration of new music.[2] Such an
investigation, restricting itself essentially to two independent
protagonists, can even be founded within the subject of music
itself. For only in such extremes can the essence of this music be
defined; they alone permit the perception of its content of truth.
"The middle road," according to Schoenberg in his Foreword to
the *Three Satires for Mixed Chorus* [*opus* 28, nos. 1–3], "is the
only one which does not lead to Rome." It is for this reason and
not in the illusion of grand personality that only these two

1. G. W. F. Hegel, *The Philosophy of Fine Art*, trans. F. P. B.
Osmaston, London, 1920, Vol. IV, 349.
2. Walter Benjamin, *Ursprung des deutschen Trauerspiels*, in *Schriften*,
ed. Theodor Adorno, Frankfurt, 1955, Vol. I, 163.

3

composers—Schoenberg and Stravinsky—are to be discussed. For if the total product of new music—as defined by its inner qualities rather than by chronology—were to be scrutinized in its entirety, including all transitions and compromises, these same extremes would again be encountered. The basic concern, after all, is not simply a matter of description or professional evaluation. Nor are we thereby necessarily passing judgment on the value or even on the representative importance of what lies between the extremes. The best works of Béla Bartók, who in many respects attempted to reconcile Schoenberg and Stravinsky, are probably superior to those of Stravinsky in density and richness.[3] The second neo-classic generation—names such as Hindemith and Milhaud—has acquiesced to the collective tendency of the times even less consciously than has Stravinsky himself. In so doing, they at least seem to reflect this tendency with greater fidelity than the master of the school of absurdity. But a study of this intermediate generation would necessarily lead to an analysis of the two innovators—not simply because they are deserving of historical priority and because the second generation is derivative—but because the innovators by virtue of their uncompromising consistency have driven forward to the point that the impulses present in their works have become legible as concepts of the object of investigation itself. This came about in the specific configurations resulting from their compositional procedures, not in the general outline of styles. While these styles are heralded by loudly resounding cultural watchwords, they permit, in their generality, falsifying ameliorations which prevent the consequence of the unprogrammatic concept inherent in the object. The philosophical investigation of art, however, is concerned precisely with this concept and not with ideas on style, regardless of the degree to which the two may be connected. Truth or untruth—whether Schoenberg's or Stravinsky's—cannot be determined by a mere discussion of categories, such as atonality, twelve-tone technique, or neo-classicism; but only in

3. Cf. René Leibowitz, "Belá Bartók or the Possibility of Compromise in Contemporary Music," (in French) *Les Temps Modernes* (October, 1947), II:25, 705–734.

the concrete crystallization of such categories in the structure of music itself. The predetermined stylistic categories pay for their accessibility not by revealing the true nature of form, but by hovering meaninglessly over the surface of aesthetic form. If neo-classicism, on the other hand, is to be treated in connection with the question of what necessity inherent in the composition forces it into this style, or of what the relationship is between the stylistic ideal to the material of the composition and its structural totality, then the problem of the stylistic legitimacy is also virtually determinable.

NEW CONFORMISM

Whatever resides between the extremes is today actually no longer in need of an interpretative relationship to those extremes. Rather, in fact, its very indifference makes speculation super-fluous. The history of modern music no longer tolerates a "meaningful juxtaposition of antitheses." Viewed in its totality since the heroic decade—the years surrounding the First World War—it has been nothing more than the history of decline, a retrogression into the traditional. The liberation of modern painting from objectivity, which was to art the break that atonality was to music, was determined by the defensive against the mechanized art commodity—above all, photography. Radical music, from its inception, reacted similarly to the commercial depravity of the traditional idiom. It formulated an antithesis against the extension of the culture industry into its own domain. To be sure, the transition to the calculated manufacture of music as a mass-produced article has taken longer than has the analogous process in literature or the fine arts. The non-conceptual and non-objective element in music which, since Schopenhauer, has accounted for music's appeal to irrational philosophy, has served only to harden it against the market-place mentality. Not until the era of the sound film, the radio, and the singing commercial began was its very irrationality expropriated by the logic of the business world. Just as soon as the industrial

5

management of all cultural goods had established itself as a totality, it also gained power over whatever did not aesthetically conform. Because the monopolistic means of distributing music stood almost entirely at the disposal of artistic trash and compromised cultural values, and catered to the socially determined predisposition of the listener, radical music was forced into complete isolation during the final stages of industrialism. For those composers who want to survive, such isolation becomes a moral-social pretense for a false peace. This has given rise to a type of musical composition—feigning unabashed pretensions of "modernity" and "seriousness"—which has adjusted to mass culture by means of calculated feeble-mindedness. Hindemith's generation still had talent and skill to offer. Their moderation confirmed itself above all in its intellectual submissiveness, which committed itself to nothing, composing according to the whims of the times; and liquidating in their compositions, as in their despicable artistic credo, everything which was musically uncomfortable. All they achieved was a respectably routined neo-academicism. This accusation cannot be leveled at the third generation. Such conciliation to the listener, masking as humaneness, began to undermine the technical standards attained by progressive composition. That which was valid before the break—the structure of musical relationships through tonality—has been irretrievably lost. The third generation does not believe in the academic triads which its exponents so fleetingly write, nor have their threadbare means the power to produce anything but a shallow sound. They prefer to withdraw themselves from the consequences of the new idiom which rewards with gross failure on the market the most sincere effort of artistic conscience. This has been proven unsuccessful; historical force, the "rage and fury of destruction," prohibits an aesthetic compromise, just as it would prohibit compromise in the political sphere.[4] On the one hand, these exponents seek refuge in the traditional and time-tested, claiming to have their fill of what the language of non-comprehension called experi-

4. Hegel, *The Phenomenology of Mind,* trans. J. B. Baillie, London, 1964, 604.

mentation; on the other hand, they senselessly surrender themselves to what seems most terrifying of all—anarchy. The search for times past does not simply bring them home, but deprives them, rather, of every consistency. Arbitrary preservation of the antiquated endangers that which it wishes to maintain, and, with a bad conscience, opposes everything new. These impotent late heirs to a traditional hostility towards true originality resemble one another everywhere in their feeble mixture of compositional facility and helplessness. Shostakovich, unjustly reprimanded as a cultural Bolshevist by the authorities of his home country; the facile pupils of Stravinsky's pedagogical supervision; the triumphant meagerness of Benjamin Britten—all these have in common a taste for tastelessness, a simplicity resulting from ignorance, an immaturity which masks as enlightenment, and a dearth of technical means. In Germany the National Socialist Chamber of Music (Reichsmusikkammer) has left behind a total rubbish heap. The commonplace, everyday style following the Second World War has become the eclecticism of a destroyed and shattered nation.

FALSE MUSICAL CONSCIOUSNESS

Stravinsky also asserts his right to an extreme position in the modern music movement. The capitulation of this movement can be measured in his compositions both in terms of their specific individual character and the progression from work to work. Today, however, an aspect has become evident for which he cannot directly be blamed, and which is only latently indicated in the changes in his compositional procedures: the collapse of all criteria for good or bad music, as they had been codified during the early days of the bourgeois era. For the first time, dilettantes everywhere are launched as great composers. Musical life, which is now by and large economically centralized, forces the public to recognize them. Twenty years ago the trumped-up glory surrounding Elgar seemed a local phenomenon and the fame of Sibelius an exceptional case of critical igno-

7

rance. Phenomena of such a niveau, even if they are at times more liberal in their use of dissonances, are the norm today. From the middle of the nineteenth century on, good music has renounced commercialism altogether. The consequence of its further development has come into conflict with the manipulated and, at the same time, self-satisfied needs of the bourgeois public. The pathetically small number of connoisseurs was gradually replaced by all those who could afford the price of a ticket and wished to demonstrate their culture to others. An abyss developed between public taste and compositional quality. Works of quality established themselves in the repertoire only through the strategy of the composer—in itself not always in the best interest of his work—or through the enthusiasm of competent musicians and critics. Radically modern music could no longer count on this support. Quality may be determined according to the same standards in advanced works as well as in traditional works—perhaps even more easily—despite the limitations of these standards. The prevailing musical language no longer removes the burden of accuracy and integrity from the shoulders of the composer. At the same time, the self-appointed mediators have sacrificed their capacity to make such judgments. Since the compositional procedure is gauged simply according to the inherent form of every work—not according to tacitly accepted, general demands—it is no longer possible to "learn" definitively what constitutes good or bad music. Whoever would pass judgment must face squarely the immutable questions and antagonisms of the individual compositional structure, about which no general music history can teach. No one could be better suited to this task than the progressive composer, whom discursive reasoning most eludes. He can no longer depend upon mediators between himself and the public. Critics live literally according to the "high reason" expressed in the song by Gustav Mahler: they evaluate according to what they do and do not understand.[5] Performing musicians, however—particularly conductors—allow themselves to be guided altogether by those characteristics which are the most obviously effective and com-

5. A reference to the song "Lob des hohen Verstandes."—Trans.

8

prehensible in the composition to be performed. Consequently, the opinion that Beethoven is comprehensible and Schoenberg incomprehensible is an objective deception. The general public, totally cut off from the production of new music, is alienated by the outward characteristics of such music. The deepest currents present in this music proceed, however, from exactly those sociological and anthropological foundations peculiar to that public. The dissonances which horrify them testify to their own conditions; for that reason alone do they find them unbearable. Exactly the opposite is the case of the all-too-familiar, which is so far removed from the dominant forces of life today that the public's own experience scarcely still communicates with that for which traditional music bore witness. Whenever they believe to understand, they perceive really only a dead mould which they guard tenaciously as their unquestionable possession and which is lost precisely in that moment that it becomes a possession: an indifferent show piece, neutralized and robbed of its own critical substance. Actually, it is only the coarsest vulgarities and easily remembered fragments—ominously beautiful passages, moods, and associations—which find their way into the comprehension of the public. Musical continuity, the true basis of meaning in the composition, is no less hidden from the radio-trained listener in an early Beethoven sonata than in a Schoenberg quartet, which at least reminds him that his sky does not consist entirely of clouds with silver linings upon whose radiance he can forever feast his eyes. This is not to say, by any means, that a work may be immediately accessible only in its own epoch and after that time must necessarily fall victim to depravity and historicism. There is a sociological collective tendency which has burned out of the consciousness and unconsciousness of men that humanity which once lay at the foundations of today's residue of commercial musical supply. This tendency permits only an irresponsible echo of the idea of humanity in the empty ritual of the concert, whereas the philosophical heritage of good music has become the province of those forces scorned by the heirs of this heritage. The music industry, which further degrades this musical supply by galvan-

izing it into a shrine, merely confirms the state of consciousness of the listener, for whom the harmony of Viennese classicism—attained through bitter sacrifice—and the bursting
longing of Romanticism have both been placed upon the market
as household ornaments. In actuality, much more effort is required to listen adequately to a piece by Beethoven, whose
themes the average man in the street might whistle to himself,
than to a piece of the most advanced music: but to achieve this,
the concert hall performance veneer of false interpretations
and stereotyped audience reaction patterns must be destroyed.
Since the culture industry has educated its victims to avoid
straining themselves during the free time allotted to them for
intellectual consumption, they cling just that much more stubbornly to the external framework of a work of art which conceals its essence. The prevailing, highly polished style of interpretation, even in the field of chamber music, willingly makes
concessions in that direction. It is not only that the ears of the
public are so flooded with light music that any other form of
musical expression strikes them as "classical"—an arbitrary
category existing only as a contrast to the other. And it is not
only that the perceptive faculty has been so dulled by the
omnipresent hit tune that the concentration necessary for responsible listening has become permeated by traces of recollection of
this musical rubbish, and thereby impossible. Rather, sacrosanct
traditional music has come to resemble commercial mass production in the character of its performances and in its role in the
life of the listener and its substance has not escaped this influence. Music is inextricably bound up with what Clement
Greenberg called the division of all art into kitsch and the
avant-garde, and this kitsch—with its dictate of profit over
culture—has long since conquered the social sphere. Therefore,
considerations concerning the revelation of truth in aesthetic
objectivity make reference only to the avant-garde, which is cut
off from official culture. The philosophy of music is today possible only as the philosophy of modern music. The only hope is
that this culture will herald its own demise: it only contributes

to the advancement of barbarism, about which it in turn becomes enraged. There is a temptation to regard the most educated listeners as the worst: those who promptly react to Schoenberg with "I do not understand"—an utterance whose modesty masks anger as expertise.

"INTELLECTUALISM"

Among the reproaches most obstinately repeated by these critics, the most widely spread is that of intellectualism: modern music has its origins in the brain, not in the heart or the ear; it is in no way conceived by the senses, but rather worked out on paper. The inadequacy of these clichés is evident. The critics present their arguments as though the tonal idiom of the last 350 years had been derived from nature, and that to go beyond these firmly established theoretical principles were a violation thereof; whereas these ossified principles themselves are actually the very evidence of social pressure. The idea that the tonal system is exclusively of natural origin is an illusion rooted in history. This "second nature" owes the dignity of its closed and exclusive system to mercantile society, whose own dynamics stress totality and demand that the elements of tonality correspond to these dynamics on the most basic functional level. The stimulus inherent in the older forms of expression has given rise to the new language of music; yet at the same time, a significant qualitative distinction is also to be noted. The feeling that, in contrast to traditional music, the conception of modern composition is more intellectual than sensory is nothing but evidence of incomprehension. Schoenberg and Berg surpassed the orgies of the impressionists in lush harmonic color whenever it was demanded, as in the chamber ensemble *Pierrot Lunaire* [op. 21], and in the orchestration of *Lulu*. What is labelled as emotion by musical anti-intellectualism— the necessary complement in art to the business-world rationality—yields without resistance to the mainstream of current

11

social logic: how absurd that the ever-popular Tchaikovsky, who portrays despondency with hit tunes, should be considered an expression of emotion superior to the seismograph of Schoenberg's *Erwartung* [op. 17].[6] On the other hand, the objective consequence of the basic musical concept, which alone lends dignity to good music, has always demanded alert control via the subjective compositional conscience. The cultivation of such logical consequence, at the expense of passive perception of sensual sound, alone defines the stature of this perception, in contrast to mere "culinary enjoyment." Insofar as modern music as an intellectual conception contemplates anew the logic of consequence, it falls into the tradition of the art of the fugue, as practiced by Bach and even by Beethoven and Brahms. In any discussion of intellectualism, the first person to be accused would be that moderate modernist constantly in search of the proper mixture of enticement and banality. He is far more guilty of intellectualism than the composer who obeys the integral laws of musical structure, from the single pitch to the drive inherent in the total form, even if—and precisely if—the automatic perception of the individual moments is hindered

6. The appetite of the consumer is, to be sure, less concerned with the feeling for which the work of art stands than with the feeling which it excites, namely, the sum of pleasure which he hopes to garner. The pragmatic value of art as emotions has always been insisted upon by arm-chair enlightenment. Hegel spoke the final word about this point and its Aristotelian overtones: "From such a point of view writers have asked what kind of feelings art ought to excite—take fear, for example, and compassion—with the further question how such can be regarded as pleasant, how, in short, the tendency of reflection dates for the most part from the times of Moses Mendelssohn, and many such strains of reasoning may be found in his writings. A discussion of this kind, however, did not carry the problem far. Feeling is the undefined obscure region of spiritual life. What is felt remains cloaked in the form of the separate personal experience under its most abstract persistence; and for this reason the distinctions of feeling are wholly abstract; they are not distinctions which apply to the subject matter itself. . . . Reflection upon feeling is satisfied with the observation of the personal emotional state and its singularity, instead of penetrating and sounding the matter for study, in other words the work of art, and in doing so bidding good-bye to the wholly subjective state and its conditions." Hegel, *Fine Art*, Vol. I, 43–44.

in so doing. In spite of everything, the accusation of intellectualism is so stubbornly meted out that more ground is gained by including the circumstances upon which it is based in the total perspective. Certainly, nothing is achieved by any resigned attempt to counter stupid arguments with more clever ones. On the conceptual level, the most questionable and least unarticulate ideas of the common mind harbor—alongside the lie— that trace of negativity concealed in the thing itself which the definition of the object cannot dispense with. Today art in its entirety, and music in particular, feels the shattering effects of that very process of enlightenment in which it participates and upon which its own progress depends. Hegel demands of the artist "a liberal education . . . in which every kind of superstition and belief which remains restricted to certain forms of observation and presentation should receive their proper subordination as merely aspects or phasal moments of a larger process; aspects which the free human spirit has already mastered when it once and for all sees that they can furnish it with no conditions of exposition and creative effort which are, independently for their own sake, sacrosanct."[7] In this light, anger over the alleged intellectualism of the spirit liberated from the self-evident premise of its object, as well as from the absolute truth of traditional forms, places upon the artist the burden—viewed as misfortune or guilt—for whatever happens objectively and out of necessity. "We have, however, no reason to regard this simply as a misfortune which the chances of events has made inevitable, one, that is to say, by which art has been overtaken through the pressure of the times, the prosaic outlook and the dearth of genuine interest. Rather it is the realization and progress of art itself, which, by envisaging for present life the material in which it actually dwells, itself materially assists on this very path, in each step of its advance, to make itself free of the content which is presented."[8] The advice that artists would do better not to think too much—though precisely their freedom indicates the irrevocable necessity of such thought—is

7. Hegel, *Fine Art*, Vol. II, 394.
8. *Ibid.*

13

nothing more than commercialized mourning for the loss of naïvete, as designed by mass culture. In the present age this arch-romantic motive results in the command to avoid all critical reflection and thus humble oneself before the subject matter and the formal categories prescribed by tradition, even if they belong hopelessly to the past. For it is by no means a one-sided decadence (curable through organization—in itself a rational approach) that is being lamented, but rather only the shadow of progress. The negative aspect of progress is so visibly dominant in the current phase of development that art is summoned against it, even though they both stand under the same sign. Fury over the avant-garde is so immoderate and extends so far beyond its role in the late stage of industrial society—indeed, far beyond its role in the drama of cultural ostentation—because in modern art the intimidated conscience, seeking to escape from total enlightenment, finds the door bolted. Art today, insofar as it is at all deserving of substantiality, reflects without concessions everything that society prefers to forget, bringing it clearly thereby into conscious focus. From this relevant source, modern art designs irrelevance—offering nothing more to society. The compact majority appropriates for its own use Hegel's tremendously sober interpretation of an historical current: "In the very fact that we have an object set before our ocular or spiritual vision, whether it be by Art or the Medium of Thought, with a completeness which practically exhausts it, so that we have emptied it, and nothing further remains for our eyes to discover or our souls to explore, in that alone the vital interest disappears."[9] It was precisely this kind of absolute interest which had confiscated art in the nineteenth century, when the total claim of philosophical systems had followed the demands of religion into Hades: Wagner's Bayreuth is the most outspoken testimony of such a *hubris* born of necessity. The more significant exponents of modern art have freed themselves from this conception, avoiding that mystic obscurity about whose permanance Hegel—himself thoroughly

9. *Ibid.*, Vol. II, 391.

at home in this realm—felt such anxiety. For such obscurity, defeated by the progress of the intellect in ever-renewed attacks, has always succeeded in re-establishing itself in constantly changing form down to the present day. This results from the pressure which the tyrannical spirit exercises over all forms of nature—human and otherwise. Moreover, such obscurity is not simple being-in-and-for-itself as can be found, for example, in Hegel's aesthetics. But the doctrine of the phenomenology of the mind is to be applied to art; and according to this doctrine, all immediacy already represents a mediation in itself. In other words, it is only a product of domination. When the immediate self-certainty of unquestioningly accepted materials and forms has vanished from the foundations of art, then at least one region of obscurity will have healed over, will have relieved that boundless suffering whereby the substance of intellectual conception is brought to consciousness.[10] This will be not merely an episode interrupting an already perfected enlightenment, but it does obscure its most recent phase and, to be sure, its actual power makes concrete representation almost impossible. The all-powerful culture industry appropriates the enlightening principle and, in its relationship with human beings, defaces it for the benefit of prevailing obscurity. Art vehemently opposes this tendency; it offers an ever-sharper contrast to such false clarity. The configurations of that deposed obscurity are held up in opposition to the prevailing neon-light style of the times. Art is able to aid enlightenment only by relating the clarity of the world consciously to its own darkness.[11] Only in a society which had achieved satisfaction would the death of art be possible. Its demise today, which appears immanent, would only signify the triumphs of base existence over the penetrating eye of consciousness which would presume to assert itself against it.

10. Hegel, *Fine Arts,* Vol. I, 37.
11. Cf. Max Horkheimer, "Neue Kunst und Massenkultur" ("Modern Art and Mass Culture"), in *Die Umschau* (1948), III:4, 459f.

MODERN MUSIC UNPROTECTED

Nonetheless, this threat hovers over the few intransigent works of art which are still produced. Through a realization of their own intrinsic principles of enlightenment, and without regard for the crafty naïveté of the culture industry, they become antithetical—repulsive because of their truth—to the total control aimed for by industry. Yet they also assume a similarity to the essential structure of this industry and thus come into conflict with their own interests. The loss of "absolute interest" in principles inherent in the individual work concerns not only their momentary fate in society, which by now can spare itself the usual indignation—a shrug of the shoulders, dismissing such music as foolishness at best. Rather it shares the fate of political sects, which, though they would like to adhere to the progressive manifestations of theory, are driven into untruth by the disparity between the ideal and the power of the established order. Even upon achieving complete autonomy, upon renouncing any role as entertainment, the integral essence of such works is still hardly indifferent to public reception. Social isolation, a problem that cannot be overcome by art alone, is yet a mortal danger to art's success. Hegel, perhaps as a direct result of his isolation from absolute music—the most significant products of which have always been esoteric—and as a consequence of his negation of Kantian aesthetics, has cautiously stated something that is a matter of grave concern to the life of music. At the core of his argument, which is by no means free of inartistic naïveté, is the designation of music's reliance upon its own pure immanence as the decisive factor—as it is forced to do by its own law of development and by the loss of social reaction. The composer, says Hegel in the chapter where he treats of music within the "System of Individual Arts," can, "in complete indifference to such a scheme, devote himself to musical structure simply and the assertion of his genius in such architectonics. Composition, however, of this character readily tends to become defective both in the range of its conception and emotional quality, and as a rule does not imply any profound cultivation of mind or taste in other respects. And by reason of the fact that such a content is not necessary, it frequently happens that the gift of musical composition not merely will show considerable development in very early age, but composers of eminence remain their life long men of the poorest and most impoverished intellectual faculty in other directions. More penetration of character may be assumed where the composer even in instrumental music is equally attentive to both aspects of composition; in other words, the expression of a content, if necessarily less defined than in our previous mode, no less than its musical structure, by which means it will be in his power at one time to emphasize the melody, at another the depth and colour of the harmony, or finally to fuse each with the other."[12] Except that one cannot make up for "lack of thought and sensitivity" with rhythmical variations or additional content. It is an historical fact that lack of thought and sensitivity—by causing the actual decline of the idea of expression—has come to undermine music. At the same time, however, Hegel has the last word against himself; historical force extends still further than his aesthetic would proclaim. At the present level of development the artist is incomparably much less free than Hegel could ever have believed at the beginning of the liberal era. The dissolution of everything traditionally taken for granted has not resulted in the possibility of disposing all materials and technical means according to discretion—only impotent syncretism could have such ideas, and even such a magnificent conception as Mahler's *Eighth Symphony* ran aground in the illusion that such a thing was possible. But the artist has become the mere executor of his own intentions, which appear before him as strangers—inexorable demands of the compositions upon which he is working.[13] That type of freedom which Hegel ascribes to the

12. *Fine Arts,* Vol. III, 425.
13. It is highly surprising that Freud, who otherwise placed all possible emphasis on the subjective-psychological content of the work of art, hit upon this idea in one of his late works: "Unluckily an author's

composer and which found its utmost realization in Beethoven—of whom he hardly took notice—is, as always, necessarily related to the traditionally pre-established, within which framework there are manifold possibilities. On the other hand, what is simply of itself and for itself cannot be other than it is and excludes the conciliatory acts by which Hegel promised himself the salvation of instrumental music. The elimination of everything traditionally pre-established—the corresponding reduction of music to the absolute monad—causes it to ossify and affects its innermost content. As a self-sufficient domain it justifies the organization of society divided into various branches: the obstinate domination of one-sided interest, perceptible behind the disinterested manifestation of the monad.

THE ANTINOMY OF MODERN MUSIC

The fact that music as a whole, and polyphony in particular—the necessary medium of modern music—have their source in the collective practices of cult and dance is not to be written off as a mere "point of departure" due to its further progress towards freedom. Rather this historical source remains the unique sensory subjective impulse of music, even if it has long since broken with every collective practice. Polyphonic music says "we" even when it lives as a conception only in the mind of the composer, otherwise reaching no living being. The ideal collectivity still contained within music, even though it has lost its relationship to the empirical collectivity, leads inevitably to conflict because of its unavoidable social isolation. Collective perception is the basis of musical objectification itself, and when this latter is no longer possible, it is necessarily degraded almost to a fiction—to the arrogance of the aesthetic subject, which says "we," while in reality it is still only "I"—and this "I" can

---

creative power does not always obey his will: the work proceeds as it can, and often presents itself to the author as something independent or even alien" (*Moses and Monotheism. The Complete Psychological Writings of Sigmund Freud,* London, 1964, Vol. XXIII, 104).

say nothing at all without positing the "we." The discrepancy contained in a solipsistic piece for large orchestra lies not only in the disproportion between the number of performers on the platform and the empty seats before which they perform, but rather offers evidence that form as such necessarily extends beyond the mere "I," the perspective from which it is projected. Actually, music has its origin in this perspective and, portraying it in turn, cannot go beyond it in any positive sense. This antinomy detracts from the powers of modern music. Its paralysis manifests the anxiety of the composition in the face of its despondent untruth. This form convulsively attempts to escape such anxiety by submersion into its own law, which at the same time, however, consistently heightens its untruth. To be sure, significant absolute music today—namely, that of Schoenberg's school—is the opposite of that "lack of thought and sensitivity" which Hegel feared, perhaps with a side-glance at that instrumental virtuosity which had been unleashed in his day for the first time. Here there is a type of vacuity of a higher order—not completely dissimilar to Hegel's "unhappy self-consciousness": "But this self has freed content by means of its emptiness."[14] The material transformation of those elements responsible for expression in music, which—according to Schoenberg—has taken place uninterruptedly throughout the entire history of music, has today become so radical that the possibility of expression itself comes into question. In the process of pursuing its own inner logic, music is transformed more and more from something significant into something obscure—even to itself. No music today, for example, could possibly speak in the accents of "reward." Not only has the mere idea of humanity, or of a better world no longer any sway over mankind—though it is precisely this which lies at the heart of Beethoven's opera.[15] Rather the strictness of musical structure, wherein alone music can assert itself against the ubiquity of commercialism, has hardened music to the point

14. *The Phenomenology of Mind,* 789ff.
15. Adorno here refers to Florestan's expression of gratitude to Fidelio and Rocco near the beginning of Act Two of Beethoven's opera.—Trans.

that it is no longer affected by those external factors which caused absolute music to become what it is. Various devious attempts to regain this content (devious because the musical structure as such withdraws in the face of such attempts) resort mainly to the most superficial and disconnected topicality in subject matter; only Schoenberg's most recent works, which exhaustively construct modes of expression and various forms of the row according to these modes, pose again the question of "content" regarding subject matter, without pretending to achieve the organic unity of this content with purely musical procedures. Advanced music has no recourse but to insist upon its own ossification without concession to that would-be humanitarianism which it sees through, in all its attractive and alluring guises, as the mask of inhumanity. Its truth appears guaranteed more by its denial of any meaning in organized society, of which it will have no part—accomplished by its own organized vacuity—than by any capability of positive meaning within itself. Under the present circumstances it is restricted to definitive negation.

GROWING INDIFFERENTISM

Music today, like all other expressions of the objective spirit, is accused of creating a schism between the intellectual and the physical, between the work of the mind and that of the hands: the guilt of privilege—Hegel's dialectic of master and servant—is extended, in the final analysis, to the sovereign spirit dominant over nature. The further this creative spirit advances towards autonomy, the more it alienates itself from a concrete relationship to everything dominated by it—human beings as well as materials. As soon as it has come to terms with the last heteronomous and material factors of its own most particular realm—that of free artistic production—it begins to circle aimlessly, imprisoned within itself, released from every element of resistance, upon whose permeation it was solely dependent for its meaning. The fulfillment of freedom of mind occurs simultaneously with the emasculation of the mind. Its fetish character, its hypostatization as that of a mere form of reflection, becomes evident when it frees itself from its last dependence upon things which are not themselves mind, but which as the implicit content of all intellectual form lends "mind" its substance. Non-conforming music has no defense against the indifferentism of the mind, that of means without purpose. Undoubtedly, such music preserves its social truth through the isolation resulting from its antithesis to society. The indifference of society, however, allows this truth to wither. It is as though music were deprived of its creative stimulus, its very *raison d'être.* For even the loneliest language of the artist lives from the paradox of speaking to men precisely by virtue of its isolation, and of its renunciation of the power of communication once inherent in this language. Otherwise a crippling and destructive element enters into the creative process—no matter how courageous the attitude of the artist as such might be. Among the symptoms of such crippling, perhaps the strangest is that progressive music—repudiated through its autonomy by precisely that democratically broad public which it had once conquered through its autonomy—now recalls the institution of composition by commission. This institution, common in the era before the bourgeois revolution, by its very essence excludes such autonomy. The new ethic, however, dating back to Schoenberg's *Pierrot Lunaire,* and Stravinsky's compositions for Diaghilev, is related to it. Almost all compositions which ever achieve completion and find their way into a performance are not marketable but are paid for by patrons or institutions.[16]

16. This tendency is by no means limited to advanced composition, but is valid for everything labeled esoteric under the domination of mass culture. In America a string quartet cannot support itself unless subsidized by a university or by other wealthy interests. Here, too, the general trend affirms itself, transforming the artist, under whose feet the foundation of liberal enterprise wavers, into a salaried employee. This happens not only in music, but in all fields of the objective spirit, particularly in literature. The actual reason is growing economic concentration and the decline of free competition.

The conflict between commission and autonomy results in a reluctant and scanty production. For today, far more than in the age of absolutism, the patron, and the artist—whose relationship was always precarious—are alienated. The patron has no relation at all to the work, but places his order for it as an exceptional example of that "cultural obligation" which itself proclaims the neutralization of culture. For the artist, however, being tied down to deadlines and specific occasions is sufficient to kill off that instinctive spontaneity upon which the emancipated capacity for expression depends. A historically preestablished correlation prevails between the material reliance upon commissioned compositions which are otherwise unsaleable, and a weakening of inner tension. To be sure, this enables the composer to fulfill heteronomous tasks with the technique of the autonomous work, and these tasks are achieved with indescribable effort. But this weakening, in turn, detracts from the autonomous work. The tension, resolved in the work of art, is that between subject and object, from within and from without. Today both subject and object have been integrated into false identity under the pressure of total economic organization, along with mass acceptance of the machinery of domination. Consequently, not only tension but the productive drive of the composer disappears hand in hand with the gravitational force of his work—upon which his relationship to the work once depended. Historical force no longer stands at the service of the composer. The work has by means of total enlightenment now been purified by the "idea"—which appears as a mere ideological decoration, as the private *Weltanschauung* of the composer. As a result of its absolute intellectualization, the work is condemned to a blind existence, in glaring contrast to the unavoidable designation of every work of art as a matter of spirit. When survival offers nothing more than an example of heroic struggle, it has become worthless. There is validity in the suspicion, once expressed by Eduard Steuermann, that the concept of great music, which has today been passed on to radical music, belongs itself only to a moment in history; that man in the age of the omnipresent radio and juke box has forgotten the experience of music altogther. Once music has been refined to an end in itself, its purposelessness, or a pragmatic concern with the consumer market, causes it to atrophy. The social division of labor, concerned not with socially useful work but rather with the demand for utility— its own major interest—shows signs of questionable irrationality.[17] This is the direct result of the detachment of music not only from the critical ear, but from all internal communication with ideas, with the discipline of philosophy *per se*. Such irrationality becomes unmistakable at the moment that new music begins to concern itself with the mind—with philosophical and social subjects—and then not only shows itself to be hopelessly disoriented, but rather denies, through its ideology, those opposing drives present within it. The literary

17. In his aesthetics of music—in the third section of *Fine Arts*— Hegel contrasted dilettantes and connoisseurs, who take opposing views of absolute music. He subjected the aural perception of the layman to penetrating criticism—still of validity today—and unconditionally supported the claim of the experts. As admirable as this deviation from the healthy common sense of the bourgeoisie—which Hegel was ever eager to support in questions of this nature—might possibly be, he nonetheless overlooks the necessity of the divergence of these two types, rooted in the division of labor. Art became the heir of highly specialized artisan procedures when the artisan craftsmen were totally succeeded by mass production. Consequently, the connoisseur, whose contemplative relationship to art has always contained something of that suspicious taste which Hegel's aesthetics saw through so completely, also arrives at that state of untruth—complementary to the layman—whose only expectation from music remains that it continue to babble forth alongside his workday. He becomes an expert; his knowledge—the only thing which can still reach the object in any way—degenerates to a warehouse of information which, in turn, kills the object. He unionizes intolerance with stubborn naïveté in everything which extends beyond technique as an end in itself. While he can control all counterpoint, he has long since lost his ability to perceive the purpose of the entirety and whether there even still is a purpose: this specialized know-how is transformed into blindness; at the same time, perception into an administrative statement of accounts. In their snobbish zeal for the apologetics of the cultural commodity, the real expert and the cultivated listener are on the same footing. His attitude is reactionary: he monopolizes progress. The more this development stamps the composer as an expert, the more does the attitude of the expert as the agent of a group identified with privilege permeate the internal construction of music.

quality of Wagner's *Ring* was dubious as a crudely patched-together allegory of Schopenhauer's denial of the will to life. It is, however, beyond all doubt that the libretto of the *Ring*— its music was already considered esoteric—treats the central underlying concerns of impending bourgeois decline, offering an example of the highly fertile relationship between musical form and the nature of the ideas which objectively determine this relationship. Schoenberg's musical substance will probably some day be proven superior to that of Wagner. Not only are his texts private and casual when compared to those of Wagner (which go to extremes in both their good and bad aspects); stylistically as well they set themselves apart from the music and become mere slogans—even if only out of defiance. Such sloganeering exhibits a guilelessness which is negated by every note in the composition: for example, the triumph of love over convention. It has never been possible for the quality of music to be indifferent to the quality of the text with which it is associated: works such as Mozart's *Cosi fan Tutte* and Weber's *Euryanthe* try to overcome the weaknesses of their libretti through music but nevertheless are not to be salvaged by any literary or theatrical means. Any stage-work in which the conflict between extreme musical intellectualization and the crudity of its subject matter is exaggerated *ad infinitum*—the only hope there is for a reconciliation between the two factors—will hardly fare better in the theater than did *Cosi fan Tutte*. It is possible, in other words, for even the best modern music to sink into oblivion without necessarily justifying itself wholly through such absolute renunciation of mediocre success.

ON METHOD

It is tempting to deduce all of this in social terms directly out of the decline of the bourgeoisie, whose most unique artistic medium has always been music. Such an approach, however, is compromised by the inclination to throw an all-too rapid glance at the total picture, thereby overlooking and devaluating the individual moment present in this totality of social forces, which is determined by it and, in turn, resolved by it. This view becomes entangled with the inclination to take sides with the totality, or the mainstream, and to condemn anything which does not fit into the over-all picture. In this way, art becomes the mere exponent of society, rather than a catalyst for change in society. It thus gives official approval to that tendency of the bourgeois consciousness to degrade all intellectual formulations to a simple function, an object which can be substituted for some other object, or—in the final analysis—an article of consumption. The work of art is deduced from a society which is denied by art's own immanent logic. This derivation attempts to break through the fetishism of the work of art, that is, the ideology of its being-in-itself—and to a certain degree actually does break through it. In doing so, such deduction silently accepts the hypostatization of all matters of the mind in consumer society. The standards of consumer goods are the basis upon which the right to existence of the work of art is determined; this standard is regarded as the absolute criterion of social truth. Thus, unawares, such a process works in the service of conformism and inverts the meaning of the theory (which itself warns against applying theory in the same manner that the species would be applied to the specimen). In our totally organized bourgeois society, which has forcibly been made over into a totality, the spiritual potential of another society could lie only in that which bears no resemblance to the prevailing society. Furthermore, the reduction of advanced music to its social origins and its social function hardly ever rises above the hostilely uncritical designation that it is bourgeois, decadent, and a luxury. This is the language of philistine suppression on the level of management. The more sovereignly advanced music attaches its intellectual formulations to its own social roots the more helplessly it recoils from these roots. The dialectical method, and it is precisely the one which is placed squarely upon its feet, cannot simply treat the separate phenomena as illustrations or examples of something in the

25

already firmly established social structure and consequently ignore the kinetic force of a concept; in this way dialectic declined to a state religion. It is rather demanded that the force of the general concept be transformed into the self-development of the concrete object and that it resolve the social enigma of this object with the powers of its own individuation. In so doing the central concern is not social justification, but the establishment of social theory by virtue of explication of aesthetic right or wrong lying at the very heart of the objects which are property. The concept must submerge itself in the monad until the social essence of its own dynamics becomes evident. This accomplishes more than does the classification of the monad as a special example of the macrocosm, or as Husserl said, disposing of it "from above." A philosophical analysis of the extremes of modern music—which takes its historical situation as well as its chemistry into account—deprives itself in its very intentions of sociological responsibility just as fundamentally as from an autonomously applied aesthetic, consisting of traditional philosophical relationships. Certainly not the least among the obligations of the continuing dialectical method is that one come to terms with Hegel's statement: "Consequently, we do not require to bring standards with us, nor to apply *our* fancies and thoughts in the inquiry; and just by our leaving these aside we are enabled to treat and discuss the subject as it actually is in itself and for itself, as it is in its complete reality."[18] At the same time, the method distinguishes itself from the functions for which the subject is traditionally reserved. These functions are descriptive technical analysis, apologetic commentary, and criticism. Technical analysis is assumed at all times and often disclosed, but it needs to be supplemented by detailed interpretation if it is to go beyond mere humanistic stock-taking and to express the relationship of the subject to truth. Apologetics, more relevant than ever as an antithesis to industrialization, limits itself to the positive. Criticism, finally, limits itself to the task of deciding the worth or worthlessness of works of art. The

18. Hegel, *The Phenomenology of Mind*, 141.

conclusions of criticism enter into philosophical treatment only sporadically, as the means of theoretical stimulus to overcome negativity, revealing the necessity for occasional aesthetic failure. The idea of works of art and their relationship is to be philosophically conceived, even if this at times were to lie beyond that which is realized by the work of art. The method reveals the implications of procedures and works in terms of factors within the works.[19] Thus it attempts to determine the idea behind each of two groups of musical phenomena individually, and to pursue it until the inherent consequence of the objects is transformed into their own criticism. The process is immanent: the internal consistency of the phenomenon—in the sense that this is to be developed within the phenomenon itself—becomes proof of its truth and the ferment of its untruth. The guiding category of contradiction itself is twofold in nature: that the works formulate the contradiction and, in turn, through such formulation reveal it in the markings of its imperfections; this category is the measure of its success, while at the same time the force of contradiction mocks the formulation and destroys the works. To be sure, an immanent method of such nature assumes at all times as its opposite pole that philosophical knowledge which transcends the object. This method cannot rely—as does Hegel —upon "pure observation" which promises truth simply because the conception of the identity of subject and object supports the entire process. In so doing, the observing consciousness is all the more sure of itself the more completely it submerges itself in the object. In an historical hour, when the reconciliation of subject and object has been perverted to a satanic parody—to the liquidation of the subject in objective presentation—the only philosophy which still serves this reconciliation is one which

19. Completeness of material is not in the best interests of philosophical intention or any aesthetic epistemological theory which hopes to gain more from persistence in the face of the individual object than from the unified characteristics of many objects compared with each other. That which proved itself as most fruitful for the idea was selected. Along with many others, the works of Schoenberg's prolific youth are not discussed. The essay on Stravinsky likewise admits everything from the universally known *Firebird* to the *Symphony in Three Movements* for orchestra (1945).

27

despises this illusion of reconciliation and—against universal self-alienation—establishes the validity of the hopelessly alienated, for which a "subject itself" scarcely any longer speaks. This is the limit of the immanent process, for it can as little support itself dogmatically by means of positive transcendence as could Hegel in his time. Knowledge, like its object, remains bound to the contradiction defined.

SCHOENBERG
AND PROGRESS

> Pure insight, however, is in the first
> instance without any content; it is
> rather the sheer disappearance of
> content; but by its negative attitude
> towards what it excludes it will
> make itself real and give itself a
> content.[1]

DISTURBANCE OF THE WORK

The changes encountered in music during the last thirty years
have yet to be comprehended in their full breadth. More is involved than the much discussed crisis—a condition of chaotic
fermentation, that is, the end of which could be foreseen and
which would restore order after disorder. The concept of some
future renewal—whether in significant and highly polished works
of art, or in the blissful harmony of music with society—simply
denies events of the past and elements that can be suppressed,
but not eradicated. Under the coercion of its own objective consequences music has critically invalidated the idea of the polished
work and disrupted the collective continuity of its effect. To be
sure, no crisis has been able to put a stop to public musical life
—neither the economic crisis nor the cultural crisis, in whose
concept the idea of prevailing reconstruction is already contained. Even in music the concept of the monopoly of the fittest

1. Hegel, *Phenomenology*, 561.

has survived. Even in the face of highly cacophonous sound, which flees from the web of organized culture and its consumers, the fraud of today's culture becomes obvious. Its management suppresses the emergence of a more valid culture, placing the blame for this situation on the lack of "achievement." All those outside the sphere of management are path-finders, trail-blazers, and—above all—tragic figures. Those who come after them are to have a better lot; if they conform, they are granted entry. But these outsiders are in no sense the pioneers of future works. They challenge the concept of production and the works produced. The apologist of actual radical music—who would support his arguments by pointing to the prolific output of the Schoenberg school—already denies precisely what he wishes to support. Today the only works which really count are those which are no longer works at all. This is to be recognized from the relationship of the current accomplishments of the school with the achievements of their early period. The monodrama *Erwartung* [*opus* 17], which develops the eternity of the second in four hundred bars, and the rapidly revolving pictures of *Die glückliche Hand* [*opus* 18], which takes back a life unto itself before it has a chance to find its place in time—are the sources of Berg's great opera *Wozzeck*. And to be sure, it is a great opera. It resembles *Erwartung* in detail as well as in conception —as the portrayal of anxiety; it resembles *Die glückliche Hand* in the insatiable successive strata of harmonic complexes, and the allegory of the multilateral character of its psychological subject. But Berg would have been uneasy at the thought that he had fulfilled in *Wozzeck* that which was indicated as a mere possibility in Schoenberg's Expressionistic works. The composed tragedy has to pay the price for its extensive depth and contemplative wisdom of its structure. The fleeting sketches of the Expressionistic Schoenberg are here in Berg transformed into new pictures of affects. The security of form establishes itself as a medium for shock absorption. The suffering of the helpless soldier Wozzeck in the machinery of injustice attains a composure upon which the style of the opera is based. This suffering is encompassed and assuaged. The erupting anxiety becomes a suitable subject for the music drama and the music which reflects this anxiety finds its way back into the scheme of transfiguration in resigned agreement.[2] *Wozzeck* is a masterpiece—a work of traditional art. That startling thirty-second note motiv, so very reminiscent of *Erwartung,* becomes a leit-motiv which is both repeatable and repeated. The more openly it appears in the course of the opera, the more willingly does it renounce its claim to be taken literally: it establishes itself as a vehicle of expression, and repetition softens its effect. Those who praise *Wozzeck* as the first lasting product of modern music do not know the extent to which their praise compromises a composition which in turn suffers from such sophistry. With experimental boldness, Berg before any other composer tried out such modern means over long periods of time. The richly varied supply of musical figures is inexhaustible and the greatness of the architectual dispositions proves to be equal to this supply. Courageous defeatism triumphs in the restrained sympathy of the sound. Nevertheless, *Wozzeck* negates its own point of departure precisely in those moments in which it is developed. The impulses of the composition—alive in its musical atoms—rebel against the work proceeding from them. These impulses do not permit lasting

2. The soothing quality comes totally to the surface in the opera *Lulu.* It is not only that the accents of the music have transformed Alwa into an ecstatic German youth, thereby revealing the possibility of reconciling Berg's Romantic origins with his mature intentions in the most touching manner possible. The text itself, moreover, has been idealistically distorted: Lulu has been simplified to a female creature of nature whom civilization itself outrages. Wedekind would have reacted sardonically to this twist. Berg's humanism makes the affair of the prostitute his own; in so doing he removes the irritating thorn which the prostitute represents from the flesh of bourgeois society. The principle according to which she is saved is itself a bourgeois principle: that of false sublimation of the sexual. In the second of the two dramas by Wedekind upon which Berg based his libretto, *Pandora's Box,* the closing lines of the dying Geschwitz are: "Lulu! My angel! Let me look at you once more! I am close to you! I'll stay close to you— in eternity! O accursed!" (She dies.) The decisively final words "O accursed" were eliminated by Berg. Geschwitz dies a death of love, a *"Liebestod."*

resolution. The dream of permanent artistic possessions is not only destroyed from the outside by the threatening social condition; the historical tendency present in musical means renounces this dream. The procedural method of modern music questions what many progressives expect of it: structures perfected within themselves which might be exhibited for all time in museums of opera and concert.

INHERENT TENDENCY OF MUSICAL MATERIAL

The assumption of an historical tendency in musical material contradicts the traditional conception of the material of music. This material is traditionally defined—in terms of physics, or possibly in terms of the psychology of sound—as the sum of all sounds at the disposal of the composer. The actual compositional material, however, is as different from this sum as is language from its total supply of sounds. It is not simply a matter of the increase and decrease of this supply in the course of history. All its specific characteristics are indications of the historical process. The higher the degree of historical necessity present within these specific characteristics, the less directly legible they become as historical indications. In that very moment when the historical expression of a chord can no longer be aurally perceived, it demands that the sounds which surround it give a conclusive account of its historical implications. These implications have determined the nature of this expression. The meaning of musical material is not absorbed in the genesis of music, and yet this meaning cannot be separated from it. Music recognizes no natural law; therefore, all psychology of music is questionable. Such psychology—in its efforts to establish an invariant "understanding" of the music of all times—assumes a constancy of musical subject. Such an assumption is more closely related to the constancy of the material of nature than psychological differ-

32

entiation might indicate. What this psychology inadequately and noncommitally describes is to be sought in the perception[3] of the kinetic laws of matter. According to these laws, not all things are possible at all times. To be sure, a unique ontological law is by no means to be ascribed either to the material of tones itself or to tonal material which has been filtered through the tempered system. This, for example, is the typical argumentation of those who—either from relationships of harmonic tones or from the psychology of the ear—attempt to deduce that the triad is the necessary and universally valid condition of all possible comprehension and that, therefore, all music must be dependent upon it. This argumentation, which even Hindemith has appropriated for himself, is nothing but a superstructure for reactionary compositional tendencies. Its deception is revealed by the observation that the trained ear is able to perceive harmonically the most complicated overtone relationships as well as less complex relationships. The listener, thereby, feels no particular urgency for a "resolution" of the alleged dissonances, but rather spontaneously resists resolutions as a retrogression into less sophisticated modes of listening. Similarly, in the thorough-bass era, the progression by fifths was suspected to be a type of archaic regression. The demands made upon the subject by the material are conditioned much more by the fact that the "material" is itself a crystallization of the creative impulse, an element socially predetermined through the consciousness of man. As a previous subjectivity—now forgetful of itself—such an objectified impulse of the material has its own kinetic laws. That which seems to be the mere self-locomotion of the material is of the same origin as is the social process, by whose traces it is continually permeated. This energy pursues its course in the same sense as does actual society, even when energy and society have become totally unaware of each other and have come into conflict with each other. Therefore, the altercation of the com-

3. The German word is *"Erkenntnis,"* —Trans.

33

poser with his material is the same as an altercation with society, precisely to the extent that it finds expression in his work, and does not simply face his product as consumer or opponent—a mere external and heteronomous factor. The instructions directed to the composer by the material and, in turn, transformed by his obedience to them are formulated in the inherent interplay of this altercation. It is clear, of course, that in the earlier stages of a technique, its later developments cannot be anticipated but at best subjectively envisioned. The reverse is also true. All the tonal combinations employed in the past by no means stand indiscriminately at the disposal of the composer today. Even the more insensitive ear detects the shabbiness and exhaustion of the diminished seventh chord and certain chromatic modulatory tones in the salon music of the nineteenth century. For the technically trained ear, such vague discomfort is transformed into a prohibitive canon. If all is not deception, this canon today excludes even the medium of tonality—that is to say, the means of all traditional music. It is not simply that these sounds are antiquated and untimely, but that they are false. They no longer fulfill their function. The most progressive level of technical procedures designs tasks before which traditional sounds reveal themselves as impotent clichés. There are modern compositions which occasionally scatter tonal sounds in their own context. It is precisely the triads which, in such context, are cacophonous and not the dissonances! As a substitute for dissonances, these triads at times might even be justified. Impure style is, however, not alone responsible for the impropriety of their employment. Rather the technical horizon, against which the tonal sounds are glaringly conspicuous, today encompasses all music. If a contemporary composer restricts himself exclusively to tonal sounds —in the manner of Sibelius—these sound just as false as if they were enclaves within the atonal field. This statement, to be sure, must be qualified. The isolated appearance of chords does not in itself decide their correctness or incorrectness. These are to be judged only from the perspective of the level of technique adhered to at a given time. The diminished seventh chord, which rings false in salon pieces, is correct and full of every possible expression at the beginning of Beethoven's *Sonata* [*opus* 111].[4] This chord is not just superimposed and merely a result of the structural disposition of the movement. Rather it is the total *niveau* of Beethoven's technique which gives the chord its specific weight. The components of this technique include the tension between the most extreme dissonance possible for him and consonance, the harmonic perspective which includes all melodic events, and the dynamic conception of tonality as a whole. But the historical process, through which this weight has been lost, is irreversible.[5] This chord itself, as an obsolete form,

4. The same is true for modern music. In the domain of twelve-tone technique chords essentially employing octave doublings sound incorrect. Their exclusion was at first viewed as one of the most significant limitations of the technique in comparison with free atonality. But—strictly speaking—the prohibition pertains only to the state of material today and not to older works. The numerous octave doublings of *Die glückliche Hand* are in every case still correct. They were technical necessities because of the excessive tonal richness in the stratified structure of harmonic sound levels upon which the construction of the work is based. For the most part they are neutralized, since the doubled tones in themselves belong to different sub-complexes; they are not directly related to each other and nowhere do they suspend the effect of the one "pure" chord, which is not even sought here. At the same time, they have their identity in the quality of the material. In free atonality there are effects which are related to those of the leading tone. This results in a tonal residue—the understanding of the goal-tone as a "lead basic tone." This gives rise to the possibility of octave doublings. There is no mechanical pressure—not even the highest precision of aural perceptions—which leads to twelve-tone technique. It is rather the tendencies of the material (which by no means correspond to the tendencies of the individual work and often enough even contradict them) which do so. Furthermore, twelve-tone composers are undecided as to whether, in the future, they will avoid all octave doublings for the sake of the purity of the composition or whether they ought to readmit them for the sake of clarity in the work.

5. In cases where the developmental tendency of Occidental music has not been purely developed—as in many agrarian regions in southeast Europe—the use of tonal material has been permitted down to the most recent past. This was not a matter of disgrace. Janaček and Bartók come to mind. Janaček's art is extra-territorial, but nonetheless magnificent in its consequences. Many of Bartók's compositions, in spite of his folkloristic inclinations, are nonetheless among the most progressive in European musical art. The legitimation of such music on the periphery lies foremost in its ability to formulate a technical canon which is in itself both correct and selective. In contrast to the

35

represents in its dissolution a state of technique contradictory as a whole to the state of technique actually in practice. Even if, therefore, the truth or falsity of all musical detail is dependent upon such a total state of technique, this level will be evident only in the specific configurations of the compositional tasks. No chord is false "in itself," simply because there is no such thing as a chord in itself and because each chord is a vehicle of the total context—indeed, for the total direction. But precisely for this reason, the faculty of the ear to perceive what is right or wrong is unequivocally dependent upon this single chord and not upon abstract reflection regarding the total *niveau* of technique. But at this point the picture of the composer is also transformed. He loses that freedom on a grand scale which idealistic aesthetics is accustomed to grant to the artist. He is no longer a creator. It is not that the times and society impose external restrictions upon him; it is rather the rigid demand for compositional accuracy made upon him by his structure which limits him. The state of technique appears as a problem in every measure which he dares to conceive: with every measure technique as a whole demands of him that he do it justice and that he give the single correct answer permitted by technique at any given moment. The compositions themselves are nothing but such answers—nothing but the solution of technical picture puzzles—and the composer is the only one who is capable of reading his compositions and understanding his own music. He works on an infinitely small scale. His efforts find fulfillment in the execution of that which his music objectively demands of him. But such obedience demands of the composer all possible disobedi-

---

blood-and-soil ideology—a party-line tenet of National Socialism—truly extra-territorial music (the material of which, even though it is familiar, is organized in a totally different way from that in the Occident) has a power of alienation which places it in the company of the avant-garde and not that of nationalistic reaction. The external exertion of this force comes to the aid of inner-musical cultural criticism as is expressed in radical modern music itself. Ideological blood-and-soil music, on the other hand, is always affirmative and holds to "tradition." It is precisely the tradition of every official music, however, which is suspended by Janáček's diction—patterned after his language—in the midst of all triads.

ence, independence, and spontaneity. This is the dialectical nature revealed in the unfolding of the musical material.

SCHOENBERG'S CRITICISM OF ILLUSION AND PLAY

Today this process has turned against the self-sufficient work of art and everything determined thereby. The illness which has befallen the idea of the work might well have its roots in a social condition which reflects nothing binding and affirmative enough to guarantee the internal harmony of the work sufficient unto itself. The prohibitive difficulties of the work are, however, evident not only in the reflection upon it, but in the dark interior of the work itself. If one thinks of the most conspicuous symptom—namely, the shrinking of the expansion in time—which in music is only an external factor of the work, then it must be stated that only individual impotence, incapacity for structural formulation—not sparseness—is to be made responsible for the lack of success of a given work. No works could exhibit greater concentration and consistency of formal structure than Schoenberg's and Webern's shortest movements. Their brevity is a direct result of the demand for the greatest consistency. This demand precludes the superfluous. In so doing this consistency opposes expansion in time, which has been the basis for the conception of the musical work since the eighteenth century, certainly since Beethoven. The work, the age, and illusion are all struck by a single blow. Criticism of the extensive scheme is interlocked with criticism of the content, in terms of phrase and ideology. Music, compressed into a moment, is valid as an eruptive revelation of negative experience. It is closely related to actual suffering.[6] In this spirit of compression modern music

6. Cf. Friedrich Holderlin's poem "Brevity":
"Why so brief now, so curt? Do you no longer, then,
  Love your art as you did? When in your younger days,
    Hopeful days, in your singing
      What you loathed was to make an end!"

Like my joy is my song. —Who in the sundown's red

destroys all decorative elements and, therewith, symmetrically extended works. Among the arguments which would attempt to relegate the disquieting phenomenon of Schoenberg into the past of Romanticism and individualism (in order to be able to serve the operations of modern collectives with a better conscience), the most widely spread is the one which brands him as an "*espressivo* composer" and his music as an "exaggeration" of a decayed mode of expression. It is neither necessary to deny his origin in the Wagnerian *espressivo* style nor to overlook the traditional *espressivo* elements in his earlier works. These compositions, nonetheless, prove their ability to come to terms with this barren emptiness. At the same time, Schoenberg's *espressivo* style since the break—if not from the very beginning, at least since the *Piano Pieces* [*opus* 11] and the George songs, *Das Buch der hängenden Gärten* [*opus* 15]—differs in quality from Romantic expression precisely by means of that intensification which thinks this *espressivo* though to its logical conclusion. The expressive music of the West, since the beginning of the seventeenth century, assumed an expressiveness which the composer allotted to his musical structures in much the same way as the dramatist did to his theatrical figures, without the expressed emotions claiming to have immediate presence and reality within the work. Dramatic music, just as true *musica ficta,* from Monteverdi to Verdi presented expression as stylized communication —as the representation of passions.[7] Whenever this music extended beyond this, laying claim to a substantiality beyond the appearance of expressed feelings, this claim hardly restricted itself to specific musical emotions, reflecting in turn such emotions of the soul. This claim was validated only by the totality of the form, which exercises control over the musical characters and their correlation. The process is totally different in the case

---

    Glow would happily bathe? Gone it is, cold the earth,
      And the bird of the night whirs
        Down, so close that you shield your eyes.
Poems and Fragments, tr. Michael Hamburger (Ann Arbor, 1967), 45.
    7. *Musica ficta:* In the music of the tenth to sixteenth centuries, the theory of the chromatic or, more properly, non-diatonic tones other than those in the diatonic scale. —Trans.

of Schoenberg. The actual revolutionary moment for him is the change in function of musical expression. Passions are no longer simulated, but rather genuine emotions of the unconscious—of shock, of trauma—are registered without disguise through the medium of music. These emotions attack the taboos of form because these taboos subject such emotions to their own censure, rationalizing them and transforming them into images. Schoenberg's formal innovations were closely related to the change in the content of expression. These innovations serve the breakthrough of the reality of this content. The first atonal works are case studies in the sense of psychoanalytical dream case studies.[8] In the very first publication on Schoenberg, Vassily Kandinsky called the composer's paintings "acts of the mind." The scars of this revolution of expression, however, are the blotches which have become fixed in his music as well as in his pictures, as the heralds of the id against the compositional will.[9] They destroy the surface and are as little to be removed by subsequent correction as are the traces of blood in a fairy tale. Authentic suffering has implanted these in the work of art as a sign that the autonomy of the work is no longer recognized by this suffering. The heteronomy of the scars—and the blotches—challenges music's façade of self-sufficiency. This façade is based on the fact that in all traditional music the formally defined elements are employed as if they were the inviolable necessity of this one individual case; or that this façade appears as though it were identical with the alleged language of form. Since the beginning of the bourgeois era, all great music has founded its sufficiency in the illusion that it has achieved an unbroken unity and justified through its own individuation the conventional universal legality to which it is subject. This is contradicted by modern music. The criticism directed towards decorative elements, towards convention, and towards abstract universality of musical language

8. This concept is a recurrent motive in Adorno's study, reflecting the indebtedness of the Frankfurt school to the work of Freud. The translation emphasizes this aspect through reliance upon the term "case study." —Trans.

9. The tremolo passage in the first piano piece from *opus* 19 or measures 10, 269, and 382 of *Erwartung* are examples of such blotches.

39

are all of one mind. If music is privileged above all other forms by the absence of illusive imagery—the fact that it does not paint a picture—then it nonetheless has participated energetically in the illusory character of the bourgeois work of art; this it does by means of its specific interests with the domination of conventions. Schoenberg declared his independence from this type of art by seriously heeding precisely that expression whose inclusion in the universal trend towards conciliation determines the most basic principle of musical illusion. His music officially denies the claim that the universal and the specific have been reconciled. Regardless of the indebtedness of this music in its origins to parallel principles exhibited in nature, and regardless of the similarity of its formal irregularities to organic forms—in no way does it present an organic totality. Even Nietzsche in one of his occasional remarks has pointed out that the essence of the great work of art lies in the fact that it might be totally different in any of its given moments. The definition of the work of art in terms of its freedom assumes that conventions are binding. Only at the outset where such conventions guarantee totality beyond all question could everything in actuality be different: precisely because nothing would be different. Most compositions by Mozart would offer the composer far-reaching alternatives without forfeiting anything. The positive position taken by Nietzsche on aesthetic conventions is consistent with this possibility of constant change and his highest wisdom is the ironic play with forms whose substantiality has diminished. Anything which does not lend itself to this play was in his eyes suspect as plebian and protestant: a strong touch of this flavor is definitely discernible in his polemic against Wagner. But not until Schoenberg has music accepted Nietzsche's challenge.[10] Schoenberg's composi-

10. The origin of atonality as the fulfilled purification of music from all conventions contains by its very nature elements of barbarism. In Schoenberg's outbursts—often hostile to culture—this purification repeatedly causes the surface to tremble. The dissonant chord, by comparison with consonance, is not only the more differentiated and progressive; but furthermore, it sounds as if it had not been completely subdued by the ordering principle of civilization—in a certain respect, as if it were older than tonality itself. In the midst of such chaos the

tions are the first in which nothing actually can be different: they are case studies and construction in one. There is in them no trace of convention which guarantees any freedom of play. Schoenberg's attitude towards play is just as polemic as is his attitude towards illusion. He turns just as sharply against the New Objectivity music-makers and their collective retinue as he does against the decorative elements of Romanticism.[11] He has formulated both attitudes in his theoretical writings: "Music is not to be decorative; it is to be true," and "Art does not arise out of ability but rather out of necessity."[12] With the negation of illusion and play music tends towards the direction of knowledge.

DIALECTICS OF LONELINESS

This knowledge is founded upon the expressive substance of music itself. What radical music perceives is the untransfigured

style of Florentine *Ars Nova*—the combining of voices without concern for harmony, accomplished merely through the senses of untrained musicians—can easily be confused with many thoughtless products of "linear counterpoint." At first the complex chords strike the naïve ear as "false," as an inability to do things correctly, in the same manner that the layman finds radical graphics "misdrawn." Progress itself in its passionate protest against conventions has something of the child —a regressive tendency. Schoenberg's earliest atonal compositions— particularly the *Piano Pieces* [opus 11]— shocked the audience much more through primitivism than through their complexity. In the midst of all proliferation, Webern's works retain a thoroughly primitive complexion, precisely through the help of proliferation. Stravinsky and Schoenberg are for a second tangential in this impulse. In Schoenberg the primitivism of the revolutionary phase is related to the content of expression. The expression of unmitigated suffering, bound by no convention whatsoever, seems ill-mannered: it violates the taboo of the English governess who took Mahler along to a parade, and warned him: "Don't get excited!" The international resistance to Schoenberg, in its innermost motivation, is not at all so different from that directed towards Mahler in his strict tonality. (Cf. Max Horkheimer and Theodor W. Adorno, *Dialektik der Aufklarung*, Amsterdam, 1947, 214.)

11. "New Objectivity": an artistic movement in the years after the first war; in German "*die neue Sachlichkeit*." —Trans.

12. Arnold Schoenberg, *Probleme des Kunstunterrichts* (*Problems of Art Instruction*), Musikalisches Taschenbuch, Vienna, 1911.

suffering of man. His impotence has increased to the point that it no longer permits illusion and play. The conflicting drives, about whose sexual genesis Schoenberg's music leaves no doubt, have assumed a force in that music which has the character of a case study—a force which prohibits music from offering comforting consolation. In the expression of anxiety as "forebodings," the music of Schoenberg's Expressionistic phase offers evidence of this impotence. The monodrama *Erwartung* has as its heroine a woman looking for her lover at night. She is subjected to all the terrors of darkness and in the end comes upon his murdered corpse. She is consigned to music in the very same way as a patient is to analysis. The admission of hatred and desire, jealousy and forgiveness, and—beyond all this—the entire symbolism of the unconscious is wrung from her; it is only in the moment that the heroine becomes insane that the music recalls its right to utter a consoling protest. The seismographic registration of traumatic shock becomes, at the same time, the technical structural law of music. It forbids continuity and development. Musical language is polarized according to its extremes: towards gestures of shock resembling bodily convulsions on the one hand, and on the other towards a crystalline standstill of a human being whom anxiety causes to freeze in her tracks. It is this polarization upon which the total world of form of the mature Schoenberg—and of Webern as well—depends. The intensification of musical "communication"—not even suspected by this school in the beginning—the difference between theme and development, the constancy of harmonic flow, and the unbroken melodic line are destroyed by this polarization. There is not one of Schoenberg's technical innovations which cannot be traced back to that polarization of expression, and which does not reveal traces of this polarization even beyond the sphere of influence of expression. This might well offer insight into the interdependency of form and content in all music. For one thing, it is foolish to proscribe exaggerated technical articulation as formalistic. All forms of music, not just those of Expressionism, are realizations of content. In them there survives what is otherwise forgotten and is no longer capable of speaking directly. What once sought refuge in form now exists without definition in the constancy of form. The forms of art reflect the history of man more truthfully than do documents themselves. Every ossification of form insists that it be interpreted as the negation of the severity of life. That the anxiety of the lonely becomes the law of aesthetic formal language, however, betrays something of the secret of that loneliness. The reproach against the individualism of art in its later stages of development is so pathetically wretched simply because it overlooks the social nature of this individualism. "Lonely discourse" reveals more about social tendencies than does communicative discourse. Schoenberg hit upon the social character of loneliness by developing this lonely discourse to its ultimate extreme. From the musical perspective, his "drama with music" *Die glückliche Hand* is perhaps his most significant work: the dream of a totality, all the more valid because the dream is never realized as a total symphony. The text —inadequate expedient that it might be—cannot be separated from the music. It is precisely the coarse compactness of this text which gives the music its compressed form and, therewith, its depth and effectiveness. Consequently, the criticism of just this coarseness of the text strikes at the very core of Expressionistic music. The subject of the drama is Strindberg's lonely man who experiences the same failures in his erotic life as in his work. Schoenberg disdains the interpretation which sees this subject as the "social-psychological" product of industrial society. But he has noted how subjects and industrial society relate to each other in a perennial contradiction, which communicates through anxiety. The third scene of the drama takes place in a workshop. "Several workers at their jobs in realistic dress" are seen. "One is filing, another sits at the machine, a third is hammering." The hero enters the workshop. With the words "That can be done more simply" (measures 101ff., Scene III)— a symbolic criticism of the superfluous—he produces with a single magic blow from a piece of gold the piece of jewelry for the manufacture of which the other workers needed complicated procedures dictated by the division of labor. "Before he raises his hammer to strike, the workers jump up, preparing to attack him. In the meantime he observes his raised left hand, without noticing the threat. . . . As the hammer falls, the faces of the workers freeze in astonishment: the anvil splits in the middle and the gold falls into the resulting crevice. The man bends over and picks it up with his left hand. Slowly he raises it up. It is a diadem, richly decorated with precious jewels." The man sings, "That's how jewelry is made." —He declaims this "simply, without emotion." "The faces of the workers becoming threatening, then contemptuous. They start talking with each other and seem to be planning a new attack on the man. With a laugh the man throws them the jewelry. They are about to attack him. He has turned away and does not see them." Thereupon the scene changes. The objective naïveté of these procedures is no other than that of the man who "does not see the workers." He is alienated from the actual process of production in society and is no longer able to recognize any relationship between labor and economic system. The phenomenon of labor strikes him as an absolute. The realistic appearance of laborers in stylized drama corresponds to the anxiety of the individual alienated by material production in the very face of it. It is the anxiety of being forced to awaken—the fear which totally dominated the Expressionistic conflict of dream-theatre and reality. Because the individual caught in this dream-state is above viewing the laborers realistically, he thinks that this threat of conflict comes from them and not from the total system, which has driven him and the worker apart. The chaotic anarchy in human labor relationships, which results from the system itself, finds expression by placing the burden of guilt upon the victims. In reality, however, the workers' threat is not their offense, but rather their answer to the universal injustice which threatens their existence with every new invention. The masking of this injustice, which does not permit the subject to "see," is itself of an objective nature; it is the ideology of the class. In this respect, the chaotic aspect of *Die glückliche Hand*—allowing the obscure to remain obscured—affirms that upright intellectual honesty which Schoenberg represents in opposition to illusion and play. But the reality of chaos is not the total reality. Chaos defines the law according to which market-society blindly reproduces, with no consideration for the individual. It includes the continuing growth of power in the hands of those in command over all others. The world is chaotic in the eyes of the victims of the law of market value and industrial concentration. But the world is not chaotic "in itself." It is the individual—oppressed inexorably by the principles of this world—who considers it such. The forces which make the world chaotic in the eyes of the individual in the end assume responsibility for the reorganization of chaos because the world is at the mercy of these forces. Chaos is the function of the cosmos—disorder before order. Chaos and system belong together, in society as well as in philosophy. The world of values, conceived in the midst of Expressionistic chaos, bears traits of a new force of domination on the horizon. The man in *Die glückliche Hand* sees the woman he loves as little as he sees the workers around him. He elevates his self-pity to a secret realm of the mind. He is a leader. The music depicts his strength—the text, his weakness. The criticism of hypostatization which he represents is reactionary in the same sense as was the criticism of Wagner in his own day. This criticism is directed not against the social conditions of production, but rather against the division of labor. Schoenberg's compositions suffer from his own application of such division of labor between music and text. They are encumbered by poetic experiments with which he supplements the highest measure of specialized skill in music. Here also, a Wagnerian tendency collapses. What was still unified and progressive in Wagner's composite work of art (*Gesamtkunstwerk*)—unified by the rational organization of the artistic processes of production—is broken up into disparate entities in Schoenberg's compositions. He, as a competitor, remains true to the existing order. "That can be done more simply" than the others do it. Schoenberg's man has "a rope around his waist as a belt upon which two Turksheads hang," and holds "an unsheathed bloody sword in his hand." No matter how poorly he fares in the world, he is nonetheless the man of power. But the mythical animal of anxiety, which buries its teeth in the back of his neck, forces him

45

to obedience. This helpless man learns to live with his helplessness, doing to others precisely that injustice which is done unto him. Nothing could more vividly underscore his historical ambiguity than the stage direction according to which the scene "represents something between a mechanic's shop and a goldsmith's studio." The hero, prophet of the New Objectivity, is, as an artisan craftsman, supposed to save the magic of old means of production. His one simple gesture, in opposition to the superfluous, is sufficient to produce a diadem. Siegfried, his model, had at least forged a sword. "Music is not to be decorative, but rather to be true." But then again the work of art has only art as its object. It cannot aesthetically escape the context of deception to which it socially belongs. The radically alienated and absolute work of art, in its blindness, relates tautologically only to itself. Its symbolic nucleus is the realm of art. And thus this work of art becomes hollow. The emptiness that is manifested in the New Objectivity permeates this nucleus at the height of Expressionism. What Expressionism anticipates of the New Objectivity, it shares with *Art Nouveau* (*"Jugendstil"*) at the same time and with the development of commercial art, both of which preceded it. To these two movements *Die glückliche Hand* is indebted in its use of color symbolism. The return to illusion becomes so easy for the Expressionistic protest because the movement originated in illusion—in the illusion of individuality itself. Expressionism remains—against its will—that which art had openly professed around 1900: loneliness as style.

LONELINESS AS STYLE

Erwartung contains a musical quotation towards the end at one of its most celebrated spots, accompanying the words "thousands of people march past" (measures 411f., cf. 401f.). Schoenberg has taken this quotation from an earlier tonal song, whose theme and counterpoint are woven into the freely moving vocal texture of *Erwartung* with greatest artistry, and without destroying its atonality. The song is entitled "Am Wegrand" and belongs to the group of *opus* 6, number 6, all of which are based upon poems from the *Art Nouveau* movement. The words are by John Henry Mackay, who wrote the biography of Max Stirner.[13] The words define the point of intersection between *Art Nouveau* and Expressionism, as does the composition of this song itself, which, in the use of Brahmsian technique of piano composition, disturbs tonality by independent chromatic auxiliary tones and contrapunctal conflicts. The text reads:

> Thousands of people march past,
> The one for whom I long,
> He is not among them!
> Restless glances fly past
> And ask the one in haste,
> Whether it is he. . . .
> But they ask and ask in vain.
> No one answers:
> "Here I am. Be still."
> Longing fills the realms of life,
> Left empty by fulfillment,
> And so I stand at the edge of the road,
> While the crowd flows past,
> Until—blinded by the burning sun—
> My tired eyes close.

Herein lies the formula of the style of loneliness. This loneliness is a common one: that of city dwellers who are totally unaware of each other. The gesture of the lonely person offers a basis for comparison. And consequently, this gesture can be quoted: the Expressionist reveals loneliness as universal.[14] He continues

13. Mackay (1864–1933) was born in Scotland, but lived in Germany from earliest childhood. In 1898 he published the definitive biography of Max Stirner (1806–1856). Stirner, himself a student of Hegel in Berlin, was a dominant voice of social and economic criticism in the nineteenth century; his theories anticipate many of those of the Frankfurt School. He was one of the earliest advocates of anarchy. —Trans.

14. In the case of Alban Berg, in whose works the tendency towards stylization of expression dominates and who never completely emancipated himself from the *Art Nouveau* movement, the art of quotation moved more and more into the foreground after *Wozzeck*. Thus the

47

to quote even where the quote is not a literal one: the spot "Beloved, beloved, morning is coming" (*Erwartung*, measures 389f.) can be traced back to "Hark, beloved" from the second act of *Tristan* following Brangäne's warning to the lovers. As in all other areas of knowledge, the quotation represents authority. The anxiety of the lonely person who is quoting seeks support in what is currently valid. Anxiety has emancipated itself from the bourgeois taboos on expression in its Expressionistic case studies. In its emancipated state it is no longer prevented from aligning itself with the stronger party. The position of the absolute monad in art is twofold: resistance to association with bad company and a readiness to association with still worse.

EXPRESSIONISM AS OBJECTIVITY

The sudden transformation necessarily takes place. This arises from the fact that the content of Expressionism—the absolute subject—is not absolute. Society is reflected in the isolation of the Expressionist movement. The last of Schoenberg's six pieces for male chorus [*opus* 35] offers simple proof thereof. "Deny that you also belong to this—you are not alone—." Such a "bond," however, reveals itself in that pure expressions in their state of isolation liberate those elements of the intra-subjective and therewith the elements of aesthetic objectivity. Every Expressionistic consequence which challenges the traditional category of the work brings new demands of organization—demands of a consistency in terms of being-thus-and-not-being-able-to-be-otherwise. Expression polarizes musical continuity according to

---

Lyric Suite duplicates, tone for tone, a spot from the *Lyric Symphony* of Alexander Zemlinsky (Viennese composer and conductor; Schoenberg was his friend, pupil, and—subsequently—his brother-in-law), as well as the beginning of Wagner's *Tristan*. Likewise, a scene in *Lulu* quotes the first measures of *Wozzeck*. By divesting the autonomy of form of its power in such a quotation, its monadological depth is immediately recognized as illusory. Proving oneself sufficient in the singular form is tantamount to the perfection of that which has been assigned to all other forms. The quoting Expressionist defers to communication.

its extremes; this results in turn in the determination of continuity according to the succession of the extremes. Contrast, as a law of form, is no less binding than was transition in traditional music. It would even be possible to define twelve-tone technique in its later stages as a system of contrasts, as the integration of those elements which are unconnected. As long as art preserves its distance from the immediacy of life, it is not able to step beyond the shadow of its autonomy and its immanence of form. Expressionism, in itself hostile to the concept of the work, is able to do this even less precisely because of this hostility. Precisely in its renunciation of communication, the movement insists upon its autonomy, guaranteed only by consistency within works of art. It is this unavoidable contradiction which makes it impossible to continue steadfastly according to the principles of Expressionism. In that the aesthetic object is to be designated as pure here-and-now, it goes beyond the pure here-and-now—by virtue of this negative designation—renouncing all that extends beyond it, under whose law the aesthetic object falls. The absolute liberation of the particular from the universal renders it universal through the polemic and principal relationship of the universal to the particular. What has once been defined is, by force of its own definition, more than the mere result of individuation as it is delineated as being. Even the gestures of shock in *Erwartung* take on a certain resemblance to this formula—as soon as they have made their first reappearance—and therewith give contour to the form which encompasses them: the final chorus is a true finale. If the drive towards well-integrated construction is to be called objectivity, then objectivity is not simply a counter-movement to Expressionism. It is the other side of the Expressionistic coin. Expressionistic music had interpreted so literally the principle of expression contained in traditionally Romantic music that it assumed the character of a case study. In so doing, a sudden change takes place. Music, as a case study in expression, is no longer "expressive." What is no longer expressed hovers over music at an undefined distance, and consequently music is deprived of that reflected splendor of infinity. As soon as music has clearly and sharply defined what

49

it wishes to express—its subjective content—this content becomes rigid under the force of the composition, manifesting precisely that objective quality the existence of which is denied by the purely expressive character of music. In its case-study disposition towards its object, music itself becomes "matter-of-fact." With its expressive outbursts the dream of subjectivity explodes, and along with it all conventions. These chords—reflecting the character of the case study—blast the subjective illusion. Thereby, however, these chords invalidate their unique expressive function. What they portray as their object—no matter how precisely this might be done—becomes a matter of indifference: it is, after all, the same subjectivity, whose magic dissolves before the exactness of the penetrating eye cast upon it by the work. Thus the case study chords become the material of construction. This happens in *Die glückliche Hand*. It is at one and the same time a document of orthodox Expressionistic theory and a concrete work of art. It professes architectural form through its employment of a reprise with ostinato, reposing harmonies, and lapidary thematic trombone chords in the final scene (measures 214f., 248 and 252). Such architecture negates musical psychologism, which nevertheless finds its perfection in this architecture. In so doing music does not—like the text— simply drop below the Expressionist level of knowledge, but simultaneously surpasses this level. The categorization of the work as a flawless and cohesive totality is not bound up in that illusion which Expressionism brands as a lie. The category itself is of a double nature. If the work reveals itself to the isolated and totally alienated subject as a deception of harmony (a deception of reconciliation within itself and with other works), then it is at the same time that instance which puts this false individuality back into its proper bounds—an individuality which has its proper place in bad company. If this individuality takes a critical stand upon the work, the work in turn becomes critical of this individuality. If the contingency of individuality protests against the repudiated social law which once gave rise to this individuality, then the work designs schemata intended to overcome this very contingency. The work represents the truth of society against the individual, who recognizes its untruth and is himself this untruth. Only works of art manifest that which transcends limitations of subject and object to the same degree. As illusory reconciliation, these works are the reflection of actual reconciliation. In its Expressionistic phase music rescinded any claim to totality. But Expressionistic music did remain "organic": it was a language; it was subjective and psychological.[15] These factors drove music again in the direction of totality. Perhaps Expressionism was not sufficiently radical in its position on superstitions regarding the organic. Nevertheless, the elimination of the organic resulted in a renewed crystallization of the concept of the work of art; the works necessarily become heirs to the expressionistic heritage.

TOTAL ORGANIZATION OF THE ELEMENTS OF MUSIC

The possibilities indicated above would seem to be without limitation. All restricting principles of selection in tonality have been discarded. Traditional music had to content itself with a highly limited number of tonal combinations, particularly with regard to their vertical applications. It had further to content itself with rendering the specific continuously by means of configurations of the general, which these configurations para-

15. In its attitude towards the organic, Expressionism distinguishes itself from Surrealism. The "inner strife" of Expressionism is a result of its organic irrationality. This strife is definable in terms of opposites: sudden gesture and motionlessness of the body. Its rhythm is patterned after that of waking and sleeping. Surrealistic irrationality, on the other hand, assumes that the physiological unity of the body has collapsed—Paul Bekker once called Schoenberg's Expressionism "physiological music." Surrealism is anti-organic and rooted in lifelessness. It destroys the boundary between the body and the world of objects, in order to convert society to a hypostatization of the body. Its form is that of montage. This is totally alien to Schoenberg. With regard to Surrealism however, the more subjectivity renounces its right over the world of objects, aggressively acknowledging the supremacy of that world, the more willing it is to accept at the same time the traditionally established forms of the world of objects.

doxically present as identical with the unique. Beethoven's entire work is an exegesis of this paradox. Today, in contrast, chords are tailored to the non-changeable demands of their concrete usage. No conventions prevent the composer from using the sound which he needs in a specific spot. No convention forces him to acquiesce to traditionally universal principles. With the liberation of musical material, there arose the possibility of mastering it technically. It is as if music had thrown off that last alleged force of nature which its subject matter exercises upon it, and would now be able to assume command over this subject matter freely, consciously, and openly. The composer has emancipated himself along with his sounds. The various dimensions of Western tonal music—melody, harmony, counterpoint, form, and instrumentation—have for the most part developed historically apart from one another, without design, and, in that regard, according to the "laws of nature." Even in those instances where the one assumed the function of the others —as did melody, for example, that of harmony during the Romantic period—the one did not actually proceed out of the other; they simply came to resemble one another. Melody "circumscribed" the harmonic function; harmony differentiated itself in the service of melodic valor. But melody itself, in its liberation from its old triadic character by means of the Romantic art song—the *Lied*—remains within the framework of harmonic common practice. The blindness with which the development of the productive forces of music has proceeded, particularly since Beethoven, has resulted in incongruities. Whenever an isolated aspect of artistic material has developed within an historical span, other aspects of this material have been left behind. With regard to the unity of the work, these more progressive aspects have been accused of deception by the more regressive elements. During the Romantic era this was, above all, valid for counterpoint. It was only a decoration upon the homophonic composition. It confined itself either to the superficial combination of homophonically worked-out themes, or to a simple embellishing decoration of a harmonic "chorale," the seeming contrapuntal nature of which is only an illusion. From this perspective Wagner, Strauss, and Reger resemble each other. At the same time, however, all counterpoint by its own definition insists upon the simultaneity of independent voices. If this is ignored, then inferior counterpoint results. Drastic examples thereof are to be found in the "all-too-good" contrapuntal works of late Romanticism. They are melodically and harmonically conceived. In such cases the given voices would appear to function as leading voices where they at best might function as motivic fragments in the total structuring of the voices. Consequently, they obscure the progression of voices and disavow the construction through obtrusively song-like pretensions. Such incongruities do not, however, remain restricted to technical details. They become the historical forces of the whole. For the further the individual aspects of musical material are developed, the more that many of them are blended together—as, for example instrumental sound and harmony in Romanticism—and the more clearly does the idea of rational total organization of the total musical material define itself. This idea eliminates those incongruities. It already was an important element in the Wagnerian composite work of art; but its full realization comes with Schoenberg. In his music it is not only that all dimensions are developed to an equal degree, but further that all of them evolve out of one another to such an extent that they all converge. Schoenberg has visions of such a convergence even in his Expressionistic phase; an example of this is to be found in his concept of the "*Klangfarbe*" melody.[16] He implies that the mere instrumental change of coloration of identical sounds can assume melodic force, without alteration of the melodic realm in the old sense. In a later development a common denominator is sought for all musical dimensions. This is the origin of the twelve-tone technique, which finds its cul-

16. "*Klangfarbenmelodie*": a term suggested by Schoenberg in his *Harmonielehre* in a discussion of the possibility of composing "melodically" with varying tone colors, on a single pitch level as well as with varying pitch, duration and intensity. The term attempts to establish timbre as a structural element comparable in importance to pitch, duration, and so forth (cf. *Harvard Dictionary*, 455). —Trans.

53

mination in the will towards the suspension of that fundamental contrast upon which all Western music is built—the contrast between polyphonic fugal structure and homophonic sonata-form. This was Webern's point of departure in his last string quartet [*opus* 28]. Schoenberg was once viewed as a synthesis of Brahms and Wagner. In the later works of Schoenberg and Webern still higher goals are sought. The alchemy of these works would appear to seek to unite the most fundamental impulses of Bach and Beethoven. This is the direction taken by the restitution of counterpoint. But such a restitution vanishes, in turn, in the utopia of that synthesis. The specific essence of counterpoint, its derivation from traditional *cantus firmus,* becomes untenable. The concept of counterpoint is at any rate no longer to be found in Webern's late chamber music: his sparse sounds are precisely those remnants which the fusion of the vertical and the horizontal have left behind —that is to say, they are the monuments of music which have grown mute in indifference.

TOTAL DEVELOPMENT

It is the contrast to the idea of the rational total organization of the work, the contrast to the "indifference" of the material dimensions towards each other in the work, which reveal the reactionary nature of the compositional procedures of Stravinsky and Hindemith. And to be sure, these procedures are technically reactionary, regardless of the position in society of these two composers. This pseudo-musicianship is a clever manipulation involving one isolated aspect of musical material in place of a constructive consequential procedure which subjects all aspects of this material to the same law. Such cleverness, in its hard-headed naïveté, has today become aggressive. The integral organization of the work of art, which is in opposition to the work itself—the only possible objectivity for the work of art today—is precisely the product of that subjectivity denounced by this pseudo-musicianship for what they term its "accidental nature." To be sure, the conventions destroyed today were not always of such superficial significance in their relationship to music. Experiences which were once vital have imprinted themselves in these conventions and have thus fulfilled a certain function fairly well. This function was essentially organizational. Conventions were deprived of this function, however, by autonomous aesthetic subjectivity, which strove to organize the work freely from within itself. The transition of musical organization to autonomous subjectivity is completed by virtue of the technical principle of the development. It was at the beginning, in the eighteenth century, a minor element in sonata-form. Experimentation with subjective illumination and dynamics were conducted with the themes once they had been stated and their existence could be presumed. In Beethoven, however, the development—subjective reflection upon the theme which decides the fate of the theme —becomes the focal point of the entire form. It justifies the form by engendering it anew and spontaneously, even in such cases where the form is nothing more than an assumption of convention. Of assistance in this regeneration of form is an older, likewise residual, means which has revealed its latent possibilities only in this later phase. It often happens in music that remnants of the past surpass the state of technique which it currently manifests. Development recalls the procedure of variation. In music before Beethoven—with very few exceptions—the procedure of variation was considered to be among the more superficial technical procedures, a mere masking of thematic material which otherwise retained its essential identity. Now, in association with development, variation serves the establishment of universal, concretely unschematic relationships. The procedure of variation becomes dynamically charged with newly gained dynamic qualities. In variation, as developed up to this point, the identity of the thematic material remains firmly established—Schoenberg calls this material the "model." It is all "the same thing." But the meaning of this identity reveals itself as nonidentity. The thematic material is of such a nature

55

that to attempt to secure it is tantamount to varying it. It really does not in any way exist "in itself" but only in view of the possibility of the entirety.[17] Fidelity to the demands of the theme signifies a constantly intervening alteration in all its given moments. By virtue of such non-identity of identity music achieves a completely new relationship to the time within which a given work takes place. Music is no longer indifferent to time, since it no longer functions on the level of repetition in time, but rather on that of alteration. However, music does not simply surrender to time, because in its constant alteration it retains its thematic identity. The concept of the classic in music is defined by this paradoxical relationship to time. This relationship involves at the same time, however, the limitation of the principle of development. Music through its powers of evocation is able to hold the pure force of time at a distance only as long as the development is not absolute, only as long as it is something not totally subjected to music, but rather—in Kantian terms—an *a priori* musical "*Ding an sich*" (an object "in and for itself"). Therefore this intervening variation, in the most tightly constructed works of Beethoven's "classicism"—as, for example, the *Eroica* —contents itself with the sonata-development as only a "portion" of the totality, respecting therein the exposition and reprise. At a later stage, however, the empty passage of time becomes more and more threatening to music, precisely due to the increasing preponderance of the dynamic forces of subjective expression, which destroy conventional remnants. The subjective moments of expression liberate themselves from the continuum of time. They can no longer be held in check. To counter this, the variational development is extended over the entire sonata. The problematic totality of the sonata is to be reconstructed by the all-encompassing function of development. In Brahms the development—as the execution and transformation of the thematic material—took possession of the sonata as a whole. Subjectification and objectification are intertwined.

17. Cf. Theodor Adorno, "The Radio Symphony," *Radio Research 1941* (New York, 1941), *passim.*

Brahms' technique unites both tendencies, forcing the lyric intermezzo and academic structure into meaningful union. While still composing within the total framework of tonality, Brahms by and large rejects conventional formulae and fundamentals, producing a unity of the work which—out of freedom—is constantly renewed at every moment. He consequently becomes the advocate of universal economy, refuting all coincidental moments of music, and yet developing the most extreme multiplicity—the result from thematic materials the identity of which has been preserved. This indeed is his great accomplishment. There is no longer anything which is unthematic; nothing which cannot be understood as the derivative of the thematic material, no matter how latent it may have become. Schoenberg develops the tendencies of Beethoven and Brahms; in so doing he can lay claim to the heritage of classic bourgeois music—in a sense very similar to that in which dialectical materialism is related to Hegel. The epistemological energy of modern music finds its legitimacy not in that it relates back to the "great bourgeois past"—to the heroic classicism of the revolutionary period—but rather in that it neutralizes in itself romantic differentiation in terms of technique and, thereby, according to its substantiality. The subject of modern music, upon which the music itself presents a case study, is the emancipated, isolated, concrete subject of the late bourgeois phase. This concrete subjectivity and the material which is radically and thoroughly formulated by it furnishes Schoenberg with the canon of aesthetic objectivism. The depth of his work is thereby discernible. In Beethoven and still more completely in Brahms the unity of the motivic-thematic manipulation is achieved in a type of balance between subjective dynamics and traditional—"tonal"—language. The subjective approach to composition forces the conventional language to speak again, without varying it by means of its intervention as language. The alteration of language was accomplished along Romantic-Wagnerian lines at the expense of objectivity and the binding force of the music itself. This alteration has shattered motivic-thematic unity in the art song and substituted for them leitmotiv and programmatic content. Schoenberg was the first to reveal the principles of universal unity and economy of material which Wagner had discovered as new, subjective, and emancipated. His works offer definite proof that the more consequently adhered to the nominalism of musical language inaugurated by Wagner, the more perfectly this language is to be mastered by rational means. It is to be mastered by the force of tendencies dwelling within the language itself, not by means of counterbalancing tact and taste. This is most clearly recognizable in the relationship between harmony and polyphony. Polyphony is the means best suited for the organization of emancipated music. In the era of homophony, organization was perfected by chordal conventions.[18] However, once these conventions have disappeared—and, along with them, tonality—then every sound which merely serves to form a chord becomes subject to coincidence, so long as it is not validated by the course of voice leading—that is to say, by polyphonic means. Late Beethoven, Brahms, and, in a certain sense, even Wagner have paid their respects to polyphony, if only to compensate for the fact that tonality has sacrificed its constructional force and grown rigid as an empty formula. Schoenberg, finally, asserts the principle of polyphony no longer simply as a heteronomous principle of emancipated harmony, which for the moment awaits reconciliation with harmony. He reveals it as the essence of emancipated harmony itself. The inherent properties of a single chord—which in the classic-Romantic tradition, as the subjective vehicle of expression, represented the opposite pole to polyphonic objectivity—are discerned in its own polyphony. The means by which this is accomplished is no other than that extreme means of Romantic subjectifica-

18. Triadic harmonies are to be compared to the occasional expressions of language and, even more so, to money in economics. Their abstractness qualifies them to assume a mediating role at any point and their crisis is deeply ingrained in the crisis of all functions of mediation in the present phase. Berg's musical-dramatic allegory alludes to this fact. In *Wozzeck* as well as in *Lulu* the C-major triad appears in contexts otherwise detached from tonality, as often as money is mentioned. The effect is that of pointed banality and, at the same time, of obsolescence. The little C-major "coin" is denounced as counterfeit.

tion: dissonance. The more dissonant a chord, the more sounds contained—sounds effective by virtue of their differentiation from each other and in the quality of the differentiation itself —the more "polyphonic" is this chord; or, as Erwin Stein once stated, the more each individual sound assumes the character of "voice" in the simultaneity of the accord. The predominance of dissonance seems to destroy the rationally, "logical" relationships. Dissonance is nevertheless still more rational than consonance, insofar as it articulates with great clarity the relationship of the sounds occuring within it—no matter how complex—instead of achieving a dubious unity through the destruction of those partial moments present in dissonance, through "homogenous" sound. Dissonance and its related categories of melodic construction by means of "dissonant" intervals are, however, the actual vehicles of expressive character which again manifest the nature of a case study. Consequently, the subjective drive and the longing for self-proclamation without illusion, become the technical organ of the objective work. On the other hand, the reverse is true as well; it is the rationality and the unification of the material which makes the subjected material tractable to the forces of subjectivity. In any music, in which every single tone is transparently determined by the construction of the whole work, the difference between the essential and the coincidental disappears. Such music maintains in all its moments the same distance from a central point. In so doing, the conventions of form, which had once regulated the proximity and distance from this central point, lose their meaning. There is no longer any unessential transition between the essential moments, between the "themes"; consequently, there are no longer themes at all and, in the strictest sense, not even a "development." This has already been observed in works in disjunct atonal style. "In the instrumental music of the nineteenth century, one may trace everywhere a tendency to construct the form of the music out of the means afforded by the symphony. Beethoven, as one of the pioneers, knew how to rise with the help of small figures to a powerful climax which grew out of one germ-motive, the stimulus of the idea. The

59

principle of contrast, which is dominant in all art, first comes into its own when the effect of the idea of the germ-motive has ceased. The period before Beethoven knew nothing of such construction in the symphony. The themes of Mozart, for example, often contained within themselves the principle of contrast; they are compact first sections followed by freer second sections. This principle of a direct effect of contrast, and of a juxtaposition of contrasting figures in the course of the theme, is revived by Schoenberg in the works of his later style."[19] This process of thematic formation originated in the case study character of music. The moments in the course of events of music are placed disjointedly alongside one another, similarly to psychological impulses—first of all as shocks and secondly as contrasting figures. The continuum of subjective time-experience is no longer entrusted with the power of collecting musical events, functioning as a unity, and thereby imparting meaning to them. The resulting discontinuity destroys musical dynamics, to which it owes its very being. Once again music subdues time, but no longer by substituting music in its perfection for time, but by negating time through the inhibition of all musical moments by means of an omnipresent construction. Nowhere does the secret agreement between incidental and progressive music prove itself more conclusively than here. Late Schoenberg shares with jazz—and moreover with Stravinsky—the dissociation of musical time.[20] Music formulates a design of the world, which —for better or for worse—no longer recognizes history.

THE CONCEPT OF TWELVE-TONE TECHNIQUE

The sudden transition from musical dynamics to statics—the dynamics of musical structure (not simply a change in the

19. Egon Wellesz, *Arnold Schonberg*, trans. W. H. Kerridge, New York, 1969, 116.
20. Cf. Theodor W. Adorno's review of Wilder Hobson's *American Jazz Music* and Winthrop Sargeant's *Jazz Hot and Hybrid*, in *Studies in Philosophy and Social Science* (1941), 9:1, 173.

degree of intensity) which naturally continues to recognize crescendo and decrescendo—explains the uniquely determined systematic character which Schoenberg's compositional technique assumed in its later phase, as a result of the twelve-tone technique. The tool of compositional dynamics—the procedure of variation—becomes absolute. In assuming this position variation frees itself from any dependence upon dynamics. The musical phenomenon no longer presents itself involved in its own self-development. The working out of thematic materials is reduced to the level of a preliminary study by the composer. Variation, as such, no longer appears. Everything, yet nothing, is variation; the procedure of variation is again relegated to the material, preforming it before the actual composition begins. Schoenberg hints at this when he refers to the twelve-tone structure of his late works as his own private affair. Music becomes the result of processes to which the materials of music have been subjected and the perception of which in themselves is blocked by the music. Thus music becomes static.[21] Twelve-tone technique must not be misunderstood as a "technique of composition" as was, for example, the technique of Impressionism. All efforts to employ it as such result in absurdity. It can be more correctly compared to the arrangement of colors on a palette than to the actual painting of a picture. The compositional process actually begins only when the ordering of the twelve tones is established. Therefore, this ordering has made composition not simpler but, rather, more difficult. The twelve-tone technique demands that every composition be derived from such a "fundamental structure" or "row," no matter whether it is a single phrase or a work consisting of several movements. This refers to an arbitrarily designated ordering of the twelve tones available to the composer in the tempered half-tone system, as, for example, c♯-a-b-g-a flat-f♯-b flat-d-e-e

21. In his tendency to conceal the working-out in the phenomenon itself, Schoenberg carries an old impulse of all bourgeois music to its logical conclusion. Cf. Theodor W. Adorno, "Essay on Wagner," in *Versuch uber Wagner*, Berlin and Frankfurt, 1952, 107.

61

flat-c-f in the first of Schoenberg's published twelve-tone compositions.[22] Every tone of the composition is determined by this row: there is no longer a single "free" note. This does not mean, however—with the exception of a few very early cases as they appeared in the earliest days of the technique— that this particular row runs its course unaltered throughout the entire composition, revealing only minor alterations of the row and of rhythmic figures. The Austrian composer Josef Hauer developed such a procedure independently of Schoenberg.[23] The results were of the most barren meagerness.[24]. In contrast to Hauer, in a radical gesture Schoenberg absorbs the classic and, to a still larger degree, archaic techniques of variation into the twelve-tone materials. For the most part he employs the row in four ways: as the basic row; as the inversion thereof, that is to say, by substituting for each interval of the row the same interval but in the reverse direction (according to the pattern of the "fugue at the inversion"— for example the one in G major from the first volume of the *Well-Tempered Clavier*); as a "crab" in the sense of earlier contrapuntal practice, so that the row begins with the final tone and ends with the first; and as the inversion of the crab.

22. The last of the *Five Piano Pieces* [*Opus* 23]. —Trans.

23. Josef Hauer (1883–1959), Austrian composer; developed a system of composition according to "tropes" or patterns, without repeated notes and aggregating to thematic formations of twelve notes. The true development of the method, with full use of contrapuntal and canonic devices, did not appear until Schoenberg laid its foundations about 1924. —Trans.

24. It is hardly a coincidence that the mathematical techniques of music originated in Vienna, the home of logical positivism. The inclination towards numerical games is as unique to the Viennese intellect as is the game of chess in the coffee house. There are social reasons why this is so. While productive intellectual forces in Austria developed to the highest level of capitalist technique, material forces did not keep pace. For this very reason controlling calculation became the dream image of the Viennese intellectual. If he wanted to be a part of the process of material production, he had to seek a position in industry in Germany. If he stayed at home, he became a doctor or a lawyer, or else he kept to the numerical game as a phantasm of monetary power. The Viennese intellectual wants to prove this to himself as well as to others: "*bitte schön!*"

These four procedures can then, for their own part, be transposed, beginning with each of the twelve tones of the chromatic scale, so that the row offers itself in forty-eight different forms for a given composition. Furthermore, "derivations" may be formulated out of the rows by means of symmetrical arrangements of specific pitches, resulting in new, independent rows, which at the same time retain their relationship to the basic row. Berg employed this procedure extensively in *Lulu*. On the other hand, a concentration of tonal relationships can be accomplished by subdividing the row into partitions which in turn are related to each other. Finally, a composition, instead of basing itself only upon a single row, may use two or more as a point of departure, by analogy with the double and triple fugue (for example, Schoenberg's *Third String Quartet, opus* 30). The row is by no means presented only melodically, but harmonically as well, and every tone of the composition, without exception, has its positional value in the row, or in one of its derivatives. This guarantees the "indifference" of harmony and melody. In simple cases the row is distributed among vertical and horizontal structures and, as soon as the twelve tones have appeared, the row is repeated or replaced by one of its derivations; in more complicated cases the row is employed "contrapuntally"—that is to say, simultaneously in various transformations or transpositions. As a rule, in the case of Schoenberg, the compositions in a simpler style—as, for example, the *Accompaniment to a Cinematographic Scene* [*opus* 34], are in their twelve-tone structure less complicated than those composed in a more complex style. Thus the *Variations for Orchestra* [*opus* 31] is inexhaustible in its row combinations. In twelve-tone technique octave registrations are also "free"; whether the second tone of the basic set of the waltz, a, appears a minor sixth above or a major third below the first tone, c-sharp, is determined by the demands of the composition. Furthermore, the total rhythmic configuration is liberated, as a matter of principle, from the individual motive to the total structure. The rules are not arbitrarily designed.

They are configurations of the historical force present in the material. At the same time, these rules are formulae by which they adjust themselves to this force. In them consciousness undertakes to purify music of the decayed organic residue. These rules fiercely wage the battle against musical illusion. However, even the boldest manipulations of the twelve-tone system are a reflection of the technical level of material. This is true not only for the integral principle of variation of the whole, but even for the row—the microcosmic matter of twelve-tone itself. The row rationalizes what is instinctive in every conscientious composer: sensivitity towards the too-early recurrence of the same pitch, except for cases in which it is immediately repeated. The contrapuntal prohibitions against a double climax and the feeling of weakness in view of the bass voice leading in a harmonic setting—which arrive again too quickly at the same note—underscore this experience. The composer's sense of urgency increases, however, once the system of tonality has vanished, validating the preponderance of individual tones over other tones. Anyone who has worked with free atonality is familiar with the diverting force of a melodic or bass tone which appears a second time before all others have appeared. Such a tone threatens to disrupt the melodic-harmonic flow. Static twelve-tone technique actualizes the sensitivity of musical dynamics in the face of the unconscious recurrence of the same.[25] This technique makes such a sensitivity sacrosanct. The tone which recurs too early, as well as the tone which is "free" or coincidental in the face of the totality, becomes taboo.

MUSICAL DOMINATION OF NATURE

A system by which music dominates nature results. It reflects a longing present since the beginnings of the bourgeois era:

25. In his use of the phrase "recurrence of the same" Adorno undoubtedly plays upon Nietzsche's coinage and use of this concept. It is a basic formula in Nietzsche's thought on the myth. —Trans.

to "grasp" and to place all sounds into an order, and to reduce the magic essence of music to human logic. Luther calls Josquin des Pres, who died in 1521, "the master of notes who compelled the notes to bend to his will, in contrast to other composers, who bent to the will of the notes."[26] The conscious disposition over the material of nature is two-sided: the emancipation of the human being from the musical force of nature and the subjection of nature to human purposes. In Spengler's philosophy of history the principle of blatant domination breaks through at the end of the bourgeois era. This principle was inaugurated by the bourgeoisie itself. Spengler has an affinitive feeling for the terror of domination and for the relationship between its dispositional rights of both the aesthetic and political fields: "The means of the present are, and will be for many years, parliamentary—elections and the press. He may think what he pleases about them, he may respect them or despise them, but he *must command them*. Bach and Mozart *commanded* the musical means of their times. This is the hallmark of mastery in any and every field, and statecraft is no exception."[27] When Spengler prophesies about the late-stage of Western science that it would ". . . bear all the marks of the great art of counterpoint. . . ," and when he calls the ". . . *infinitesimal music of the boundless world-space . . . the deep unresting longing . . .*" of Western culture,[28] there twelve-tone technique, retrogressive in itself, infinitely static by virtue of its total independence of any historical forces, approaches that ideal more closely than Spengler or even Schoenberg ever imagined to be possible.[29]

26. Quoted by Richard Batka in *Allgemeine Geschichte der Musik*, Stuttgart, n.d., Vol. 1, 191.
27. Oswald Spengler, *Decline of the West*, trans. C. P. Atkinson, New York, 1926, Vol. 2, 477.
28. *Decline of the West*, Vol. 1, p. 428.
29. One of the most outstanding characteristics of Schoenberg's later style is that it no longer permits conclusions. Furthermore, since the dissolution of tonality, cadential formulae no longer exist in harmonic context. Now they are eliminated on the level of rhythm as well. With increasing frequency the closing of a work falls upon the weak beat of the measure. It becomes no more than a breaking-off.

At the same time, however, this technique further approaches the ideal of mastery as domination, the infinity of which resides in the fact that nothing heteronomous remains which is not absorbed into the continuum of this technique. Infinity is its pure identity. It is, however, the suppressing moment in the domination of nature, which suddenly turns against the subjective autonomy and freedom itself, in the name of which this domination found its fulfillment. The number game of twelve-tone technique and the force which it exercises borders on astrology and it is not merely a fad of those adept in the technique who have succumbed to its appeal.[30] Twelve-tone rationality approaches superstition *per se* in that it is a closed system—one which is opaque even unto itself—in which the configuration of means is directly hypostatized as goal and as law. The legitimacy of the procedure in which the technique fulfills itself is at the same time merely something imposed upon the material, by which the legitimacy is determined. This determination itself does not actually serve a purpose. Accuracy or correctness, as a mathematical hypothesis, takes the place of that element called "the idea" in traditional art. This "idea," to be sure, degenerated to an ideology in late Romantic art, to the assertion of metaphysical substantiality by means of the crude and material preoccupation of music with the eschatological—with last and final things—even if this concern

30. Music is the enemy of fate. Since earliest times the force of protest against mythology has been ascribed to it. This is equally true in the image of Orpheus and in Chinese musical theory. Only since Wagner, however, has music attempted to imitate fate. The twelve-tone composer resembles the gambler; he waits and sees what number appears and is happy if it is one offering musical meaning. Berg spoke emphatically of such joy when tonal contexts were coincidentally produced by the rows. With the augmentation of this character of gambling, twelve-tone technique once again communicates with mass music. Schoenberg's first twelve-tone dances are of a game-like nature, and during the time in which the new technique was being defined, Berg was actually offended by them. Walter Benjamin insisted upon the differentiation between illusion and play, pointing to the death of illusion. Illusion, as superfluous, is also rejected by twelve-tone technique. In play, however, that mythology, rejected as illusion, is reproduced along with the technique.

did not manifest itself concretely in the pure structure of the work of art. Schoenberg—whose music secretly contains an element of that positivism upon which the essence of his counterpart Stravinsky is based—has, as a consequence of the availability of music for case-study expression, extirpated "meaning" insofar as meaning, in the tradition of Viennese classicism, lays claim to being present purely in the context of the technical structure. Structure as such is to be correct rather than meaningful. The question which twelve-tone music asks of the composer is not how musical meaning is to be organized, but rather, how organization is to become meaningful. What Schoenberg has produced during the last twenty-five years are progressive attempts to answer this question. In the final analysis the intention is imbedded—almost with the fragmentary force of allegory—in an emptiness which extends into the innermost cells of the work of art. The dominating quality of such a late gesture, however, is a reflection of that dominating essence of the system inherent in its origins. Twelve-tone precision treats music according to the schema of fate, divesting itself of any implication of meaning present in the musical object itself, as if such meaning were a matter of illusion. Fate and the domination of nature are not to be separated. The concept of fate might well be patterned after the experience of domination, proceeding directly from the superiority of nature over man. The concrete is stronger than the abstract. Man has thereby learned to become stronger himself and to master nature, and in the process fate has reproduced itself. Fate develops inevitably in steps: inevitably, because the previous superiority of nature dictates every step of the way. Fate is domination reduced to its pure abstraction, and the measure of its destruction is equal to that of its domination; fate is disaster.

LOSS OF FREEDOM

Music, in its surrender to historical dialectics, has played its role in this process. Twelve-tone technique is truly the fate of music. It enchains music by liberating it. The subject dom-inates music through the rationality of the system, only in order to succumb to the rational system itself. In twelve-tone technique the actual process of composition—the productivity of variation—is returned to the basic realm of musical ma-terial. On the whole, the freedom of the composer undergoes the same experience. This technique is realized in its ability to manipulate the material. Thus the technique becomes the designation of the material, establishing itself as alien to the subject and finally subduing the subject by its own force. If the imagination of the composer has once made this material pliable to the constructive will, then the constructive material cripples the imagination. The New Objectivity submissive-ness, a remnant of the Expressionistic subject, remains below the level of this technique. This subject denies its own spon-taneity by projecting rational experiences, out of its altercation with historical content, upon this content itself. From the procedures which broke the blind domination of tonal material there evolves a second blind nature by means of this regulatory system. The subject subordinates itself to this blind nature, seeking protection and security, which it indicates in its despair over the impossibility 'of fulfilling music out of itself. The Wagnerian hypothesis upon the rule which one establishes for oneself and then follows reveals its fateful aspect. No rule proves itself more repressive than the self-determined one. It is precisely its subjective origin which, as soon as it establishes itself in a positive way with regard to the subject, exercising a regulatory function, results in the coincidental nature of any arbitrary assumption. The force to which man is subjected by mass-music continues to live on as a socially opposite pole in that music which totally withdraws from man. To be sure, among the rules of twelve-tone technique there is not one which does not proceed necessarily out of compositional experience—out of the progressive illumination of the natural material of music. But this experience had assumed a defensive character by virtue of its subjective sensibility that no note appear which does not fulfill its motivic function within the structure of the entire work; that no harmony be employed which is not conclusively identified at a specific spot. The truth of all these desiderata rests in their incessant confrontation with the concrete form of music to which they are applied. These desiderata indicate a factor to be approached with caution, but do not indicate how this factor is to be approached. Disaster ensues as soon as the desiderata are elevated to the level of norms and are dispensed from that confrontation. The content of the norm is identical with that of spontaneous experience. However, once this content becomes concrete, it is transformed into a self-contradiction. What once found a highly perceptive ear has been distorted to a concocted system wherein musical correctness supposedly can be gauged in the abstract. This explains the readiness of so many young musicians—particularly in America where the empirical roots of the twelve-tone technique are totally lacking—to compose in the "twelve-tone system," and it also explains the jubilation over having found a substitution for tonality, as though it were not even possible to survive aesthetically in this freedom and that it were necessary underhandedly to substitute a new compliance for tonality. The total rationality of music is its total organization. By means of organization, liberated music seeks to reconstitute the lost totality—the lost power and the responsibly binding force of Beethoven. Music succeeds in so doing only at the price of its freedom, and thereby it fails. Beethoven reproduced the meaning of tonality out of subjective freedom. The new ordering of twelve-tone technique virtually extinguishes the subject. The truly great moments in late Schoenberg have been attained despite the twelve-tone technique as well as by means of it—by means of it because music becomes capable of restraining itself coldly and inexorably, and this is the only fitting position for music following its decline; and despite twelve-tone technique because the spirit which thought it out remains sufficiently in self-control to penetrate repeatedly the structure of its technical components and to cause them to come to life, as though the spirit were ready, in the end, to destroy catastrophically the technical work of art. The failure

69

of the technical work of art, however, is not only a failure in terms of the aesthetic ideal behind such a work, but a technical failure as well. In the final analysis the radicalism with which the technical work of art destroys aesthetic illusion makes illusion responsible for the technical work of art. Twelve-tone music has a streamlined aspect. In reality, technique should serve purposes which lie beyond its own context. Where such purposes are absent, it becomes an end unto itself and substitutes a superficial "merging" for the substantial unity of the work of art. Such a displacement of gravitational center is responsible for the fact that the fetish-character of mass music has suddenly affected even advanced and "critical" production. In spite of any and all material justification, one cannot overlook the distant relationship of this movement with those theatrical productions which incessantly present mechanical works—indeed, tendentiously attempt to resemble machines without fulfilling their function, simply standing there as an allegory of the "technical age." All New Objectivity secretly threatens to fall into the hands of that which it most bitterly opposes: the ornament. The interior-design charlatans, sitting in full view in their streamlined club chairs, publicly confess what the loneliness of constructivist painting and twelve-tone music grasped as a matter of necessity. Illusion vanishes from the work of art as soon as the work begins to define itself in its battle against the ornament; in the process the position of the work of art in general gradually becomes untenable. Everything having no function in the work of art —and therefore everything transcending the law of mere existence—is withdrawn. The function of the work of art lies precisely in its transcendence beyond mere existence. Thus the height of justice becomes the height of injustice: the consummately functional work of art becomes consummately functionless. Since the work, after all, cannot be reality, the elimination of all illusory features accentuates all the more glaringly the illusory character of its existence. This process is inescapable. The dissolution of the illusory features in the work of art is demanded by its very consistency. But the process of dis-

70

solution—ordained by the meaning of the totality—makes the totality meaningless. The integral work of art is that work which is absolutely paradoxical. The common view projects Schoenberg and Stravinsky as being diametrically opposed. Stravinsky's masks and Schoenberg's constructions actually present a slight similarity. Yet it can very well be imagined that some day Stravinsky's unrelated juxtaposed chords and the succession of twelve-tone sounds—the connecting threads of which are severed, as it were, by the command of his system —will some day no longer strike the ear as so distinct from one another as they do today. It is rather that they designate different levels of consequence within the same realm. Common to both, by virtue of their command over atomized minutiae, is their claim to responsibility and necessity. The aporia of unconscious subjectivity becomes apparent to both and assumes the form of an unconfirmed norm which is nonetheless dominant. In the works of both men objectivity is represented subjectively—though, to be sure, on totally different levels of formulation and with unequal powers of realization. In the works of both, music threatens to ossify in space. In the works of both, all musical minutiae are predetermined by the totality, and there is no longer any interaction between the whole and the part. The commanding disposition over the totality banishes the spontaneity of the moment.

TWELVE-TONE MELOS AND RHYTHM

The failure of the technical work of art is evident in all dimensions of composition. Enchaining music by virtue of unchaining it—a liberation which grants it unlimited domination over natural material—is a universal process. The definition of the row in terms of the twelve tones of the chromatic scale is proof of this process. There is no apparent reason why such a basic formulation should contain all twelve tones without omission and only these twelve, without repeating one more frequently than another. As Schoenberg was developing the row technique in *Serenade* [*opus* 24], he was actually operating with

71

rows of even fewer than twelve tones. There is good reason for the fact that he later uses all twelve tones consistently. The limitation of the entire piece to the intervals presented in the row recommends that these be comprehensively deployed so that the tonal space be narrowed as little as possible, and that the greatest possible number of combinations be realized. However, that the row uses no more than twelve tones is a result of the endeavor to give to none of the tones, by means of greater frequency, any emphasis which might render it a "fundamental tone" and thereby evoke tonal relationships. Although there may be a tendency towards the number twelve, its binding force can in no way be derived from the number itself. The hypostatization of the number is partially responsible for the difficulties to which twelve-tone technique leads. Twelve-tone melody is indebted to this hypostatization for its liberation not only from the preponderance of the single pitch, but also from the false natural force of the effect of the leading tone and of an automated cadence. Free atonality had preserved chromaticism and that which is implicit therein—the moment of dissonance—by virtue of the predominance of the minor second and its derivative intervals—the major seventh and the minor ninth. These intervals no longer have any priority over the others, unless the composer wishes to design such a priority retrospectively via the construction of the row. The melodic form itself assumes a validity which it hardly possessed in traditional music, and which it had to borrow from traditional music through the circumscription of harmony. The more closely melody approaches the end of the row, the more unified it becomes—assuming that it coincides with the row, as it does in most of Schoenberg's themes. With every new pitch the choice of remaining pitches diminishes, and when the last one is reached, there is no longer any choice at all. The force exerted by this process is unmistakable. It is exerted not only by calculation, but the ear participates spontaneously in its perfection. At the same time, however, it is a crippling exertion. The compactness of melody makes it too dense. Every twelve-tone theme—though this might be something of an exaggeration—has an element of a rondo, of a refrain. It is significant that in Schoenberg's twelve-tone compositions the antiquated and non-dynamic rondo form and an emphatically harmless alla-breve figure—related in essence to the rondo form—is quoted with such pleasure, either literally or figuratively. The melody is too complete, and the terminal force present in the twelfth tone can be overcome by the energy of rhythm, but hardly by the gravitation of the intervals themselves. The recollection of the traditional rondo functions as a stop-gap for the immanent flow which has been cut off. Schoenberg pointed out that the traditional theory of composition has essentially treated only beginnings and closings but never once the logic of continuation. Twelve-tone melody exhibits a similar shortcoming. Each of its continuations reveals a moment of arbitrariness. It is only necessary to compare at the beginning of Schoenberg's *Fourth String Quartet* [*opus 37*], the continuation of the main theme through its inversion (measure six, second violin) and crab (measure ten, first violin) with the sharply delineated entrance of the first theme, to become aware of the necessity of this continuation. It intimates that the continuation has no desire within itself whatever to proceed further with the twelve-tone row once it has been concluded, and that it is driven on only by the external configurations of the row. The necessity for continuation is all the greater since the continuation itself is dependent upon the basic row which has exhausted itself as such, and for the most part, only insofar as its first appearance actually coincides with the theme constructed from it. As mere derivation, continuation disavows the inescapable claim of twelve-tone music that it is equidistant in all its moments from a central point. In the majority of the existing twelve-tone compositions the continuation sets itself apart from the thesis of the basic row just as fundamentally as consequence of inspiration in late Romantic music sets itself apart from inspiration itself.[31] Meanwhile, the

31. The reason for this is the incompatibility of the concrete melody of song, towards which Romanticism strove as the seal of subjectivity, with the "classic" idea of integral form, as found in Beethoven. Brahms

pressure of the row engages in far worse disaster. Mechanical patterns befall the melos.[32] The true quality of a melody is

who foreshadows Schoenberg in all questions of construction which go beyond mere chordal material, offers a blatant example of what will later develop into the discrepancy between row exposition and continuation, namely, the break between the theme and the next consequence to be developed from it. A striking example is the beginning of the *String Quartet in F-major*. The concept of "*Einfall*" was defined in order to distinguish the theme as a matter of organic essence from its creative transformation in the work as a matter of abstract, hypothetical ordering. "*Einfall*" is not just a psychological category, a matter of "inspiration," but a moment in the dialectical process manifest in musical form. This moment marks the irreducibly subjective element in this process and, by means of its inexplicability, further designates this aspect of music as its essence, while the "working out" represents the process of objectivity and the process of becoming, which, to be sure, contains this subjective moment as a driving force. On the other hand, as essence, "*Einfall*" is also possessed of objectivity. Since Romanticism music has been based upon conflict and synthesis of these moments. It appears, however, that they resist unification just as strongly as the bourgeois concept of the individual stands in perennial contrast to the totality of the social process. The inconsistency between the theme and what happens to it reflects such social irreconcilability. Nevertheless, composition must keep a firm grasp on the "*Einfall*" if the subjective moment is not to be lost. This would make the composition a parable of fatal integration. If Beethoven's genius was able to manage without this "*Einfall*," which in his day had been developed to an incomparable degree by the masters of early Romanticism, Schoenberg, on the other hand, adhered to the "*Einfall*"—to thematic plasticity—in cases where this had long lost the qualities which would permit its unification with formal structure. In such instances Schoenberg undertook formal construction from the perspective of this worn-out contradiction instead of striving for tasteful reconciliation. (The German word "*Einfall*" with which Adorno here works is impossible to translate; it involves the idea of a decisive inspirational occurrence bordering upon revelation which becomes the basis for a work of art. —Trans.)

32. In no way is this to be attributed to a decline of individual compositional power, but rather to the weighty handicap of the new technique. When Schoenberg in his mature years worked with earlier, random material—for example in the *Second Chamber Symphony* [*opus* 38]—the spontaneity and the melodic character resulting in these works are in no way inferior to the most inspired pieces of his youth. On the other hand, however, an obstinate insistence in many twelve-tone compositions—the magnificent first movement of the *Third Quartet* is actually a formulation of this principle—is by no means an external decoration upon Schoenberg's musical essence. Such obstinacy is rather the mirror image of undeterred musical consequence: just as Schoenberg

always to be measured by whether or not it succeeds in transforming the spatial relations of intervals into time. Twelve-tone technique destroys this relationship at its very roots. Time and interval diverge. All intervallic relationships are absolutely determined by the basic row and its derivatives. No new material is introduced into the progression of intervals, and the omnipresence of the row makes it unfit in itself for the construction of temporal relationships, for this type of relationship is based upon differentiations and not simply upon identity. Consequently, however, the melodic relationship is relegated to a non-melodic means—autonomous rhythmics. The row is non-specific by its very omnipresence, and the melodic specification falls to established and characteristic rhythmic figures. Definite and constantly recurring rhythmic configurations assume the role of themes.[33] Since the melodic space of these rhythmic themes is determined in each case by the row, and since they must content themselves at all costs with those tones at their disposal, they take on an obstinate rigidity. In the final analysis, melos is the victim of thematic rhythm. The thematic and motivic rhythms return, totally unconcerned about the content of the row. In Schoenberg's rondos it is evident how he brings

---

could not eliminate from his mind the neurotic weakness of anxiety through his will towards emancipation. Particularly the tonal repetitions, which in twelve-tone music often have something obstinate and stubborn about them, appear in an elemental form much earlier in Schoenberg—though, to be sure, usually with a particular intent of characterization, as in "Vulgarity" in *Pierrot Lunaire* (song no. 16 of the cycle). Even the first movement of the *Serenade* [*opus* 24], which is not twelve-tone, shows signs of this same coloration, which is at times reminiscent of the musical idiom of Beckmesser in Wagner's *Meistersinger*. Frequently, Schoenberg's music speaks as though it were trying to justify itself at any price before an imaginary court of justice. Berg consciously avoided such gesticulations; in so doing, of course, he in turn contributed against his will to the smoothing and leveling.

33. Berg was pressured in this direction by the technique of variation even before Schoenberg discovered twelve-tone technique. The tavern scene in the third act of *Wozzeck* is the first example of a melodically abstract rhythm which becomes thematic. This serves a drastic theatrical intention. In *Lulu* this has developed into a large form, which Berg calls monoritmica.

75

into the thematic rhythmic pattern, with every statement of the rondo theme, a different melodic form of the row, thereby accomplishing variation-like effects. The concrete event in music, however, is a matter of rhythm, and of rhythm alone. Whether emphatic and overly precise rhythm includes this or that interval is a matter of little concern. At best, the most that can be understood is that the intervals now stand in relationship to the thematic rhythmic patterns in a way different from their first presentation; melodic modification, however, no longer gives the barest indication of meaning. Consequently, the specifically melodic factor in rhythm is devaluated. In traditional music a minimal intervallic deviation not only had a decisive effect upon the expression of a specific spot, but even upon the formalistic meaning of an entire movement. Twelve-tone music, by contrast, manifests total crudity and impoverishment. At one time, all musical meaning was unequivocally determined by intervals: the not-yet, the now, and the afterward; the promise, the fulfillment, and the omission; moderation and squander; and the permanence of form and transcendence of musical subjectivity. Now intervals have become nothing more than building stones, and all experiences which are encompassed in their differentiation are seemingly lost. To be sure, means of emancipation from step-progression by seconds and the uniformity of musical consonances have been found; to be sure, the tritone, the major seventh, and those intervals which extend beyond the octave have gained equal rights, but at the price of being placed upon the same level as the older intervals. In traditional music it might well be difficult for the ear—restricted by tonality—to understand extreme intervals as melodic moments. Today there are no longer any such difficulties—those which have been overcome merely share the monotonous fate of others which have long since been accepted. Melodic detail, however, sinks to the level of mere consequence of the total construction, without having the slightest power over it. This detail is the image of that type of technical progress with which the world abounds. And even that which might still thrive melodically—Schoenberg's creative power again and again renders the impossible possible —is destroyed in the recurrence of a once-heard melody. In such recurrence, the melody relentlessly presents the same rhythmic patterns with different intervals—intervals frequently lacking not only any connection to the fundamental intervals, but even to the rhythm itself. A certain type of melodic approximation in this process is highly suspect. The outlines of the old melody are preserved; an interval of like proportions is made to correspond to a large or small leap at the analogous rhythmic spot, but only in categories of the large or small interval. Whether the characteristic leap is a major ninth or a tenth is of no concern whatever. In Schoenberg's middle period such questions were totally irrelevant, because all repetition was excluded. The restoration of repetition, however, goes hand in hand with the lack of regard for what is repeated. To be sure, even from this perspective twelve-tone technique is by no means the rationalistic source of disaster, but is much more the executor of a tendency stemming from Romanticism. The manner in which Wagner interpolates motives—which are so defined that they contradict the procedure of variation—is a precursor of Schoenberg's compositional procedure. It leads to the decisive technical antagonism of music since Beethoven: the antagonism between traditional tonality—which is in constant need of reconfirmation—and the substantiality of the individual. If Beethoven developed a musical essence out of nothingness in order to be able to redefine it as a process of becoming, then Schoenberg in his later works destroys it as something completed.

DIFFERENTIATION AND COARSENING

If musical nominalism—the elimination of all recurrent formulae —is carried through to its logical conclusion, then differentiation itself crumbles. In traditional music the here-and-now of the composition in all its elements is continually in conflict with the tonal scheme. The specification was limited by a matter of convention which was, to a large degree, external. The specific was liberated by the solution to the problem: right down to the restorative counter-attack of Stravinsky, musical progress was a matter of progressive differentiation. Deviations from the prescribed scheme of traditional music, however, exerted a meaningful and decisive influence. The more binding the scheme, the more refined does the possibility of modification become. That which gave the initial impulse could no longer be detected in emancipated music. Consequently, traditional music permitted far subtler nuances than when every musical event exists of and for itself. Refinement, in the final analysis, is paid for with coarsening. This is to be traced to the tangible phenomena of harmonic perception. When in tonal music the Neapolitan sixth chord in C major with d-flat in the soprano part is followed by the dominant seventh chord with b in the soprano part, then, by virtue of the force of the harmonic schema, the step from d-flat to b—which is called a "diminished third"—by abstract measurement represents the interval of a second: it is understood as a third, particularly in relation to the omitted C which lies between them equidistantly. Such an immediate perception of an "objective" interval of a second is impossible beyond tonality: it assumes a coordinate system, and defines itself by its differentiation from this system. That which is valid up to the point where acoustic phenomena become almost material attains true validity only when applied to higher, musical organization. In the subordinate theme of Weber's *Der Freischütz* overture —taken from Agatha's aria—the interval which leads to the climactic g in the third measure is a third. In the coda of the total composition this interval is expanded first to a fifth and finally to a sixth, and in relation to the initial tone of the theme—upon which an understanding of this interval must be based—the sixth actually forms a ninth. By extending beyond the range of the octave this ninth attains an expression of superabundant jubilation. This is possible only through the comprehension of the interval of the octave as a unit of measure —a concept inherent in tonality. If this range is exceeded, its significance is thereby enhanced to an extreme, suspending the balance of the system. In twelve-tone music, however, the octave has lost the organizing force which it once had by virtue of its identity with the root of the triad. A quantitative, but not a qualitative difference allegedly prevails between those intervals which are larger or smaller than the octave. Therefore, the effects of melodic variation are no longer possible, as in the example from Weber and in numerous other cases, and above all in Beethoven and Brahms. Expression itself, which necessitated this process, is threatened because it can no longer be conceptualized after the disappearance of all ingrained relationships and all qualitative distinctions between intervals, sounds, and form fragments. What once attained its meaning from the difference in the schema was devalued and levelled in the collective dimensions of composition—not only in melody and harmony. Within the traditional schema of modulation, form had above all a normative system according to which it could be developed through the most minute alterations—in the case of Mozart, at times, even through a single indication of transposition. If larger forms are to be articulated today, it will be necessary to resort to far cruder means: drastic contrasts of register, dynamics, compositional procedures, and timbre. And finally, the formulation of themes becomes dependent upon ever more striking qualities. The foolish reproach of the layman against the monotony of modern music contains, in contrast to the wisdom of the expert, a grain of truth: whenever the composer scorns brutal contrasts such as those between high and low, loud and soft, to any great degree, the result is a certain monotony. Differentiation is only of any force when it distinguishes itself from that which is already implicitly established, while the more highly differentiated means themselves—simply placed alongside one another —come to resemble each other and become indistinguishable. It was one of the greatest accomplishments of Mozart and Beethoven that they were able to avoid simple contrasts and achieve multiplicity in the most subtle transitions, often only by means of modulation. This achievement was already endangered during the Romantic era. The themes of Romanticism —gauged according to the ideal of integral form in Viennese classicism—were for the most part all too lacking in a direct relationship, thus threatening to dissolve the form into episodes. Precisely in the most serious and responsible music of today, the means of most minute contrast have been lost. Even Schoenberg can salvage this means only as an illusion, to the extent that once again he provides the themes with that course of progression—for example, in the first movement of the *Fourth Quartet*—which in Viennese Classicism was called main theme, transition, and second-theme group. Schoenberg does not permit the evaluation of these characteristics—which still fluctuated in Beethoven and Mozart—according to the total harmonic construction. Thus these characteristics assume an impotent and noncommittal cast, as if they were the death masks of the profiles of instrumental music, perfected by Viennese Classicism. If the composer foregoes such rescue attempts as are indicated by the force present in the material, he becomes dependent upon exaggerated contrasts inherent in the raw material of sound. The nuance results in the act of violence —symptomatic perhaps for the historical changes inevitably taking place today in all categories of individuation. If tonality were to be restored today or replaced by other systems of relationships, such as that formulated by Scriabin—in order to regain with this footing the lost wealth of differentiation—then such maneuvers would be frustrated by the same isolated subjectivity which it would hope to conquer. Tonality would be, as with Stravinsky, nothing but a game with tonality, and schemata, such as Scriabin's, are limited to chordal types of a dominant function, to such an extent that they are totally without effective contrast. Twelve-tone technique, as the mere preformation of material, is wisely on guard against manifestation as a system of relationships; although such reservation excludes the concept of nuance. In so doing, however, it thereby carries out the sentence passed upon it by liberated, unchained subjectivity.

80

HARMONY

There are objections against the arbitrariness of twelve-tone music which are of greater immediacy: for example, that in spite of all rationality, it relegates harmonics—and, to be sure, not just the individual chord—as well as the succession of sounds to coincidence; that it regulates succession abstractly, but is totally unaware of any forceful harmonic necessity. The objection is too superficial, however. For nowhere does the order of twelve-tone technique proceed more rigorously out of historical tendencies of the material than in harmony, and if schemata of twelve-tone harmony were to be worked out, the beginning of Wagner's Prelude to *Tristan* could probably be viewed more simply in this perspective than in the function of a-minor. The law of vertical dimension of twelve-tone music might well be called the law of complementary harmony. Precursory forms of complementary harmony are found less in Schoenberg's middle period than in Debussy and Stravinsky. They are to be found above all where there is no harmonic progress in terms of the rules of thorough bass, but rather static levels of sound which permit only a selection from the twelve tones and then suddenly change into new levels of sound which provide for the remaining tones. In complementary harmony every sound is complexly constructed: it contains its individual pitches as independent and differing moments of the whole, without causing their differences to disappear, as would be the case in triadic harmony. Within the range of the twelve tones the experimenting ear cannot withdraw from the chroma of experience, whereby each complex sound fundamentally demands for completion those pitches of the chromatic scale which are not present in the sound itself. This demand can be fulfilled simultaneously or successively. Tension and release in twelve-tone music are always to be understood in the perspective of the individual sounds of the twelve tones viewed comprehensively. The single complex chord becomes capable of attracting musical

81

forces unto itself which formerly had meaning only within entire melodic lines or harmonic structures. At the same time, complementary harmony, through sudden transformation, is able to cause these chords to radiate in such a manner that all their latent power is revealed. The change from one harmonic stratum, defined by chord, to the next complementary stratum, produces harmonic effects of depth—a type of perspective that traditional music has often sought, and attempted, for example, in Bruckner; but hardly ever achieved.[34] If one is to take Lulu's twelve-tone death chord as the integral totality of complementary harmony, then Berg's allegorical genius proves itself within a historical perspective which makes the brain reel: just as Lulu in the world of total illusion longs for nothing but her murderer and finally finds him in that sound, so does all harmony of unrequited happiness long for its fatal chord as the cipher of fulfillment—twelve-tone music is not to be separated from dissonance. Fatal: because all dynamics come to a standstill within it without finding release. The law of complementary harmony already implies the end of the musical experience of time, as this was heralded in the dissociation of time according to Expressionistic extremes. This law proclaims, even more vehemently than any other symptoms, that condition characterized by a loss of historical perspective in music. Today it is still undecided whether this condition is dictated by the horrible fixation of society within the present structures of domination or whether it points to the end of antagonistic society, which finds its historical basic precisely in the pre-production of its antagonisms. However, this law of complementary harmony is actually valid only in harmonic terms. It is paralyzed by the indifference between the horizontal and the vertical. The supplementary pitches are the desiderata of "voice-leading" within the complexly constructed chords, which are delineated according to their

34. The early works of twelve-tone technique preserve the principle of complementary harmony most clearly. Harmonically conceived passages—such as the coda of the first movement (measures 200ff.) of Schoenberg's *Woodwind Quintet* or the conclusion of the first chorus of *opus* 27 (measures 24f.)—show this tendency, as it were, in didactic clarity.

voices, just as all harmonic problems—even in tonal music—proceed from the demands of voice-leading. On the other hand, all contrapuntal problems result from demands of harmony. Thereby the actual harmonic principle is simultaneously destroyed at its very foundation. In twelve-tone polyphony the chords actually constructed hardly ever stand in a complementary relationship. They are rather "results" of voice-leading. Due to the influence of Kurth's book on linear counterpoint, there was a widely accepted opinion that harmony in modern music is a matter of indifference and that the vertical, in contrast to polyphony, is no longer of any value.[35] This assumption was dilettante: the unification of various musical dimensions does not simply imply the disappearance of one of them. Thus in twelve-tone music it can gradually be seen that even this unification threatens to devalue each single material dimension and thereby, to be sure, the harmonic dimension as well. Passages constructed according to complementary harmony are the exception—as a matter of necessity. For the compositional principle, whereby the row "collapses" into simultaneous sounds, demands that each individual tone identify itself as a segment of the row horizontally as well as vertically. This makes the pure complementary relationship between the vertical sounds a matter of rare good fortune. The actual identity of dimensions is not as much guaranteed by the twelve-tone schema as hypothesized by it. This identity remains hidden in every moment of the composition, and the arithmetical "correctness" is no proof whatever whether identity has been achieved—whether, that is, the "result" is harmonically justified by the tendency of the sounds. The majority of all twelve-tone compositions simulates that coincidence simply by numerical accuracy. To a large extent harmonies allegedly result from that which takes place in the voices, and result in absolutely no specifically harmonic meaning. It is necessary only to compare arbitrary chords or even harmonic progressions from twelve-tone compositions (a crass example of harmonic break-down is found in the slow move-

35. Ernst Kurth, *Grundlagen des linearen Kontrapunkts: Bachs melodische Polyphonie*, Bern, 1917. —Trans.

83

ments of Schoenberg's *Fourth Quartet,* measures 636–637), with a truly harmonically perceptible spot of free atonality (*Erwartung,* measures 196ff., for example) to become aware of the coincidental nature of twelve-tone harmony, the way things simply fit together. The "basic drives of the sounds" are suppressed. It is not only that the pitches are numbered at the outset; the primacy of the lines permits the sounds to atrophy. The suspicion cannot be totally avoided that the entire principle of the indifference between melody and harmony is an illusion as soon as it is seriously tested. The origin of such rows in themes— their melodic meaning—resists harmonic reinterpretation, which can be done only at the price of their specifically harmonic relationship. While complementary harmony, in its pure form, binds the successive chords more closely to one another than ever before, these chords become alienated from each other through the totality of twelve-tone technique. This is the reason that Schoenberg, in one of his most magnificent twelve-tone compositions thus far—the first movement of the *Third Quartet*— employs the technique of ostinato which he had carefully excluded up to that time. This technique is intended to create a relationship which no longer exists from sound to sound, nor hardly in the individual sound. The elimination of the tendency of the leading tone, which continued into free atonality as a tonal residue, leads to a loss of relationship and to a rigidity of the successive moment—which not only penetrates Wagner's "Treibhaus," the third of the *Wesendonck Songs,* as a frigid corrective—but also contains the threat of specifically musical meaninglessness, of the liquidation of continuity. This meaninglessness is not to be confused with the difficulty of understanding that which has not yet been subsumed. It should rather be ascribed to the new subsumption. Twelve-tone technique replaces the drive-like character of the leading tone—the "transition" viewed as "mediation"—with conscious construction. The atomization of sounds is the terribly high price paid for such construction. The freeplay of forces in traditional music, in which the totality is produced from sound to sound without preformation, is replaced by the "deployment" of sounds alienated from one another. There is no longer any anarchistic desire for union on the parts of sound, there is only the absence of any monadic relationship between them and a calculating domination over them all. It is at this point that coincidence truly results. If a totality had previously found its realization behind the scene of single events, it now becomes fully conscious. The individual events, however, —the concrete relationships—are sacrificed to this totality. Even the sounds as such are defeated by coincidence. The sharpest dissonance, the minor second, which was used with the greatest caution in free atonality, is now employed as though it meant nothing at all—in choruses, often, to the disadvantage of the movement.[36] On the other hand, open sounds of the fourth and fifth—and their urgent need for mere existence is quite clear—push their way more and more into the foreground: dull chords, lacking in tension, hardly different from those loved by the neo-classicists, Hindemith above all. Neither the frictions nor the open sounds are sufficient for the compositional purpose: both demonstrate the sacrifice of the music to the row. Tonality suggestions crop up everywhere; apart from the will of the composer—alert criticism could eliminate this phenomenon in free atonality. They are understood not according to twelve-tone, but according to tonality. There is nothing within the force of composition which allows the historical implications of the material to be forgotten. Free atonality spread dissonance universally throughout music with its taboo triadic harmony. Consequently, only dissonance prevailed. The restorative moment of twelve-tone technique is perhaps nowhere more strongly manifested than in the tentative re-admission of the consonance. It might be argued that the very universality of dissonance has suspended the concept itself, that dissonance was possible only in tension leading to consonance, and now dissonance is simply transformed into a multi-toned complex as soon as it is no longer contrasted with consonance. This, however, simplifies the circumstances, for in a sound consisting of several tones, dissonance is suspended only in the sense of an

36. Cf. Schoenberg, *opus* 27, no. 1, measure 11, soprano and alto, and the corresponding measure 15, tenor and bass.

Hegelian double meaning. The new sounds are not the harmless successors of old consonances, that is, new syntheses arising from old antitheses. Rather, they are distinguished from these by the fact that their unity is totally articulated within the sounds themselves; by the fact that the individual pitches of the accords are brought together in the chord-figure, but within the chord-figure each of them is differentiated from all the others. Thus they continue to "dissonate"; to be sure, not in contrast to the consonances which have been eliminated, but within themselves. In so doing, however, they retain the historical picture of dissonance. Dissonances arose as the expression of tension, contradiction, and pain. They take on fixed contours and became "material." They are no longer the media of subjective expression. For this reason, however, they by no means deny their origin. They become characters of objective protest. It is the mysterious good fortune of these sounds that they have come to master the suffering which they once proclaimed, precisely by means of their transformation into material—and, thus, by the retention of suffering. Their negativity is true to utopia: it includes within itself the concealed consonance. Hence the passionate sensitivity of modern music against the resemblance of sound to consonance. Schoenberg's jest, that the "Moon Spot" in *Pierrot* was written according to the rules of strict counterpoint—he permitted consonances only in passing and at that only in unaccented beats—, reflects almost directly the fundamental experience. Twelve-tone technique evades this experience. Dissonances become mere quantities, without quality, without differentiation, and therefore suitable for use wherever the schema demands. These are what Hindemith designated with the horrifying expression "raw material" in his *Craft of Composition*.[37] Thus the material regresses to mere nature, back to physical tone relationships, and it is precisely this regression which subjects twelve-tone music to the force of nature. Not only does the attracting force of the material disappear; its resisting force vanishes as well. The sounds incline only as slightly

37. Paul Hindemith, *Craft of Musical Composition*, trans. Arthur Mendel, New York, 1942.

towards the totality represented by the world as they incline towards each other. In the ordering of the sounds, that musical spatial depth disappears which complementary harmony seemed at the very point of revealing. They have become so totally indifferent that the consonantal environment no longer disturbs them. The triads at the end of *Pierrot* made dissonances aware, with a shock, of their unattained goal, and their hesitant contradiction resembled that green horizon faintly dawning in the east. In the theme of the slow movement of the *Third Quartet,* consonances and dissonances stand disinterestedly beside each other. They no longer even sound out-of-tune.

INSTRUMENTAL TIMBRE

The decline of harmony is not to be attributed to the lack of harmonic consciousness, but to the gravitational force of twelve-tone technique. This may be deduced from that dimension which was ever closely related to the harmonic dimension and which exhibits as well now as in Wagner's time the same symptoms as harmony: the decline of instrumental timbre. The total construction of music permits constructive instrumentation to a surprising degree. The Bach arrangements by Schoenberg and Webern, which convert the most minute motivic relationships of the composition into relationships of color—thus realizing them for the first time—would not have been possible without twelve-tone technique.[38] The postulate of clarity in instrumentation, as stated by Mahler, becomes capable of realization only thanks to the achievements of twelve-tone; that is, without reliance upon doublings and sustained horn pedals. Just as the dissonant chord absorbs each sound contained within it and thereby retains its differentiated character, the instrumental timbre now makes possible the realization of the balance of all voices in relationship to one another and, at the same time, the retention of the

38. Schoenberg orchestrated two choral preludes and one organ prelude and fugue by Bach; Webern transcribed the six-part fugue of Bach's *Musical Offering* for orchestra. —Trans.

87

contour of each. Twelve-tone technique absorbs the entire wealth of compositional structure and transforms it into the structure of color. Such a technique, however, never places itself despotically before the composition, as had the technique of late Romanticism. It becomes the obedient servant of the composition. Yet in the final analysis, this restricts technique to the point that it contributes less and less to the comp on, and the dimension of timbre—as the produ tive dimension of composition, as it had been defined by the Expressionistic phase —disappears. In the compositional theory of Schoenberg's middle period, *Klangfarbe* melody had its definitive function. It was thereby intended that the changes of color were to become a compositional event in themselves and to determine the course of the composition. Instrumental timbre appeared as the yet-untouched level which the compositional imagination now approached. The third of the *Five Pieces for Orchestra* [*opus* 16], as well as the music for the light-storm of *Die glückliche Hand,* are examples of such a tendency. Twelve-tone music has achieved nothing of this sort and it is to be seriously doubted whether it ever could. This orchestral piece, after all, with its "changing chord," presumes a substantiality of harmonic event which is negated by twelve-tone techniques. The latter technique regards as outrageous the concept of a color fantasy as contributing to the composition from its own resources. The timidity before doublings of color, excluding everything which does not narrowly depict the composition, confirms not only a hatred towards the evil realm of late Romantic coloration but also the ascetic will to strangle everything which penetrates the defined space of twelve-tone composition. This simply no longer allows colors merely to "occur." Timbre, no matter how differentiated, approaches again that which it once was, before subjectivity took hold of it: a simple matter of registration. Once again the early day of twelve-tone technique is exemplary: Schoenberg's *Woodwind Quintet* [*opus* 26] resembles an organ score, and the fact that it is scored precisely for woodwinds might well be related to the concept of organ registration. It is no longer specifically scored like Schoenberg's earlier chamber music. In the *Third Quartet,* furthermore, all the colors which Schoenberg extracted from the strings in the first two quartets are sacrificed. The quartet's timbre becomes solely a function of compositional scoring, intensified to the utmost, particularly in the exploitation of wide ranges. Later, beginning with the *Variations for Orchestra* [*opus* 31], Schoenberg began to revise his position and allowed coloration a wider range. The priority of clarinets in particular, which had demonstrated this particular registrational tendency most decisively, is no longer asserted. But the coloristic palette of the late works shows traces of concession. This is founded less in the structure of twelve-tone itself than in the "hypothesis"—that is, in the concern for clarity. This interest itself is, however, of a double nature. It excludes all the musical levels in which, according to the requirement of the compositions, it is not clarity which is demanded, but rather the opposite. This interest unconditionally takes possession of the New Matter-of-Fact postulate, namely, "impartiality towards material." Twelve-tone technique itself, in its relationship to the row, approaches the material fetish character of such a postulate. While the colors of Schoenberg's orchestration in his later works illuminate the compositional structure—just as the sharply defined photograph illuminates its objects—these colors themselves are prevented from "composing." The result is a dazzlingly hermetic sound with unrelentingly changing lights and shadows, bearing a certain similarity to a highly complicated machine, which remains firmly fixed in one place in spite of the dizzying movement of all its parts. The sound becomes as clear and polished as positivistic logic. It reveals the moderation concealed by the severity of twelve-tone technique. The colorfulness and the secure balance of this timbre anxiously denies the chaotic outburst from which twelve-tone fought its way forth; and offers an image of a new order, contradicted by all the genuine impulses of modern music, yet which, by force, it has to prepare. The case study of the dream formulates itself as the hypothesis of a case study.

TWELVE-TONE COUNTERPOINT

Counterpoint is unquestionably the actual beneficiary of twelve-tone technique. It has attained primacy in composition. Contrapuntal logic is superior to harmonic-homophonic logic because it has always liberated the vertical from the blind force of harmonic convention. It never really lost respect for the latter. However, it indicated to all simultaneous musical events the basis of their meaning in the uniqueness of the composition, by defining the other voices completely in terms of their relationship to the melodic leading voice. By virtue of the universality of the relationships between rows, twelve-tone technique is contrapuntal in origin—for in it all simultaneous sounds are equally independent, because all are integral components of the row—and its precedence over the arbitrariness of traditional "free composition" is also contrapuntal in nature. Since the establishment of homophonic music in the thorough-bass era, the most searching experiences of composers have indicated the inadequacy of homophony for the cohesive constitution of concrete forms. Bach's recourse to older polyphonic forms (for example, the most structurally advanced fugues, such as that in c-sharp minor from the first volume of the *Well-Tempered Clavier,* the six-voiced fugue from the *Musical Offering,* and the later ones from the *Art of the Fugue,* come to resemble the ricercare) and the polyphonic sections in Beethoven's last works are the greatest monuments to such experience. For the first time, however, since the waning of the Middle Ages—and in an incomparably more rational disposition over the means—twelve-tone technique has crystallized into a genuine polyphonic style. This has swept aside not only the external symbiosis of polyphonic schemata and harmonic logic, but also the impurity which results from the contrasting effects of harmonic and polyphonic forces, tolerated by free atonality in disparate co-existence. In the polyphonic advances of Bach and Beethoven there was an earnest seeking after a balance between thorough-bass chorale and true polyphony. This was to represent a balance between subjective

90

dynamics and concrete objectivity. Schoenberg proved his abilities as an exponent of the most mysterious tendencies in music in that he no longer imposed polyphonic organization upon the material but rather derived it from the material itself. This alone placed him among the great composers. It is not just that he worked out a purity of style equal to those stylistic models once unconsciously prescribed in composition. The legitimacy of a stylistic ideal had, after all, become the subject of grave doubt. But, in the present day, something bordering on counterpoint again exists. Twelve-tone technique has taught the composer to design several independent voices simultaneously and to organize them into a unity without reliance upon harmonic logic. It has definitely put an end to the disorganized and irresponsible use of counterpoint by many composers of the era following the First World War and to neo-German ornamental counterpoint as well. The new polyphony is "actual." In Bach, tonality answers the question how is polyphony possible as harmonic polyphony? For this reason, Bach is actually what Goethe considered him to be: a harmonist. With Schoenberg, tonality has renounced the validity of that answer. Schoenberg directs his question regarding the polyphonic tendency of the chord to the ruins of tonality. Thus he is a counterpuntist. The unperfected aspect of Schoenberg's work with the twelve-tone technique is harmony; exactly the reverse is the case in Bach, where the harmonic scheme of independent voices marks the boundary which was transcended only by the speculation of the *Art of the Fugue*. In twelve-tone technique, however, harmonic aporia effects counterpoint as well. Composers have always found it a gigantic feat to overcome contrapuntal problems, as accomplished in the notorious "arts" of the Netherlands school and the later intermittent return to them. And rightly so, for contrapuntal acrobatics always proclaim the victory of the composition over the sluggishness of harmony. The most abstract designs of crab and mirror canons are schemata which enable music to outwit the purely formal elements of harmony by using common chords to disguise the total predetermination of the course of the voices. The importance of this accomplishment diminishes, however, when the harmonic stumbling block is removed; when the formation of "correct" chords is no longer the basic test of counterpoint. The only valid standard is now the row. It is responsible for the closest possible interrelationship of the voices, the relationship of contrast. Twelve-tone technique literally realizes the desideratum to place note against note. The heteronomy of the harmonic principle regarding the horizontal was withdrawn from this wish. Now that the external pressure of prescribed harmonies is broken, the unity of voices can be developed strictly out of their differentiation, without the connecting link of "relationship." In truth, therefore, twelve-tone counterpoint actually resists imitation and canonic treatment. The use of such means by Schoenberg, in his twelve-tone phase, has the effect of over-definition, of tautology. They organize anew a continuity already pre-established by twelve-tone technique. The principle which forced the rudimentary foundation for all imitation and canonic treatment is developed to its extreme. This explains the heterogeneous and alien element in the techniques developed out of traditional contrapuntal practice. Webern knew quite well why he attempted in his late works to derive a canonic principle out of the structure of the row itself, while Schoenberg apparently demonstrated anew a sensitivity towards all such ingenuity. The old connecting means of polyphony functioned only in the harmonic realm of tonality. These means strive to connect the voices with one another with the result that one line reflects another and that the force of conscious harmonic progression—in itself alien to the voices—is neutralized beyond the actual level of the voices. Imitation and canon presume a consciousness of progression or at least a tonal "modus" with which the twelve-tone row—operating behind the scenes—is not to be confused. For only the apparent tonal or modal order, in the hierarchy of which every step assumes its position once and for all, allows repetition. Such repetition is possible only in an articulated system of relationships. Such a system defines the events within a pervasive generality above and beyond the unrepeatable individual case. The relationships of this system—steps and cadences—imply at the outset a continuation, a certain dynamic force. Repetition within such relationships does not, however, automatically imply arrival at a standstill. At the same time, they relieve the work from the responsibility for continuation. Twelve-tone technique is unsuited for this responsibility. In no way is it a substitute for tonality. A row, valid only for one specific work, does not possess that pervasive generality which is assigned a function to the repeated event by means of a schema. The event does not fulfill this function solely through the repetition of its individual features. Furthermore, the interval succession of the row does not influence repetition to the extent that the repeated element undergoes any significant change of meaning. If, by the same token, twelve-tone counterpoint—particularly in Schoenberg's earlier twelve-tone pieces and throughout Webern's works—makes use of imitation and canon in the broadest measure; this usage contradicts, rather, the specific ideal of the twelve-tone procedure. The return to archaic-polyphonic means is, to be sure, no mere display of bravado on the part of these combinatorial elements. Such inherently tonal procedures were excavated precisely because twelve-tone technique as such does not accomplish what is expected of it and is achieved, in the final analysis, only through recourse to the tonal tradition. The loss of the specifically harmonic as a structural element evidently becomes suspiciously perceptible, that the pure twelve-tone counterpoint as such is no longer sufficient as organizational compensation. Indeed, it is not even sufficient contrapuntally. The principle of contrast collapses. To be sure, one voice is never freely added to another, but it appears, rather, only as a "derivation" of an earlier voice. Events in one voice are left totally void in the other voice, which thus becomes the negation of the first. The voices are thereby brought into a reflective relationship, in which the tendency latently dwells, to suspend the independence of the voices from each other and thereby to suspend the entire counterpoint to an extreme completely in the total complex of the twelve sounds. Imitation might well appear as a counteractive force. Its discipline wishes to preserve that freedom endangered by its own consequence—pure contrast. The voices, brought into total

93

accord with each other, are identical as products of the row; they are, however, totally alien to each other and, in their accordance, actually hostile to each other. They have nothing in common with each other, yet everything in common with a third force. Imitation is unconsciously evoked in order to reconcile the alienation of the all-obedient voices.

FUNCTION OF COUNTERPOINT

In light of all this, the most recent polyphonic achievements reveal a questionable aspect. The unity of the twelve-tone voices, inherent in the row, contradicts probably the deepest impulse of more recent counterpoint. What schools of composition call good counterpoint—smooth, independently meaningful voices which, however, do not aggressively obscure the leading voice; harmonically flawless progression; the skilled joining of heterogeneous lines by means of a cleverly contrived added part—gives only the barest glimmer of the idea by misusing it as a formula. The concern of counterpoint was not the successful and supplemental addition of voices, but the organization of music in such a way that is had an absolute need of each voice contained within it—that each voice and each note fulfill a precise function within the texture. The structure must be so conceived that the relationship of the voices to each other determines the progression of the entire composition and, ultimately, its form. It is the skillful manipulation of such relationships, and not the fact that he wrote such good counterpoint in the traditional sense of the word, that constitutes Bach's true superiority in the realm of polyphonic music. It is not the linear aspect as such, but rather its integration into the totality of harmony and form. From this perspective, *The Art of the Fugue* knows no equal. This concern is renewed in Schoenberg's emancipation of counterpoint. However, it is questionable as to whether twelve-tone technique—to the extent that it carries the contrapuntal idea of integration to an absolute—does not actually abolish the principle of counterpoint by means of its own

94

totality. In twelve-tone technique there is no longer anything which is differentiated from the texture of the voice, neither a prescribed *cantus firmus* nor specific harmonic weight. In Western music, counterpoint itself could be understood as the expression of the differentiation of dimensions. Counterpoint strives to overcome this differentiation by giving it formation. In the case of total organization, counterpoint in the narrower sense would have to disappear and be replaced by the simple addition of one independent voice to another. It has its right to existence only in the overcoming of something not absorbed within it, and thus resisting it, to which it is "added." Where there is no longer any such priority of a musical essence *per se* by which counterpoint can be measured, it becomes a futile struggle and vanishes in an undifferentiated continuum. Counterpoint shares to a degree the lot of an all-contrasting rhythmic structure which forms the basis of every part of a given measure in differentiated voices which supplement each other. Precisely therein, rhythmic monotony results. Webern's most recent works are consequent in that they designate the liquidation of counterpoint. The contrasting tones are grouped into monody.

FORM

The inappropriateness of all repetition in the structure of twelve-tone music, as this becomes evident in the intimacy of imitative detail, defines the major difficulty of twelve-tone form—form in the specific sense of the musical theory of form, not in the comprehensive aesthetic sense. The desire in Expressionism to reconstruct the large form above and beyond the criticism of aesthetic totality is as questionable as is the "integration" of a society in which the economic basis of alienation continues to exist unchanged while the justification of antagonisms is denied by suppression.[39] An element of this paradox is inherent in in-

39. The assertion made in a programmatic essay written by Erwin Stein in 1924 and continually repeated since then remains unproven: namely, that in free atonality larger orchestral forms are not possible. *Die glückliche Hand* is perhaps closer to such a possibility than any

tegral twelve-tone technique. Only that, in the technique, the antagonisms cannot be so convincingly shaken off as in a society which is not only reflected by modern art but at the same time cognitively perceived and thus criticized by it. This is perhaps true in all cultural phenomena which assume a completely new gravity in an age of total planning of substructure. The phenomena achieve this by denouncing such planning. The reconstruction of the large form by twelve-tone technique is not merely questionable as an ideal, but also in terms of its own success. It has often been noted—and particularly by musical reactionaries —that the forms of twelve-tone composition resort eclectically to the "pre-critical" large forms of instrumental music. Sonata form, rondo, and variation appear either literally or figuratively: for example—as in the finale of the *Third Quartet*—with great effort to harmlessly and naïvely forget not only the genetic implications of meaning in this music but, further, glaringly to distinguish itself from the complicatedness of each individual rhythmic and contrapuntal factor by the simplicity of its total disposition. The inconsistency is readily apparent, and Schoenberg's most recent instrumental works are, above all, attempts to overcome it.[40] It has not been seen with equal clarity, how-

other work of Schoenberg. Incompetence in larger forms had to be interpreted more narrowly than in the Philistine sense that the desire to achieve this was there; but the anarchistic material would not permit it, and therefore new principles of form had to be worked out. Twelve-tone technique does not simply prepare the material in such a way that it is finally suited for use in larger forms. It cuts through the Gordon knot. Everything which happens within the technique bears traces of an act of violence. Its invention is a *coup de main* of the type glorified by *Die glückliche Hand*. This could never have been achieved without violence, because the manner of composition—polarized to extremes—turned its critical weapon towards the idea of formal totality. Twelve-tone technique attempts to evade this responsible criticism.

40. The extremely significant *String Trio* [*opus* 45] goes furthest in this direction. In its dispersion—the construction of extreme sound—the *Trio* evokes the Expressionist phase, which it approaches in character as well, without neglecting any structural element. The insistence with which Schoenberg pursues the questions which he has once designed can only be compared with Beethoven. Schoenberg does this without ever contenting himself with one particular "style," such as, for example, the one represented in the earlier twelve-tone works.

ever, how that inconsistency necessarily has its origin in the very nature of twelve-tone music itself. Twelve-tone music has not produced any type of large form unique to itself; this is by no means coincidental, but rather the immanent revenge of a critical phase now forgotten. The construction of truly free forms, delineating the unique nature of a composition, is prevented by a lack of freedom ordained by the row technique—by the continual reappearance of the same elements. Consequently, the need to make rhythmic figures thematic and to provide them, in each case, with a content of various row figures might well result in a compulsion towards symmetry. Whenever such rhythmic formulae appear, they herald corresponding formal components, and it is these correspondences which evoke the spirits of precritical forms. And, to be sure, they are evoked only as spirits. For twelve-tone symmetries are without essence, without depth. The result is that these symmetries are produced by force, but are no longer of any purpose. Traditional symmetries are based upon symmetrical harmonic relationships which they either articulate or create. The function of the classic sonata-reprise is inseparable from the schema of modulations in the exposition and from the harmonic digressions of the development: it serves to confirm the major key area which was only "stated" in the exposition—a consequence of that process inaugurated in the exposition. In any case, it can be imagined that the sonata form retains something of this function in free atonality—after the elimination of the modulatory basis of correspondence—when, that is, the driving force of the sounds develops such powerful tendencies and counter-tendencies that the idea of the "goal" is affirmed, and that the arrival of the reprise in symmetry with the exposition does justice to the concept present in this function. This is totally out of the question in twelve-tone technique. On the other hand, such a technique—in light of its incessant permutations—is incapable of justifying any architecturally static symmetry of pre-classic structural forms. Obviously, the demand for symmetry in twelve-tone technique is as urgently voiced as it is inexorably denied. The problem of symmetry might perhaps best be solved in compositions such as the first movement of the

Third Quartet. Such pieces renounce not only the illusion of the dynamics of form but even the barest trace of such form, whose symmetry indicates harmonic relationships. These pieces operate instead with very rigid, pure, and, to a certain extent, geometric symmetries. These symmetries require no binding system of relationships of the form and serve not the idea of a goal, but rather the idea of unique balance. It is compositions of this type which most closely fulfill the objective possibility of twelve-tone technique. This quartet movement keeps the idea of development totally at a distance through its stubborn eighth-note figure, and, at the same time, produces a musical cubism through the juxtaposition of symmetrical but nonetheless distorted surfaces. The contrived row-complexes of Stravinsky merely simulate this. Schoenberg, however, does not stop at this point. If this total production in all its transitions and extremes is to be understood as a dialectical process between expression and construction, then this process has not been resolved in the New Matter-of-Factness.[41] The actual experiences of Schoenberg's generation had to shatter his ideal of the objective work of art—even its positivistically disenchanted form; likewise, the blatant emptiness of the integral composition could not escape his musical ingenuity. The most recent works pose the question: How is structure to become expression without plaintively giving in to lamenting subjectivity? The slow movement of the *Fourth Quartet*—its disposition, the double succession of disrupted recitative, its song-like refrain in closed form—resembles *Entrückung,* Schoenberg's first composition, which contains no key signature and opens the Expressionistic phase.[42] This movement, along with the march finale of the *Violin Concerto [opus 36],* is of almost exaggeratedly clear expression. No one can resist the force of such expression. It leaves the private subject far behind. But even this power is not able to close the gap—and how

41. Cf. T. W. Adorno, "Der dialektische Komponist," *Arnold Schönberg, Festschrift,* Vienna, 1934.
42. *"Entrückung"* is the text for the soprano solo in the fourth movement of the *Second Quartet [opus 10].* The poem is by Stefan George. —Trans.

should it be? These works are magnificent in their failure. It is not the composer who fails in the work; history, rather, denies the work in itself. Schoenberg's more recent compositions are dynamic. Twelve-tone technique contradicts dynamics. The technique neutralizes the dynamic impulse of the work from one sound to another; thus it does not permit any dynamic impulse of the totality to emerge. It devaluates the concepts of melos and theme, and thus eliminates the actually dynamic-formal categories of motivic development, thematic development and transition. If Schoenberg in his earlier period perceived that no "consequences" were to be drawn, in a traditional sense, from the main theme of the *First Chamber Symphony* [*opus* 9], then the prohibition contained in that perception remains valid for twelve-tone technique. Every tone is as valid a row tone as any other. But how is transition to be accomplished without detaching the dynamic categories from compositional substance? Each form of the row is "the" row with the same validity as the previous row; no row is more and no row is less. Even the form upon which the set-complex is based is a matter of coincidence. In this regard, of what possible relevance is "development"? Every tone is thematically exhausted through its relationship in the row and no tone is "free"; the various segments might produce combinations to a greater or lesser degree, but no segment can ally itself more closely with the material than does the first statement of the row. The totality of thematic working-out in the pre-formation of material makes a tautology of all visible thematic working-out in the composition itself. For this reason, development, in the final analysis, becomes illusory in the sense of strict construction; and Berg had reason to omit development in the introductory allegretto of the *Lyric Suite,* his first twelve-tone work.[43]

43. After this, Berg did not write another composition in sonata form. Those parts of *Lulu* relating to Dr. Schoen seem to be an exception. But the "exposition" and its repetition in the composition are so far removed from development and reprise that they can hardly be understood along with these as a matter of actual form: the name "sonata" refers rather to the symphonic sound of this music, to its dramatically cohesive activity, and to the spirit of the sonata in its inner musical composition, rather than to its external architecture.

It is only in the most recent works of Schoenberg that such questions of form become critical. In these compositions the disposition of surface elements is much further removed from traditional forms than it is in the earlier twelve-tone compositions. The *Woodwind Quintet* was, to be sure, a sonata, but one which was "constructed to death,"[44] which in a certain respect simply flowed into the twelve-tone technique and in which the "dynamic" formal elements are actually markings of the past. In the early days of twelve-tone technique—most openly in the works entitled "Suite" but to a degree also in the rondo of the *Third Quartet*—Schoenberg engaged in pensive games with traditional forms. The subtle detachment with which they were employed kept their demands—along with the demands of the material itself—in a state of artificial suspension. In his more recent works solutions of this type are prevented by the gravity of expression. For this reason, traditional forms are no longer evoked literally but, on the other hand, the dynamic demands of traditional forms are considered with all possible seriousness. The sonata is no longer "constructed to death," but is actually to be reconstructed without any claim to its schematic exterior. This impulse is motivated not only by stylistic considerations, but further by extremely important compositional bases. Up to this very day, official musical theory has made no attempt to offer a precise definition of the concept of continuation as a formal category. This has been ignored, although the large forms of traditional music—and those of Schoenberg as well—cannot possibly be understood without the contrast of "event" and continuation. A decisive quality regarding the value of compositions and even regarding entire formal types is dependent upon the depth, extent, and penetration of the continuational figures. Music proves its greatness in that moment of its progression in which a piece really becomes a composition—in which it is animated by its own inner weight, transcending the here-and-now of thematic definition from which it proceeds. In older music mere rhythmic movement assumed the task of that moment,

44. Cf. T. W. Adorno, "Schönbergs Blaserquintett," *Pult und Takt-stock* (1928), 5:45ff.

depriving it naturally of its joy as well. For Beethoven, in turn, this idea was the source of energy from which he sketched every measure of his compositions. In Romanticism, however, the question of this moment is faced squarely for the first time, and, consequently, at the same time it becomes unanswerable. It is the true superiority of the "great forms" that only they are able to create this moment in which music is crystallized in the composition. This moment is alien to song as a matter of principle, and therefore, according to the most rigid standard, songs are inferior. They remain caught up in that instant of creative revelation, while great music constitutes itself precisely through the liquidation of this moment of inspiration. This liquidation is accomplished in retrospect, however, and only through the animation of continuation. Schoenberg's ability in this direction is his great strength. Transitional themes, consequently—such as the one beginning at measure 25 in the *Fourth Quartet,* and transitions such as the melody of the second violin (measures 42ff.)—do not simply cast heterogenous glances through conventional formal masks. They manifest actually a will to continuation and transition. Indeed, twelve-tone technique itself, which in fact prevents dynamic form, induces a dynamic element. The impossibility of remaining in every moment at the same distance from the central point is now revealed by twelve-tone technique as the possibility of formal articulation. On the one hand, the technique contradicts the categories of theme, continuation, and mediation; on the other hand, it summons them to its aid. The contrast inherent in all twelve-tone music according to precise row expositions divides it into primary and secondary events, as was the case in traditional music. Their formation strongly resembles the relationship between theme and "working-out." At this point, however, a conflict arises. For it is obvious that the specific "figures" of the resurrected themes—which are so drastically differentiated from the pattern of earlier twelve-tone music in which they were almost indifferent—and their intentions in general, did not simply arise autonomously out of twelve-tone technique. These figures have, rather, been imposed upon the technique by the relentless will of the composer, as though with

101

highly critical insight. There is a deep relationship between the necessary exterior of this connection and the totality of the technique itself. The inexorable hermetic quality of the technique renders difficult the definition of an exact boundary. In the definitive diversity of the technique, everything which transcends it—everything which is constitutively new—is despised, and this is precisely the impassioned goal of Schoenberg's most recent works. Twelve-tone technique proceeded from the genuinely dialectical principle of variation. Its postulate was that insistence in the face of the recurrence of the same and the continual analysis of this factor in composition—all motivic working-out is analysis, for it atomizes its material—result in that which is unremittingly new. By means of variation, that which has been defined in terms of music—the "theme" in the strictest sense of the word—transcends itself. Twelve-tone technique elevated the principle of variation to the level of a totality, of an absolute; in so doing it eliminated the principle in one final transformation of the concept. As soon as this principle becomes total, the possibility of musical transcendence disappears; as soon as everything is absorbed to the same degree into variation, not one theme remains behind, and all musical phenomena define themselves without distinction as permutations of the row. In the totality of transmutation there is no longer anything which undergoes change. Everything remains as it was and twelve-tone technique approaches the paraphrase, the form of variation prior to Beethoven, which engaged in circumscription without any particular goal. This brings the tendency of the total history of European music since Haydn—and it was very closely interrelated to German philosophy of that time—to a standstill. Composition *per se,* however, is also brought to a standstill. The concept of the theme itself has been absorbed by the concept of the row; there is little hope for the rescue of the theme from the domination of the row. It is the objective program of twelve-tone composition to construct that which is new—all contours within the form—as a second level upon the row-like pre-formation of that material. But it is precisely here that it fails: the introduction of the new into twelve-tone construction is coincidental, arbitrary, and, where it counts most, decisively antagonistic. Twelve-tone technique does not permit a choice. Either it retains its formal immanence or new elements are meaninglessly superimposed upon it. Thus the dynamic features of the most recent works are by no means new. They are present in the very roots of music; they have been derived from abstractions out of pre-twelve-tone music, and, for the most part, from music which is older than free atonality. These features in the first movement of the *Fourth Quartet* recall the *First Chamber Symphony*. Of the "themes" in Schoenberg's final tonal works—and these were the last in which it is possible to speak of themes at all—only the gesture of those themes has survived, and even then, they have been detached from the material prerequisites of the gesture. This gesticulatory force is allegorically charged with the realization of that which is denied them within the tonal structure: stress and direction, the very image of eruption. This is indicated in the designations "schwungvoll," "energico," "impetuoso," and "amabile." The paradox of this compositional procedure is that in it the image of the new becomes surrepetitiously tantamount to the achievement of old effects with new means. A further result is that the rigid apparatus of twelve-tone technique strives for that which once arose more freely and at the same time with still greater necessity out of the decay of tonality.[45] The new will to expression finds its reward through the expression of the old. The figures sound like quotations and the desig-

---

45. This may aid in understanding why Schoenberg completed the *Second Chamber Symphony*—in the very late style of decaying tonality —thirty years after it was begun. In the second movement of the *Symphony* he utilizes the experiences of twelve-tone technique, just as the most recent twelve-tone compositions resort to figures of that earlier epoch. The *Second Chamber Symphony* belongs to the series of "dynamic" works of late Schoenberg. It seeks to overcome the externality of twelve-tone dynamics through recourse to a "dynamic" material— the material of chromatic tonality "modulated to death"—and to gain control over this through total employment of constructive counterpoint. An analysis of the *Symphony*, which sounded so old-fashioned to critics oriented to the style of Sibelius, would necessarily offer the most precise insight into the state of most progressive production. This obvious recourse recognizes the aporia with all possible Schoenbergian consequence.

nations employed for them reveal a secret pride that this is again possible. Nonetheless, whether this really is still possible remains open to question. The quarrel between alienated objectivity and limited subjectivity remains unsettled, and the very irreconcilability thereof reveals the fundamental truth involved. It is conceivable, however, that the inappropriateness of expression, the break between it and the construction, can still be defined as an inadequacy of the latter, as the irrationality of rational technique. For the very sake of its blind unique law this technique denies itself expression, transposing it into the sphere of past memories, thinking to find there the dream-image of the future. Faced by the gravity of this dream the constructivism of twelve-tone technique reveals its constructive weakness. This constructivism is capable only of ordering the moments, without revealing their essence in any penetrating way to each other. The newness prevented thereby is, however, nothing but the reconciliation of those moments which twelve-tone constructivism has failed to achieve.

THE COMPOSERS

The spontaneity of progressive composers is handicapped along with spontaneity of the composition itself. Composers find themselves faced by tasks which are as impossible as is the dilemma of a writer who is called upon to create a unique vocabulary and syntax for every sentence he writes.[46] The triumph of subjectivity over heteronomous tradition—the freedom of allowing every musical moment to stand for itself without imputation —is achieved at a very high cost. The difficulties involved in the necessary creation of the new idiom are prohibitive. In the first place, the composer is now burdened with a task which was previously accomplished for him, to a large degree, by the inter-

46. "The theater director who must himself create everything from the ground up, has even first to beget the actors. A visitor is not admitted; the director has important theatrical work in hand. What is it? He is changing the diapers of a future actor." Franz Kafka, *Diaries: 1914–1923*, trans. Martin Greenberg, New York, 1949, 222.

subjective language of music. Furthermore, he must—if his ear is sufficiently sharp—perceive in this self-created language those characteristics of the external and the mechanical which mark the termination of the musical domination of nature. In the act of composing he must admit to himself the fragility and irresponsibility of this idiom. His problems do not end with the creation of a new language upon which he can rely, and with the contradiction which from the very beginning marks a language of absolute alienation. Above and beyond all this, the composer has untiringly to perform acrobatic stunts to minimize the pretentiousness of a self-made language to a point where it becomes bearable. The better he speaks this language, the more obvious does this pretentiousness become. He is responsible for the delicate balance of the irreconcilable postulates of his procedure. Anything not included in these efforts is lost. Rattling idiotic systems lie in wait to devour any composer who might innocently pretend that this self-invented language had already found confirmation. The fact that the subject does not grow with them makes these difficulties all the more disastrous. The atomization of fragmentary musical moments, presumed by the self-made language, closely parallels the state of the subject. It is broken by total impotence. "That is what struck us as so new and unprecedented in Schoenberg's music: this fabulously sure course through a chaos of new sounds."[47] An anxiety is engraved in this exuberant metaphor which is expressed verbally in the title of one of Ravel's piano works which belongs to this same tradition:[48] "*Une barque sur l'océan.*" The surface possibilities would be horrifying even to a person who might be equal to them on the objective plane, even if the communication-branch of official musical life were to permit him to make use of this possibility in material terms and did not drown it out with the familiar outcry against the return of the same. No artist is able to overcome, through his own individual resources, the contradiction of enchained art within an enchained society. The most which he can

47. Karl Linke, *Arnold Schönberg,* Munich, 1912, 102.
48. "A Boat Upon the Sea," the third piece of the five which compose Ravel's *Miroirs.* —Trans.

hope to accomplish is the contradiction of such a society through emancipated art, and even in this attempt he might well be the victim of despair. It would be inexplicable if all the intentionless raw materials and levels—laid open by the energy of modern music in such a way that they seem to wait unclaimed for someone to reach out for them—were not to succeed in luring the curious. It would be even stranger if those in whom a natural affinity might have been expected—who would have surrendered themselves to the joys of the unrealized, had not most of them been so fundamentally gripped thereby that they had to forbid themselves such happiness from the very outset—had not been attracted either. For this reason, they are only resentful of this possibility. They close themselves off, not because they do not understand the new, but precisely because they do understand it. The new exposes, not only the deception of their culture, but also their incapacity for truth, which is by no means their only private incompetence. They are too weak to venture into the realm of the forbidden. If they were to follow the seductive powers of the waves of untamed sounds, these waves would simply close over them. The folkloristic neo-classic and collectivistic schools all have but one desire: to remain in the haven of safety and herald the pre-formed, which they have been able to comprehend and realize, as the new. Their taboos are directed against musical eruption, and their modernity is nothing but an attempt to tame the eruptive forces and, wherever possible, to resettle them into the pre-individualistic era of music, which as a stylish dress fits the present social phase so well. Proud of the discovery that what is interesting has begun to become boring, they convince themselves and others that boredom is interesting for this very reason. Their involvement, however, is so superficial that they do not even notice the repressive tendencies inherent in musical emancipation itself. They seem timely and applicable precisely because they are not at all interested in emancipating themselves. But even the inaugurators of modern music, who draw the necessary consequences, are struck down by that same type of helplessness and show symptoms of the same collective infection which they are forced to recognize in the hostile reaction against them. The number of compositions which can be seriously taken into consideration has diminished, and even what is composed nonetheless bears marks not only of indescribable effort but often enough also of listless fatigue. The quantitative decrease has obvious social bases. Demand has ceased to exist. Even in his Expressionistic phase Schoenberg, who composed frantically, was a radical opponent of the market. This fatigue is a result of the difficulties involved in composition itself; these stand in a pre-established relationship to the external difficulties. In the five years before World War I, Schoenberg traversed the total realm of musical material—from totally constructed tonality via free atonality, down to the beginnings of row technique. The twenty years which he has devoted to twelve-tone technique hardly bear comparison with these five. These two decades have been more concerned with disposition over the material than with works, the compositions themselves, the totality of which is to be reconstructed by the new technique. On the other hand, there certainly has been no lack of works envisaged on a grand scale. Just as the twelve-tone technique seems to instruct the composer, so there is a uniquely didactic moment present in twelve-tone works. Many of them—such as the *Woodwind Quintet* and the *Variations for Orchestra*—resemble patterns. The preponderance of doctrinal teaching offers magnificent proof of the manner in which the developmental tendency of the technique leaves the traditional concept of the work far behind. Productive interest is distracted from the individual composition and concentrated, rather, upon the typical possibilities of composition. This results in the transformation of the composition into nothing more than a mere means for the manufacture of the pure language of music. The concrete works are forced to pay the price for such a transformation. Clairaudient composers— not only the practical ones—can no longer completely trust their autonomy: it collapses. This can be clearly perceived even in works such as Berg's concert aria *Der Wein* and his violin concerto. The simplicity of the violin concerto by no means signifies a clarification of Berg's style. This simplicity is rather born of the necessity of haste and the need for understanding. The transparency is much too comfortable and the simple substance is over-determined by its exterior twelve-tone procedure. Dissonance as a symbol of disaster and consonance as a symbol of reconciliation are neo-romantic relics. There is no opposing voice which is strong enough to close the stylistic gap between the quotation from a chorale by Bach and all else. Only Berg's extra-musical power was capable of transcending this abyss. Prior to Berg it was only in the works of Mahler that the proclamation had touched upon the shaken work; in like manner, Berg transformed the insufficiency of the work into the expression of boundless melancholy. *Lulu,* however, is another matter. In this opera, Berg's mastery reaches its highest development in composition for the stage. The music is as rich as it is economical. In its lyric tone—particularly in the role of Alwa and in the finale—the opera is superior to any other work by Berg. Schumann's "Der Dichter spricht" (the final piece from the *Kinderszenen*) is transformed into the extravagant gesture of the entire opera. The orchestra sounds so seductive and colorful that absolutely any accomplishment of Impressionism or neo-Romanticism pales by comparison. If the instrumentation of the third act were ever completed, the dramatic effect would be beyond description. The work employs twelve-tone technique. But what was true of all of Berg's works since the *Lyric Suite* is doubly true of *Lulu:* every effort in the composition is aimed at rendering the technique unnoticeable. Precisely those finest parts of *Lulu* are obviously conceived in dominant functions and chromatic steps. The essential rigidity of twelve-tone construction has been softened to the point that it is unrecognizable. Also, the only factor which makes the row procedure perceptible is that Berg's insatiety, at times, did not have at its disposal the infinite supply of notes that it needed. The rigidity of the system now finds validity only in such limitations; otherwise it has been totally overcome. This is accomplished, however, rather by adjusting the twelve-tone technique to traditional music than by eliminating its antagonistic moments. Along with other means of a totally different origin—such as the leitmotiv and the compilation of large orchestral forms—the twelve-tone in *Lulu* aids in securing the consistency of the structure. It is employed largely as a protective measure and it is seldom followed through according to its own unique demands. It would be possible to conceive of *Lulu,* in its totality, completely without regard for the virtuoso twelve-tone manipulations involved, and still not require any decisive change in it. The triumph of the composer lies in his ability—along with many other qualities—to do one thing: to overlook the fact that the critical impulse of twelve-tone technique in truth precludes all the other factors which he has employed. It is Berg's weakness that he can renounce nothing at his disposal, whereas the power of all new music lies precisely in renunciation. The unreconciled in Schoenberg's later works (not simply in terms of intransigence, but also in terms of the antagonisms inherent in the music) is superior to the premature reconciliation in Berg's works, as Schoenberg's inhuman coldness is superior to Berg's magnanimous warmth. The intense inner beauty of Berg's late works is indebted for its success less to the hermetic surface structure of his works than to the basic impossibility which they embody: the hopelessness of the undertaking which is indicated in the surface of the work; and to the morbidly mournful sacrifice of the future to the past. It is for this reason that his works are opera and to be understood only through the formal laws of opera. Webern's position lies at the opposite pole. Berg attempted to break the spell of twelve-tone technique by bewitching it. Webern's desire is to force the technique to speak. All of his late works underscore his effort to lure, from the alienated, rigidified material of the rows, that ultimate secret which the alienated subject is no longer able to impart to the rows. His earliest twelve-tone compositions —particularly the *String Trio*—are undoubtedly to this very day the most successful experiment aimed at transforming the external rules of the row into concrete musical structure without displacing the row in any traditionalistic fashion or offering retrogressive substitution for it. This did not suffice for Webern. In practical composition Schoenberg actually regards the twelve-tone technique as the mere pre-formation of material. He "composes" with twelve-tone rows; he moves them about; from his

109

lofty vantage point he moves them about as if nothing had changed. Yet there are constant conflicts between the nature of the material and the compositional procedure superimposed upon it. Webern's recent compositions demonstrate a critical consciousness of these conflicts. It is his goal to conceal the demand made by the rows with the demand of the work itself. He strives to bridge the abyss between the autonomous composition and the material which demands treatment according to the rules. In actuality, however, this signifies renunciation at the point of greatest engagement: composing subjects the very existence of the composition itself to question. Schoenberg does violence to the row. He composes twelve-tone music as though there were no such thing as the twelve-tone technique. Webern realizes twelve-tone technique and thus no longer composes: silence is the rest of his mastery. In contrast to these two approaches the irreconcilability of contradictions has become a music in which twelve-tone technique unavoidably becomes enmeshed. In his late works Webern shies away from the formulation of new musical forms. It is anticipated that such forms would be external to the pure essence of the row. His final works are schemata of the rows translated into notes. He expresses his concern for the indifference between the row and the work through his particularly artistic selection of rows. The rows are structured as if they were already a composition—for example, in such a way that one row is divided into four groups of triads whose interrelationship, in turn, is definable in terms of the basic presentation of the row, its inversion, its crab, and the crab of inversion. An unparalleled density of relationships is guaranteed by this process. The ripest fruits of canonic imitation fall, as it were, of their own will into the lap of the composition, without the necessity of further efforts in this direction. At an early point, however, Berg had found fault with this technique because it questioned the possibility of large forms—a possibility which is a matter of programmatic demand. Through the subdivision of the row all relationships are forced into such a narrow framework that the possibilities of development are immediately exhausted. Most of Webern's twelve-tone compositions are restricted to the size of Expressionistic miniatures, and it might well be asked why such excessive organization was needed in cases where there was hardly anything to organize. The function of twelve-tone technique in Webern is hardly less problematic than in Berg. Thematic working-out extends itself over such minimal units that it virtually cancels itself out. The mere interval—functioning as a motivic unit—is so utterly without individual character that it no longer accomplishes the synthesis expected of it. There is a threat of disintegration into disparate tones, without this disintegration as such becoming articulate. Through a peculiarly infantile musical belief in nature, the material is vested with the power of determining musical meaning from within itself. It is precisely here that the astrological confusion reveals itself: the interval relationships, according to which the twelve-tones are ordered, are dismally honored as cosmic formulae. The self-determined law of the row truthfully becomes a fetish at that point when the conductor relies upon it as the source of meaning. The fetishism of the row is striking in Webern's *Piano Variations* [*opus* 27], and in the *String Quartet* [*opus* 28]. These compositions offer nothing more than uniform symmetrical presentations of the miraculous row; they even approach the parody of an intermezzo by Brahms as, for example, in such compositions as the first movement of Webern's *Piano Variations*. The mysteries of the row are hardly in a position to offer any consolation about half-wittedness in music: grandiose intentions—such as the blending of genuine polyphony and genuine sonata form—are to no avail even if they are successfully constructed, as long as they limit themselves to the mathematical relations of the material and are not borne out in the musical form itself. Performance, if it is to give even a shadow of meaning to the monotonous groupings of tones, must go far beyond rigid notation—and particularly notation of rhythm. The barrenness of this rhythmic notation is dictated by a belief in the natural force of the row; that is to say, it is a property of the thing itself. This excessive demand upon performance passes judgment on the music. In Webern, however, the fetishism of the row is not merely a matter of simple sectarianism—rather the dialectical

111

force is still at work. It was the most binding critical experience, which drove this significant composer towards the cult of pure proportions. He perceived the derivative, exhausted, insignificant essence of all those subjective elements which music would wish to fulfill here-and-now—that is, the insufficiency of the subject itself. One aspect of the situation is that twelve-tone music, by force of its mere correctness, resists subjective expression. The other important aspect is that the right of the subject itself to expression declines, evoking a condition which no longer exists. In its present phase the subject seems so fixed, that what it might be able to say is already said. Horror has cast its spell upon the subject and it is no longer able to say anything which might be worth saying. In the face of reality it is so impotent that the very claim to expression already touches upon vanity and, of course, there is hardly another claim to which this subject might still raise. It has become so isolated that it can hardly seriously hope for anyone who may still understand it. In Webern the musical subject grows silent and abdicates; it delivers itself up to the material which, however, can guarantee it—at most—an echo of its loss of speech. Its melancholy disappearance is the purest expression of its terrified and distrustful withdrawal before the traces of consumer goods which threaten it. However, it remains incapable of expressing the inexpressible as truth. What might be possible is not possible.

AVANT-GARDE AND THEORY

The possibility of music itself has become uncertain. It is not threatened, as the reactionaries claim, by its decadent, individual-istic, and asocial character. It is actually too little threatened by these factors. That certain freedom, into which it undertook to transform its anarchistic condition, was converted in the very hands of this music into a metaphor of the world against which it raises its protest. It flees forward into order. However, success is denied it. It is obedient to the historical tendency of its own material—blindly and without contradiction. To a certain degree

112

it places itself at the disposal of the world-spirit which is, after all, not world-logic. In so doing its innocence accelerates the catastrophe, in the preparation of which the history of all art is engaged. Music affirms the historical process and therefore history would like to reap the benefits thereof. Music is doomed, but this historical process in turn restores it to a position of justice and paradoxically grants it a chance to continue its existence. The decline of art in a false order is itself false. Its truth is the denial of the submissiveness into which its central principle —that of consistent correctness—has driven it. As long as an art, which is constituted according to the categories of mass production, contributes to this ideology, and as long as artistic technique is a technique of repression, that other, functionless art has its own function. This art alone—in its most recent and most consequent works—designs a picture of total repression but, by no means, the ideology thereof. By presenting the unreconciled picture of reality, it becomes incommensurable with this reality. In this way it expresses opposition to the injustice of the just verdict. The technical procedures of composition, which objectively make music into a picture of repressive society, are more advanced than the procedures of mass production which march beyond modern music in the fashion of the times, willfully serving repressive society. The institution of mass production and the product fashioned by it are modern in their adoption of industrial schemata—particularly in terms of distribution and expansion. However, such modernity has no effect upon the products. These products manipulate their listeners with the most modern methods of psycho-technology and propaganda. They are propagandistically constructed, but precisely for this reason they are bound to the immutability of a tradition which has become fragile and ossified. The innocent endeavors of twelve-tone composers are totally ignorant of the streamlined statistical procedures in use in the offices of the hit-tune industry. For this very reason, however, the rationality of the structures, as produced by their old-fashioned effort, is all the more advanced. The contradiction between productive forces and the conditions of production is manifested further as a contradiction

113

between the conditions of production and the products themselves. The antagonisms have increased to such an extent
that progress and reaction have lost their unequivocal meaning.
Painting a picture or composing a quartet today might well be
far behind the division of labor and experiments with technical
arrangement in the film; but the objective technical structure
of the picture and the quartet secures the possibility of the film,
a possibility which today is frustrated only by the social convention behind film production. The "rationality" of the structure—
no matter how chimerically it might be isolated within itself and
how problematic it might be in its isolation—is nonetheless of a
higher level than the rationalization of the film industry. The film
operates with objects which it assumes but which actually have
long since ceased to be. In its treatment of those objects, it only
intermittently penetrates beneath their surface; otherwise it resigns itself to superficial portrayal. Picasso, however, constructs
his objects out of the reflexes which photography helplessly
showers upon the objects depicted. Picasso's objects challenge
those reflexes. Exactly the same is true of twelve-tone compositions. Whatever escapes from the impending ice age might well
survive in their labyrinth. Forty years ago in his Expressionistic
period Schoenberg wrote: "The work of art is a labyrinth, at
every point of which the initiate knows the entrance and the
exit, without the help of guidelines. The more finely meshed
and interlaced the veins, the more certainly will he soar above
every path towards his goal. False paths, if there were such in a
work of art, would set him back on his proper course, and every
digressing turn of the road would still place him in relationship
to the direction of the essential content."[49] However, if the
labyrinth is to be made a comfortable place of residence, the
guidelines followed by the enemy would have to be removed.
For the "initiate" realizes "that the labyrinth is marked" and he
unmasks "the clarity offered by sign-posts as nothing more than
an expedient of peasant-like cleverness. The only thing which this
shopkeeper-arithmetic has in common with the work of art are

49. Arnold Schönberg, "Aphorismen," in *Die Musik* (Berlin, 1909–
1910), 9:4, 159ff.

the formulae. . . . The initiate turns quietly away and beholds how this matter reveals itself before a higher justice: it is a mathematical error."[50] If mathematical errors are not alien to twelve-tone composition, it becomes the subject of a higher justice in those factors where it is most correct. In other words, the survival of music can be anticipated only if it is able to emancipate itself from twelve-tone technique as well. This is not to be accomplished, however, by a retrogression to the irrationality which preceded twelve-tone technique and which would have to be denied today by the postulates of strict composition— by those who have been responsible for the formulation of twelve-tone technique. It is rather to be achieved through the amalgamation and absorption of twelve-tone technique by free composition—by the assumption of its rules through the spontaneity of the critical ear. Only from twelve-tone technique alone can music learn to remain responsible for itself; this can be done, however, only if music does not become the victim of the technique. The didactic exemplary character of Schoenberg's more recent works was derived from the nature of the technique. That which appears as the range of norms in these compositions is nothing more than the narrow passageway of discipline through which all music must pass, hoping to escape the curse of contingency; however, it is far from being the highly promised land of its objectivity. Ernst Krenek correctly compared twelve-tone technique to those rules of strict counterpoint abstracted by the Palestrina school, which even today remains the very best school of composition. The denial of any normative claim is present in such a comparison. The distinction between didactic rules and aesthetic norms lies in the impossibility of consistently doing justice to these rules. This impossibility is the motivating force behind the attempt to learn. It must fail and the rules, in turn, must be forgotten, if they are to bear fruit. The didactic system of strict counterpoint offers in actuality the most precise analogy to the antinomies of twelve-tone composition. Its problems—particularly those of the so-called third species—are, from the perspective of principle, insoluble for the

50. *Ibid.*

modern ear: they are to be solved only by tricks. For the rules of this school were the product of polyphonic thought, a type of thought to which progression by means of harmonic steps was unknown and which had to content itself with the analysis of a harmonic space defined by a very few continually recurring chords. Three hundred and fifty years of specifically harmonic experience is not to be ignored, however. Today the music student who undertakes problems in strict composition necessarily applies harmonic logic at the same time: for example, in a meaningful progression of chords. Harmonic and contrapuntal logic remain incompatible, and satisfying solutions apparently are to be found only where harmonic contraband has successfully been smuggled through the gate of prohibitions. Bach ignored those same prohibitions and, instead of adhering to them, forcefully brought about the validation of polyphony by means of thorough-bass. In like manner, the genuine indifference of the vertical and the horizontal is accomplished only when the composition, in critical alertness, establishes at every moment the unity of the two dimensions. This cannot be achieved until the composition rejects the prescriptions of rows and rules and persistently insists upon freedom of action. It is precisely for this freedom that music is being trained by twelve-tone technique— not so much by means of what the technique determines in compositions, but rather through what is prohibited by it. The didactic justice of twelve-tone technique—its terrible discipline as an instrument of freedom—is revealed in full measure by comparison with any other type of contemporary music which ignores such discipline. Twelve-tone technique is no less polemic than it is didactic. It is by no means any longer concerned with questions first posed by modern music in opposition to post-Wagnerian music—questions as to whether music is genuine or false, pathetic or objective, programmatic or "absolute"—but rather with the handing-down of technical standards in the face of impending barbarism. If twelve-tone technique sets up a barrier against this, then it has already accomplished enough, even if it has not yet gained entry for itself into the realm of freedom. It has at hand its instructions not to participate in this movement, even though these very instructions could possibly support its participation—such is the agreement within these instructions. With a firm grasp—merciless samaritan that twelve-tone technique is—it supports nonetheless that musical experience which threatens to collapse.

THE RENUNCIATION OF MATERIAL

The technique, however, does not exhaust itself in this process. It reduces the tonal material, before it is structured via the rows, to an amorphous substratum, totally undetermined within itself. Thereupon the commanding compositional subject imposes its system of rules and regulations. The abstractness not only of these rules, but of their substratum as well, has its origin in the fact that the historical subject is able to achieve agreement with the historical element of the material only in the region of most general definitions. Therefore, this abstractness eliminates all the qualities of the material which in any way extend beyond this region. Only in the mathematical determination through the row do the compositional will and the claim to continual permutation, which appears historically in the material of the chromatic scale—that is to say, the resistance to the repetition of tones—concur in the total musical domination of nature as the thorough organization of material. It is this abstract reconciliation which, in the final analysis, places in opposition to the subject the self-contained system of rules in the subjugated material as an alienated, hostile, and dominating power. This degrades the subject, making of it a slave of the "material," as of an empty concept of rules, at that moment in which the subject completely subdues the material, indenturing it to its mathematical logic. At this point, however, contradiction once again reproduces itself in the static condition of music which has been achieved. The subject cannot be content with its subjugation to its abstract identity in the material. For in twelve-tone technique, the rationality of the material—as the objective rationality of events—asserts itself blindly over the will of the subjects, triumphing thereby as irrationality. In other words, the objective rationality of the system cannot be concretely perfected in the sensory phenomenon of music—the only concrete manifestation which is possible for it. The correctness of twelve-tone music cannot be directly "heard"—this is the simplest name for that moment of meaninglessness in it. Only the force of the system rules; only this is perceptible. This system, however, does not become transparent in the concrete logic of the individual elements of music, nor does it permit these elements to pursue an arbitrary course of development from within themselves. All of this encourages the subject to liberate itself from its material, and this liberation conditions the innermost tendency of Schoenberg's later styles. It is evident that this growing indifference of the material, which the row technique now attacks by force, involves precisely that negative abstractness experienced in turn as self-alienation by the musical subject. At the same time, it is this indifferentiation, by virtue of which the subject escapes the suffocation in natural matter—that is to say, the domination of nature—which had until now been the basis of musical history. In its total alienation through twelve-tone technique the subject, against its will, is deprived of the aesthetic totality against which it had rebelled in vain during the Expressionistic phase, in order to reconstruct it in vain through twelve-tone technique. Musical language dissociates itself into fragments. In these fragments, however, the subject is able to appear directly—"in its significance," as Goethe might have said—while the parentheses of the material totality hold it in their spell. The subject—trembling before the alienated language of music which is no longer its own language—regains its self-determination, not organic self-determination but that of superimposed intentions. Music becomes conscious of itself as the means of perception, which great music has always been. Schoenberg once spoke out against the animalian warmth of music and its plaintiveness. In the most recent phase of music the subject succeeds in communication over and beyond the abyss of silence, which marks the boundaries of its isolation. It is precisely this phase which justifies that coldness, which as a hermetic system of mechanical function would only bring about ruin. At the same time, it justifies Schoenberg's sovereign disposition over the row in contrast to the cautious manner in which Webern submerges himself in the row for the sake of the unity of the structure. Schoenberg carefully preserves a distance between himself and the material. His coldness is that of one who has run away, glorified as "the air from other planets" at the climax of the *Second Quartet*. The sovereignty with which it capriciously treats the material manifests not only traits of the administrative attitude, it further contains the renunciation of aesthetic necessity, the renunciation of that totality installed in complete externality with twelve-tone technique. Indeed, it is this very externality which serves as the means for renunciation. Precisely because this externalized material no longer expresses anything for him, the composer forces it to mean what he wishes; and the discrepancies—particularly the astonishing contradiction between twelve-tone mechanics and expression—become the ciphers of such meaning. Even in so doing, however, the composer remains within a tradition. This is responsible for a similarity between the late works of great composers. "The caesurae . . . , the sudden interruption, which characterizes Beethoven's late works more than any other factor—are those eruptive moments; the work is silent when it has been deserted and turns its hollow interior outward. Only then does the next fragment fit itself into place, fixed in its place by order of this eruptive subjectivity and dependent for its very existence upon that which preceded it; for the secret lies between them and can be evoked only in the figure which the two of them form in union. This illuminates the contradiction involved in labeling Beethoven in his late works as being both subjective and objective. The fragmented landscape of the work is objective; the light which alone causes it to radiate is subjective. Beethoven does not bring about a harmonious synthesis of these extremes. Rather, he tears them apart as the force of dissociation, in time—in order, perhaps, to preserve them for eternity. In the history of art late works have

51. The quotation is the first line of the poem "*Entrückung*"; cf. note 42 above. —Trans.

119

always been catastrophic."[52] That which Goethe commended in his old age—the step-by-step withdrawal from the phenomenon —can be understood in artistic concepts as the process by which material becomes no more than a matter of indifference. In Beethoven's last works barren conventions—through which the compositional stream flows only hesitantly—play approximately the same role as the one performed by the twelve-tone system in Schoenberg's most recent works. Since the beginning of twelve-tone technique, this growing indifferentiation of material has manifested itself as a tendency towards dissociation. As long as twelve-tone technique has been in existence there has been a long list of "secondary works"—arrangements or compositions which do not employ twelve-tone technique, or which employ it as a mens to an end, thus making it functional. Schoenberg's iron-clad twelve-tone compositions—from the *Woodwind Quintet* down to the *Violin Concerto*—are offset by his smaller pieces, whose only significance lies in their large number. Schoenberg orchestrated works by Bach and Brahms and reworked to a large degree the B-flat major concerto of Handel.[53] The *Suite for String Orchestra* [*Kol Nidre, opus* 39] and the *Second Chamber Symphony* [*opus* 38]—along with several choral compositions—are all "tonal." The "Accompaniment to a Cinematographic Scene" is well-suited for commercial purposes; the opera *Von heute auf morgen,* and several choral compositions, manifest at least a tendency in this direction. This gives rise to the assumption that Schoenberg throughout his life had a secret pleasure in heresies against "style," the inexorable nature of which was rooted in the man himself. The chronology of his works is rich in overlappings. The tonal *Gurrelieder* were not completed until 1911—the time of *Die glückliche Hand.* It was precisely his grandiose conceptions such as *Die Jakobsleiter* and *Moses und Aron* which accompanied him throughout decades:

52. T. W. Adorno, "Spätstil Beethovens," *Auftakt* (Prague, 1937), 5/6:67.
53. Orchestral transcriptions of Brahms' G-minor *Piano Quartet* [*opus* 25] and the *Concerto for String Quartet and Orchestra* after Händel's *Concerto Grosso* [*opus* 6 no. 7]. —Trans.

the urge to bring a work to a conclusion was totally alien to him.[54] In an artist's production there is a rhythm probably more obvious in literature than it is in music, except perhaps in the late works of Beethoven and Wagner. It is common knowledge that Schoenberg in his earlier years was forced to earn his living through the orchestration of operettas. The investigation of these forgotten scores might well be worth the effort, not only because it can safely be assumed that therein he was not able completely to suppress himself as a composer but, above all, because they might possibly give evidence of that counter-tendency which emerges more and more clearly in the "secondary works" of his later years, precisely at that point in his career when he gained total command over his material. It is hardly a matter of coincidence that all of these secondary works of his later years have one thing in common: a more conciliatory attitude towards the public. There is a deep relationship between Schoenberg's inexorability and his particular manner of conciliation. His inexorable music represents social truth against society. His conciliatory music recognizes the right to music which, in spite of everything, is still valid even in a false society—in the very same way that a false society reproduces itself and thus by virtue of its very survival objectively establishes elements of its own truth. As a representative of the most progressive aesthetic perception Schoenberg approaches the very boundaries thereof,

54. "The perfected works are of less value to the great man than those fragments upon which they work throughout their lives. For only the weaker and more distraught individual finds incomparable joy in concluding a work, experiencing, in so doing, that he is granted return to his own life. To the genius in his workshop, the interruption, the severe blow of fate is the same as the gentle hand of sleep. He captures the magic circle thereof in a fragment. 'Genius is diligence.'" (Walter Benjamin, *Schriften*, Frankfurt, 1955, Vol. 1, 518). At the same time, it must not be overlooked that in Schoenberg's resistance to the completion of precisely the most grandiose works which he had planned, other motives than this cheerful one exerted themselves: the tendency towards destruction, with which he often damaged his own compositions; the unconscious, but deeply effective distrust towards the possibility of "grandiose works" in the present age, and the dubiousness of his own texts, which hardly could have remained hidden from him.

121

namely, that the right of the truth contained in this perception shatters that right which is nothing more than a matter of negative necessity. This perception determines the substance of his secondary works. The growing indifference of material permits the intermittent union of both claims. Even tonality bows to the demands of total construction, and, for Schoenberg in recent years, that for which he composes is no longer totally decisive. An artist, for whom the compositional procedure means everything—and the subject matter, on the other hand, nothing— is able to make use of what has disappeared and what even the enchained consciousness of the consumer still has an ear for. On the other hand, this enchained consciousness is, to be sure, perceptive enough to close itself off as soon as this worn-out material has been overtaken by compositional attack. This consciousness is not at all concerned with the material as such but rather, only with the traces left behind in it by the economic market. However, it is precisely these traces which are destroyed in Schoenberg's secondary works. He accomplishes this by reducing the material in these works to the blatant vehicle of meaning which he infuses into the material. It is his ability to forget— this unique "sovereignty"—which enables him to do this. There is perhaps no single factor which distinguishes Schoenberg so basically from all other composers as his ability to discard and reject what he has previously possessed. He is able to do this at any point; he has done it repeatedly and particularly at every turning point in his compositional procedure. The rebellion against the possessive character of experience can be detected among the deepest impulses of his Expressionism. The *First Chamber Symphony* [*opus* 9]—with the preponderance of the woodwinds, the excessive demands made upon the string soloists, and the compressed linear figures—sounds as if Schoenberg had never advanced beyond the lush and radiant Wagnerian orchestra, which was still so successfully employed in the *Six Orchestral Songs* [*opus* 8]. The compositions which open a new phase—the *Piano Pieces* [*opus* 11], as the herald of atonality, for example, and later the waltz from *opus* 23 as the very model of twelve-tone—offer an absolute display of the most magnificent clumsiness. Such compositions take an aggressive stand against routine and against that ominous solid music-making which the more responsible composers in Germany have repeatedly fallen victim to ever since Mendelssohn. The spontaneity of musical observation obscures everything traditional, denounces everything once learned, and recognizes only the force of imagination. This force of forgetfulness is related to that barbaric moment of hostility towards art which, by means of the immediacy of reaction at every moment, questions the intermediary role of musical culture. It is this force alone which offers a counter-balance to the masterly command over technique, thus preserving tradition as a basis for technique. For tradition is that which is forgotten for the moment, and Schoenberg's alertness is so vast that it still designs for itself a technique of forgetfulness. Thereby Schoenberg is enabled repeatedly to employ twelve-tone rows in powerfully progressive compositions or to make use of tonality for constructions patterned after the row technique. It is necessary only to compare such related works as Schoenberg's *Piano Pieces* [*opus* 19] and Webern's *Five Movements for String Quartet* [*opus* 5] to become aware of Schoenberg's sovereignty. Whereas Webern binds Expressionistic miniatures together by means of the most highly subtle motivic development, Schoenberg—who had fully developed every possible motivic device—ignores them and follows, with eyes closed, that direction indicated to him by the progression of tones. In forgetfulness, subjectivity finally extends incommensurably beyond the consequence and correctness of the structure which depends upon the omnipresent recollection of itself. Schoenberg has succeeded in preserving this force of forgetfulness in his most recent works. He denounces his fidelity to the sole domination of material—that very fidelity which he had once designed. He breaks with the concept of the hermetic clarity of the structure which had become absolute at this time—that clarity which classic aesthetics had come to call "symbolic" and which in truth did not correspond to a single measure which he

123

had composed. An arist, he wins back for mankind freedom from art, a dialectical composer, he brings dialectics to a halt.

COGNITIVE CHARACTER

Through hostility towards art, the work of art approaches knowledge. From the beginning, Schoenberg's music has hovered in the vicinity of cognition. This—and not dissonance —has been the basis upon which he has been rejected by so many: this has given rise to the strident outcry against intellectualism. The hermetic work of art was not interested in perception, but rather allowed perception to vanish within itself. It designed itself as the object of mere "observation," obscuring every loophole through which thought might evade the direct actuality of the aesthetic object. In so doing, the traditional work of art refrained from thought, renouncing its binding relationship to that which it cannot be in itself. The work of art was as "blind" as (according to Kant's doctrine) non-conceptual observation is "blind." The idea that the work of art should manifest observable clarity leads to the illusion that the dichotomy between subject and object has been overcome. Perception is based upon the articulation of this conciliation: the clarity of art itself is its illusory appearance. It is only when the work of art has been thrown into confusion that it throws off the clarity of its hermetic character, discarding the illusion of its appearance at the same time. It is established as the object of thought and participates in thought itself: it becomes the vehicle of the subject, whose intentions it communicates and defines; whereas in the hermetic work of art, the subject—by intention—is simply submerged. The hermetic work of art upholds the identity of subject and object. In the decline of the hermetic work this identity reveals itself as an illusion, underscoring the right of perception, which contrasts subject and object with each other as the greater and moral right of the work of art. Modern music absorbs the contradiction evident in its relationship to reality into its own consciousness and form. Through such action it refines itself as a means of perception. Even traditional art perceives all the more, the more deeply it expresses the contradictions present in its own material—thereby offering evidence of the contradictions in the world in which it dwells. Its depth is that of a judgment pronounced against the negative aspects of the world. The basis for judgment in music, as a cognitive force, is aesthetic form. It is only in measuring this contradiction according to the possibility of its arbitration that the contradiction is actually perceived and not merely registered. In the cognitive act performed by art, the artistic form represents a criticism of the contradiction by indicating the possibility of reconciliation and thereby emphasizing the non-absolute aspect of the contradiction—its contingency and the fact that it can be overcome. In such a process, to be sure, the aesthetic form is also transformed into the moment in which the act of perception ceases. Art, as the realization of the possible, has always denied the reality of the contradiction upon which it is based. Its cognitive character becomes radical in that moment in which art is no longer content with the role of perception. This is the threshold of modern art, which grasps its own contradictions with such depth that they can no longer be arbitrated. Modern art infuses the concept of form with such tension that the aesthetic product is forced to confess its insolvency before it. Modern art permits the contradiction to remain, revealing the original foundation of its categories of judgment—that is, of form. It discards the dignity of the judge and descends to the level of the plaintiff, the only position for which reality provides a conciliation. It is only in a fragmentary work that has renounced itself that the critical substance is liberated.[55] This

55. Benjamin's concept of the "aural" work of art corresponds by and large with that of the hermetic work. The aura present therein is the uninterrupted sympathy of the parts with the whole, which constitutes the hermetic work of art. Benjamin's theory emphasizes the manner in which circumstances are manifested as phenomena from the perspective of the philosophy of history; the "aural" content of the hermetic work of art underscores the aesthetic perspective. This con-

happens, to be sure, only in the decline of the hermetic work of art and not in the undifferentiated superimposition of doctrine and image, as represented by archaic art works. For it is only in the realm of necessity—manifested monadologically by hermetic works of art—that art is able to acquire that power of objectivity which finally makes it capable of perception. The basis of such objectivity is that the discipline, imposed upon the subject by the hermetic work of art, mediates the objective demand of the entire society, about which society knows just as little as does the subject. It is critically elevated to the position of evidence in the same moment in which the subject destroys discipline. This is an act of truth only when it includes the social demand which it negates. The subject evasively leaves the vacuity of the work at the mercy of that which is socially possible. Indications of this are to be found in Schoenberg's most recent works. The liquidation of art—of the hermetic work of art—becomes an aesthetic question, and the growing indifference of material itself brings about the renunciation of the identity of substance and phenomenon in which the traditional idea of art terminated. The role of the chorus in Schoenberg's recent works is the visible sign of such concession to knowledge. The subject sacrifices the clarity of the work, forces it to become doctrine and epigram, conceiving of itself as the representative

---

cept, however, permits deductions which the history of philosophy does not necessarily draw. The result of the decline of the aural or hermetic work of art depends upon the relationship of its own decline to epistemology. If the decline takes place blindly and unconsciously, it degenerates into the mass art of technical reproduction. It is not a mere external act of fate that the remnants of the aura remain throughout mass art; it is rather an expression of the blind obduracy of the structures, which, to be sure, results from their suppression by the present circumstances of domination. The work of art as a means of perception, however, becomes critical and fragmentary. Agreement on this fact prevails today in all works of art which have a chance for survival: the works of Schoenberg and Picasso, Joyce and Kafka, and even Proust offer unified support of this contention. This, in turn, perhaps allows further speculation in the field of the philosophy of history. The hermetic work of art belongs to the bourgeois, the mechanical work belongs to fascism, and the fragmentary work, in its state of complete negativity, belongs to utopia.

of a non-existent fellowship. The canons of late Beethoven are an analogy, and this fact in turn sheds light upon the canonic practices of Schoenberg's choral works. The choral texts are of a reflective and bluntly conceptual nature throughout. Eccentric characteristics—such as the use of anti-poetic foreign words or the inclusion of literary quotations in the *Jakobsleiter*—are most instructive about the tendency which belongs to the music itself. The condensation of meaning within the structure itself—a process conditioned by twelve-tone technique—corresponds to this. The "meaning" of music, even in free atonality, is determined solely by its inner relationships. Schoenberg went so far as to define the theory of composition as simply the theory of musical relationships, and everything in music which for any reason can be called meaningful may lay claim to this theory, because as a matter of detail it can be extended to relate to the totality. The same is true in reverse: the totality assumes within itself a definite demand upon the individual detail. Such an extension of the aesthetic partial moments beyond themselves—while they at the same time remain completely within the space of the work of art—is interpreted as the meaning of the work of art. It is understood in its aesthetic meaning to be more than a phenomenon, and at the same time to be no more than this—in other words, as the totality of the phenomenon. If technical analysis reveals that the emergent moment of meaninglessness is constituent for twelve-tone technique, it formulates thereby not only its criticism of twelve-tone technique, based on the fact that the totally constructed work of art (that is to say, the completely "integrated" work) falls into conflict with its own idea, but rather, by virtue of this incipient meaninglessness, the immanent hermetic quality of the work is discarded. This hermetic quality is based upon precisely that integration which determines meaning. After the elimination of this integration, music is transformed into protest. In these technological configurations an element is unmistakably perceptible which had been proclaimed in the era of free atonality with the force of an explosion. This force—closely related to Dadaism—is particularly evident in the truly incommensurable youthful works of Ernst

127

Krenek—above all, in his *Second Symphony*. This signifies the rebellion of music against its own meaning. The relationships in these works are the negation of relationships. Their triumph lies in the fact that music reveals itself in the antipode of verbal language, in that it is able to speak with no precise obligation towards meaning, whereas all hermetic musical works of art stand with verbal language under the sign of pseudo-morphosis. All organic music proceded out of the *stile recitativo*.[56] From the very beginning this was patterned after speech. The emancipation of music today is tantamount to its emancipation from verbal language, and it is this emancipation which flashes during the destruction of "meaning." Above all, however, this concerns expression. The theoreticians of New Objectivity considered as the essential concern the restitution of "absolute" music and its purification of the Romantic-subjective element of expression. What actually takes place is the dissociation of meaning and expression. Just as the meaninglessness of Krenek's early compositions grants them their most powerful expression—the expression of objective catastrophe—so do the superimposed characters of expression in the most recent twelve-tone compositions indicate the liberation of expression from the consistency of language. Subjectivity—the vehicle of expression in traditional music—is by no means the last substratum thereof. It is this as little as the "subject"—the substratum of all art down to the present day—is actually man himself. The beginning of music, in the same manner as its end, extends beyond the realm of intentions—the realm of meaning and subjectivity. The origin is gesticulative in nature and closely related to the origin of tears. It is the gesture of release. The tension of the face muscles relaxes; the tension which closes the face off from the surrounding world by directing the face actively at this world disappears. Music and tears open the lips and set the arrested human being free. The sentimentality of inferior music indicates in its distorted figure that which higher music, at the

56. *Stile recitativo:* vocal style designed to imitate and emphasize the natural inflections of speech, employed particularly in opera, most notably Baroque. —Trans.

very border of insanity, is yet able to design in the validity of its form: reconciliation. The human being who surrenders himself to tears and to a music which no longer resembles him in any way permits that current of which he is not part and which lies behind the dam restraining the world of phenomena to flow back into itself. In weeping and in singing he enters into alienated reality. "Tears dim my eyes: earth's child I am again"— this line from Goethe's *Faust* defines the position of music.[57] Thus earth claims Eurydice again. The gesture of return—not the sensation of expectancy—characterizes the expression of all music, even if it finds itself in a world worthy of death.

ATTITUDE TOWARDS SOCIETY

The potentiality of the most recent phase of music indicates a change in position. It is no longer the statement and image of an inner factor, but rather an attitude towards reality, perceived by music, but no longer glossed over in the images presented by music. In the extreme isolation resulting therefrom, the social character of music changes. In establishing the independence of its tasks and techniques, traditional music removed itself from its social basis and became "autonomous." (That the autonomous development of music reflected social development could never be deduced so simply, unquestioningly, as it could, for example, in the development of the novel.) It is not only that music *per se* lacks that unequivocal objective content, but rather that the more clearly music defines its formal laws and entrusts itself to them, the more, for the moment, it closes itself off against the manifest portrayal of society in which it has its enclaves. Music owes its social popularity to this process of isolation. Music is an ideology insofar as it asserts itself as an ontological being-in-itself beyond social tensions. Even Beethoven's music—bourgeois music at its very height—echoed the turmoil and the ideal of the heroic years of the middle class in merely the same way that

57. Goethe, *Faust* I, line 784. —Trans.

a morning dream echoes the noise of beginning day. It is not actual sensory listening but only the conceptually mediated perception of the elements and their configuration which assures the social substance of great music. The crude division into classes and groups is nothing more than an attempt to prove an assertion and runs the risk of becoming a puerile prank of instigation against a formalism which brands, as bourgeois decadence, everything which refuses to engage in the games of existing society. This same formalism ascribes to the remnants of bourgeois composition—enthroned upon the plush sofa of pseudo-Romantic pathos—the dignity of popular democracy. Music down to this very day has existed only as a product of the bourgeois class, a product which, both in the success and failure of its attempts at formulation, embodies this society and gives aesthetic documentation of it. In so doing, traditional and emancipated music are of the same nature. Feudalists hardly ever succeeded in producing their "own" music, but rather had it composed for them by the urban bourgeois. The proletariat was never permitted to constitute itself as a music subject; such a creative function was made impossible both in terms of its position within the system—where it was nothing more than an object of domination—and through the repressive factors which formed its own nature. Only in the realization of freedom and not under any system of domination did the proletariat achieve a creative function. Within the existing order there must be grave doubts regarding the existence of any type of music other than bourgeois. In contrast, the class membership of individual composers—or even their categorization as high or petty bourgeois—is as totally a matter of indifference as would be the attempt to derive the essence of modern music from its social reception. This reception scarcely indicates any differentiation in attitudes towards such highly divergent composers as Schoenberg, Stravinsky, and Hindemith. For the most part there is only the most coincidental and insignificant relationship between the private political attitudes of composers and the substance of their works. The displacement of social substance in radical modern music—evident in the reception of this music as nothing more than seeking refuge in the concert hall—cannot be ascribed to the commitment of this music to any particular cause. It is rather that this music—as the unmistakable microcosm of antagonistic human disposition—is today engaged in breaking down from within those walls which aesthetic autonomy had so carefully constructed. It was the class-orientation of traditional music—by means of its consistent formal immanence as well as the pleasantry of its façade—which lead to the proclamation that essentially there were no classes. Modern music cannot voluntarily involve itself in this struggle without injury to its own consistency. Consequently—as the enemies of this music well know—it occupies a position in this struggle by surrendering the deception of harmony, a position which has become untenable in the face of a reality rapidly moving towards catastrophe. The basis of the isolation of radical modern music is not its asocial, but precisely its social substance. It expresses its concern through its pure quality, doing so all the more emphatically, the more purely this quality is revealed; it points out the ills of society, rather than sublimating those ills into a deceptive humanitarianism which would pretend that humanitarianism had already been achieved in the present. This music is no longer an ideology. In such a role of pseudo-isolation, music begins to correspond to a momentous social change. In the present phase, in which the apparatus of production and domination are merged, the question of mediation between superstructure and substructure—like all other social mediation—begins to grow obsolete. Works of art—like all precipitates of the objective spirit—are the object itself. They are the concealed social essence quoted as the phenomenon. It might well be asked whether art has ever really been that mediated image of reality, as it attempts to validate itself before the power of the world. Was the attitude towards the world not, rather, founded in resistance against this power? This might help to explain the fact that in spite of all autonomy the dialectic of art is not hermetic and that the history of this dialectic is not simply a succession of questions and answers. The intense desire of the work of art to withdraw itself from the dialectic which it obeys might be viewed as its central concern. The works react to the suffering resulting from dialectical pressure. For art, this represents an incurable disease caused by necessity. At the same time, however, the formal validity of the work, which has its origin in material dialectics, establishes a defense against this necessity. Dialectics is interrupted—interrupted, however, by no force other than the reality to which it is related—that is to say, to society itself. While works of art hardly ever attempt to imitate society and their creators need know nothing of it, the gestures of the works of art are objective answers to objective social configurations. They have often been designed to meet the needs of the consumer; more frequently, they stand in a contradiction to his need. In no case, however, have they ever been sufficiently redesigned by this need. Every interruption in the creative process—every forgetfulness, every new beginning—designates a type of reaction to society. Yet the more precisely the work of art gives answer to the heteronomy of society, the more it becomes estranged from the world. The work of art does not have society in mind in terms of answering its questions, nor even necessarily in terms of the actual choice of those questions. However, it assumes a tense position against the horrors of history. At one point it is insistent, at another it forgets. It relents and grows hard. It endures or it renounces itself, hoping to outwit its doom. The objectivity of art lies in the fixation of such moments. Works of art are similar to those childish grimaces which the striking of the clock causes to become permanently fixed. The integral technique of the composition arose neither in the concept of the integral state nor in the concept of its eradication. It is, however, an attempt to hold ground in the face of reality and to absorb that universal anxiety to which the integral state corresponded. The inhumanity of art must triumph over the inhumanity of the world for the sake of the humane. Works of art attempt to solve the riddles designed by the world to devour man. The world is a sphynx, the artist is blinded Oedipus, and it is works of art of the type resembling his wise answer which plunged the sphynx into the abyss. Thus all art stands in opposition to mythology. In the elemental "material" of art, the "answer"—the only possible and correct answer—is ever present, but not yet defined. To give this answer, to express what is there, and to fulfill the commandment of ambiguity through a singularity which has always been present in the commandment, is at the same time the new which extends beyond the old, precisely by virtue of being sufficient to it. For this reason the total seriousness of artistic technique lies in continually designing schemata of the familiar for that which has already existed. This seriousness is today so much greater, since the alienation present in the consistency of artistic technique forms the very substance of the work of art. The shocks of incomprehension, emitted by artistic technique in the age of its meaninglessness, undergo a sudden change. They illuminate the meaningless world. Modern music sacrifices itself to this effort. It has taken upon itself all the darkness and guilt of the world. Its fortune lies in the perception of misfortune; all of its beauty is in denying itself the illusion of beauty. No one wishes to become involved with art—individuals as little as collectives. It dies away unheard, without even an echo. If time crystallizes around that music which has been heard, revealing its radiant quintessence, music which has not been heard falls into empty time like an impotent bullet. Modern music spontaneously aims towards this last experience, evidenced hourly in mechanical music. Modern music sees absolute oblivion as its goal. It is the surviving message of despair from the shipwrecked.

STRAVINSKY
AND RESTORATION

Nor is it of any real assistance to him that he further appropriates, so to speak, with his soul and substance a view of the world that belongs to the past, in other words tries to root himself in one of such and, let us say, turns Roman Catholic, as not a few have done in recent times for Art's sake, in order to give their soul some secure foundation, and so enable the definite lines of their artistic product to become themselves something which shall appear to have an independently valid growth.[1]

AUTHENTICITY

The historical innervation of Stravinsky and his disciples succumbed to the temptation of imagining that the responsible essence of music could be restored through stylistic procedures. The process by which music was rationalized—the establishment of integral domination over its material—coincided with its subjectification. The latter process, which Stravinsky, with his penchant for organizational mastery, has critically emphasized, appears to be a moment of arbitrariness. According to the

1. Hegel, *Fine Art*, Vol. 2, 393–394.

standards of the existing order, the progress of music towards total freedom of the subject would appear to be completely irrational insofar as (along with the more all-encompassing musical language) it by-and-large dissolves the easily comprehensible logic of superficial organization. The aged philosophical aporia maintains that the subject—as the vehicle of objective rationality—remains inseparable from the individual in his coincidental character. The markings of such coincidence, however, distort the accomplishment of such rationality, and consequently music is charged with complete responsibility for such aporia. Yet music, of course, has never attained to pure logic. The mind of a composer such as Stravinsky reacts vehemently against any impulse not visibly determined by society—actually against the trace of anything which has not been socially comprehended. Their intention is emphatically to reconstruct the authenticity of music—to impose upon it the character of outside confirmation, to fortify it with the power of being-so-and-not-being-able-to-be-otherwise. The music of the new Viennese school would hope to partake of the same power by means of infinite submersion within itself—by means of total organization: such force, however, is missing in its jagged physiognomy. Consummate unto itself, its intention is that the listener should share in the experience of this consummation, not simply reactively re-experience it. Since this music does not engage the listener, Stravinsky's consciousness denounces it as impotent and coincidental. He renounces the strict self-development of essence in favor of the strict contour of the phenomenon—in favor, that is, of his powers of conversion. The demeanor of music should not tolerate any contradiction. Once in his youth, Hindemith offered a brave definition of this concept: he envisioned a style in which everyone would have to compose in much the same manner, as was the case in the time of Bach or Mozart. As a teacher he still pursues today a similar program of conformism. Stravinsky's acrobatic cleverness and crafty mastery have been essentially free of such naïveté since the very beginning. He undertook his attempt at restoration without resentment against any drive towards levelling, and fully conscious of the dubious and delusive aspects of his experiment. Such urbane consciousness is the absolute determining force behind his efforts. This is still true, even if these efforts seem to have fallen into oblivion in the face of the sterile scores which he serves up to the public today. Stravinsky's objectivism is of so much greater value than that of all those who seek orientation in his style because, in his case, the factor of his own negativity is essentially included within this objectivism. Yet, despite all of this, it cannot be doubted that his dream-hostile work is inspired by the dream of authenticity, by a fear of emptiness—that anxiety before frustrated efforts which no longer find social resonance and are chained to the ephemeral fate of the individual. In Stravinsky, the desire of the adolescent is ever stubbornly at work; it is the struggle of the youth to become a valid, proven classicist—not a mere modernist—whose substance is consumed in the controversy of artistic party lines; and who is soon forgotten. It would be impossible to overlook the naïve aspect present in such a manner of reaction and the impotence of hopes associated with it— for no artist can exercise an influence upon that which survives in the aesthetic realm. It is just as unquestionable, however, that this attitude is based upon an experience which can be denied, least of all, by anyone aware of the impossibility of restoration. Even the most perfect song of Anton Webern remains far behind the simplest piece from Schubert's *Die Winterreise* from the perspective of authenticity. Even in the case of its most extreme success, this sort of attitude designates a state of consciousness which, as it were, has simply been accepted as absolute. And it is precisely such a consciousness that finds objectification appropriate in such a work. But this subjectification does not pass judgment on the objectivity of substance—on the truth or untruth of the state of consciousness itself. This state of objectification is Stravinsky's most immediate goal; he is not concerned with success in expressing a situation which he would much rather overlook than express. Even for his ear the most progressive music cannot sound as though it had been present since

137

the beginning of time; yet this is precisely how he wants music to sound. Our criticism of such a goal will result in an insight into various steps towards its realization.

SACRIFICE AND THE ABSENCE OF INTENTION

Stravinsky despised the easy way to authenticity. That would have been the academic way, the restriction to the approved inventory of the musical idiom which had developed during the eighteenth and nineteenth centuries, and which, for the bourgeois consciousness to which it belongs, had taken on the seal of matter-of-factness and "naturalness." Stravinsky was a student of Rimsky-Korsakov, who had corrected Mussorgsky's harmony according to conservatory rules; now he rebelled against his teacher's studio as only a Fauvist could do against the rules of painting.[2] His sense of binding responsibility found the demands made upon him intolerable—namely, when he contradicted himself by replacing the vital force exercised by tonality in the heroic age of the bourgeoisie with a mere convention which he had learned in school. The engraved precision of musical language—the permeation of each of its formulae by intentions— struck him not as a guarantee of authenticity, but as the erosion thereof.[3] If its principle is to be effective, slackened authenticity

2. "When all is said and done, the 'Sacre' is still a 'Fauvist' work, an organized 'Fauvist' work." Jean Cocteau, *A Call to Order*, trans. Rollo Myers, London, 1926, 43.

3. At an early date Nietzsche recognized the fact that musical material is permeated by intentions and, at the same time, with the potential contradiction of these intentions as well. "Music by and for itself is not so portentous for our inward nature, so deeply moving, that it ought to be looked upon as the direct language of the feelings; but its ancient union with poetry has infused so much symbolism into rhythmical movement, into loudness and softness of tone, that we now imagine it speaks directly to and comes from the inward nature. Dramatic music is possible only when the art of harmony has acquired an immense range of symbolical means, through song, opera, and a hundred attempts at description by sound. 'Absolute music' is either form *per se*, in the rude condition of music, when playing in time and with various degrees of

should be eradicated. This is brought about by the demolition of intentions. From this—and from the direct contemplation of primeval musical matter as well—he expects to find the binding responsibility. The relationship to concurrent philosophical phenomenology is unmistakable. The renunciation of all psychologism—the reduction to the pure phenomenon, as the

---

strength gives pleasure, or the symbolism of form which speaks to the understanding even without poetry, after the two arts were joined finally together after long development and the musical form had been woven about with threads of meaning and feeling. People who are backward in musical development can appreciate a piece of harmony merely as execution, whilst those who are advanced will comprehend it symbolically. No music is deep and full of meaning in itself, it does not speak of 'will,' of the 'thing-in-itself'; that could be imagined by the intellect only in an age which had conquered for musical symbolism the entire range of inner life. It was the intellect itself that first gave this meaning to sound, just as it also gave meaning to the relation between lines and masses in architecture, but which in itself is quite foreign to mechanical laws" (Friedrich Nietzsche, *Human, All-Too-Human*, in *The Complete Works*, trans. Oscar Levy, New York, 1924, Vol. 6, Part 1, 192–193). At the same time, however, the separation of sound and that which is "superimposed upon it"—meaning, for example—remains a mechanical conception. Nietzsche's postulate regarding the "*per se*" is a fiction: all modern music constitutes itself as a vehicle for meaning. Its essence, after all, involves more than existence in pure sound, and therefore it cannot be dissected into simple categories of illusion and reality. Consequently, Nietzsche's concept of musical progress as an expanding psychologization is too narrowly designed. Because the material in itself is already spirit, the dialectics of music move between the objective and subjective poles; it can in no way be stated that the subjective pole is of higher stature. The psychologization of music at the cost of the logic of its structure has proven itself faulty and is now obsolete. By means of phenomenological and *Gestalt*-theoretical categories, Ernst Kurth's psychology of music (*Musikpsychologie*, Berlin, 1931) has attempted to define this "superimposition" with somewhat more finesse. The result, however, is that he has fallen victim to the opposite extreme—to an idealistic concept of musical pan-inspiration which simply denies the heterogeneous material element in musical tone, or rather assigns it to the discipline of the "psychology of sound," thus restricting musical theory, from the beginning, to the realm of intentions. In so doing, Kurth—in spite of his understanding of the language of music—has closed himself off from any insight into the decisive basic component of musical dialectics. Spiritual-musical material necessarily contains a level which is without intention—something "natural," which obviously could not be distilled as such from music.

process reveals itself—opens up a region of "authentic" being which is beyond all doubt. In both cases, distrust of the un-original (at its utmost depth the suspicion of the contradiction between actual society and its ideology) results in the misleading hypostatization of the "remains," or what is left over after the removal of that which has allegedly been superimposed as truth. In both cases, the mind is caught up in the deception that with-in its own circle—the realm of thought and art—it might be able to escape the curse of being only mind and reflection, but by no means essence itself. In both cases, the unmediated contrast between the "thing" and mental reflection is absolutized, and for this reason the product arising from the subject is invested with the dignity of the natural. In both cases, it is a matter of the chimerical rebellion of culture against its own essence as culture. Stravinsky undertakes such a rebellion not only in the familiar aesthetic game with barbarism, but further-more in the fierce suspension of that element in music which is called culture—the suspension, that is, of the humanly eloquent work of art. He is drawn in that direction where music—in its retarded state, far behind the fully developed bourgeois subject —functions as an element lacking intention, arousing only bodily animation instead of offering meaning. He is attracted to that sphere in which meaning has become so ritualized that it cannot be experienced as the specific meaning of the musical act. The aesthetic ideal is that of unquestioned fulfillment. For Stravinsky—as for Frank Wedekind in his circus plays—"bodily art" becomes the watch-word. Stravinsky begins as the staff com-poser of the Russian ballet. Since *Petrouchka,* his scores pre-figure gesture and step, thus assuming a constantly increasing distance from empathy with the dramatic figure. They restrict themselves in their specialization, offering the most extreme contrast to the encompassing demands expressed by the Schoen-berg school in its most outspoken formulations, and as had once been stated by Beethoven in the *Eroica.* Stravinsky slyly pays tribute to the division of labor—denounced as ideology by Schoenberg's *Die glückliche Hand.* Stravinsky is fully aware of the futility of any such attempt to transcend, by means of

140

intellectualization, the boundaries of a competence defined in artisan terms. Present in this effort—alongside the timely attitude of the specialist—is an anti-ideological factor: the prime concern lies in the precise completion of an assigned task, not in the construction of a world with all means of technology—as Mahler was want to call it. As a cure for the division of labor, he suggests driving it to an extreme, and thus knocking the props out from under a culture based upon such a division. Out of this world of over-specialization he designs the specialty of music hall, vaudeville, and circus. This accomplishment is glorified in the *Parade* of Cocteau and Satie, but *Petrouchka* is already a preconception of it.[4] The aesthetic accomplishment becomes a complete *tour de force*—the beginnings of which were already to be found in Impressionism; it is further a breaking of gravitational force, the pretense of the impossible through the extreme intensification of special training. Actually, Stravinsky's harmony always remains in a state of suspension, thus evading the gravitation of the step-by-step progression of chords. Madness and the insignificant perception of the acrobat, the lack of freedom of the individual who continually repeats the same performance until the break-neck attempt succeeds—all of these factors give an objective picture of sovereignty, freedom from the force of nature, and a mastery which, although fully developed, is without intention. At the same time, it is all denounced as ideology as soon as these factors assert themselves individually. The blindly infinite success of the acrobatic act, formed with aesthetic antinomies, is celebrated as the sudden utopia of something which has far surpassed the bourgeois boundaries through the division of labor and hypostatization. The absence of intention is considered to be the promise of the fulfillment of all intention. *Petrouchka*—"neo-Impressionistic" in style—is pieced together from innumerable artistic fragments, from the minutely detailed whirring of the fair-ground down to the mocking imitation of all music rejected by official culture. *Petrouchka* has its origins in the atmosphere of the cabaret, embodying a mixture of liter-

4. *Parade*, a 1917 ballet upon a theme by Jean Cocteau with music by Erik Satie. —Trans.

141

ature and commercial art. While Stravinsky, on the one hand, remained faithful to the apocryphal aspects of the cabaret, on the other he rebelled against the elements of narcissistic elation and harlequin-like animation and he succeeded in asserting, against the Bohemian atmosphere, the destruction of everything intrinsically inaugurated by the cabaret number. This tendency leads from commercial art—which readied the soul for sale as a commercial good—to the negation of the soul in protest against the character of consumer goods: to music's declaration of loyalty to its physical basis, to its reduction to the phenomenon, which assumes objective meaning in that it renounces, of its own accord, any claim to meaning. Egon Wellsez was not entirely wrong in comparing *Petrouchka* to Schoenberg's *Pierrot*—both are continuous in their idea; the neo-Romantic transfiguration of the clown, even in those days, had already grown somewhat stale. The tragic art of the clown heralds at the same time the fact that this condemned subjectivity ironically retains its primacy. *Pierrot* and *Petrouchka*—as well as Strauss's *Till Eulenspiegel,* who is heard so clearly several times in Stravinsky's ballet—survive their own demise. But in the treatment of the tragic clown, the historical lines of modern music separate.[5] In Schoenberg, everything is based upon that lonely subjectivity which withdraws into itself. The entire third part of *Pierrot* designs a "voyage home" to a vitreous no-man's-land in whose crystalline-lifeless air the seemingly transcendent subject—liberated from the entanglements of the empirical—finds himself again on an imaginary plane. In this case, the subject benefits as much from the complexion of the music as it does from the text. The texture of the composition designs the image

5. Stravinsky in his earlier period—as Cocteau openly emphasized at that time—was far more impressed by Schoenberg than is admitted today in the conflict between the schools. This influence is evident in the *Three Japanese Lyrics* and in many details of *Le Sacre du printemps*—particularly in the introduction of the work. It could, however, be traced as far back as *Petrouchka.* The visual impact of the score in the final measures before the famous Russian dance of the first scene, for example (numbers 32ff.)—above all from the fourth measure on—would be difficult to imagine without Schoenberg's *Pieces for Orchestra* [*opus* 16].

of hope beyond hopelessness with the expression of shelter and security in desolation. Such pathos is totally alien to Stravinsky's *Petrouchka*. The latter work is by no means without subjectivistic traits, but the music tends to take the part of those who ridicule the maltreated hero, rather than come to his defense. Consequently, the immortality of the clown at the end of the work cannot be interpreted as appeasement for the collective, but rather as the threat of evil to it. In Stravinsky's case, subjectivity assumes the character of sacrifice, but—and this is where he sneers at the tradition of humanistic art—the music does not identify with the victim, but rather with the destructive element. Through the liquidation of the victim it rids itself of all intentions—that is, of its own subjectivity.

THE HAND ORGAN AS A PRIMEVAL PHENOMENON

Under the guise of neo-romanticism, such a turning against the subject has already taken place in *Petrouchka*. Lengthy passages of the work—with the exception of the second scene, almost the whole work—are simplified in their musical substance, in contrast to the intricate psychological ornamentation of the puppet who has been summoned into deceptive life. The technical simplicity of the work is to be observed particularly in the extremely subtle treatment of the orchestra. This simplicity corresponds to the position taken by the music towards its theme: it is the position of the highly entertained observer of fair-ground scenes, the portrayal of a stylized impression of hurly-burly, with the undertone of provocative joy which the individual, tired of differentiation, finds in that which he scorns. This is analogous to the position of the intellectual who enjoys films and detective novels with well-mannered naïveté, thus preparing himself for his own function within mass culture. The self-annihilation of the observer is implied for an instant in the vain suffering under knowledge. He is submerged into the tumult as a child in order to free himself from the burden of rational everyday life and, at the same time, of his own psychology. He thus escapes his own ego, seeking happiness in identification with that un-articulated mob of Le Bon-like nature whose *imago* of this crowd is contained within the clamour of the work.[6] In so doing, however, he takes the side of those who laugh: the concentration of the music on *Petrouchka* as its aesthetic subject unmasks his worthless existence as comic. The fundamental category of *Petrouchka* is that of the grotesque—as the term is frequently used as a dynamic marking in the score for the wind soli: the category of the distorted conspicuous individual delivered up to others. The impending disintegration of the subject itself is evident in this situation. Everything characteristic of *Petrouchka* is grotesque: the melismata which are misappropriated and restrained to the point of dullness. These are the only elements which are sharply defined against the giant harmonica of the acoustic whole—the photographic negative of the neo-Romantic giant harp. Wherever the subjective element is encountered, it is depraved: it is sickeningly over-sentimentalized or trodden to death. It is evoked as something which in itself is already mechanical, hypostatized, and—to a certain extent—already lifeless. The wind instruments in which this is expressed sound like the components of a hand organ: the apotheosis of mere piping. The strings are perverted into a joke and deprived of their soul-

6. It is here perhaps that the Russian element in Stravinsky is to be sought—something he has misused, for the most part, as an identification tag. It was noted long ago that the lyricism of Mussorgsky is distinguished from the German *Lied* by the absence of any poetic subject: he views each poem as does the opera composer the aria, not from the perspective of the unity of direct compositional expression, but rather in a manner which distances and objectifies every possible factor of expression. The artist does not converge with the lyric subject. In essentially pre-bourgeois Russia the category of the subject was not quite so firmly fitted together as in the Western countries. The factor of alienation—particularly in Dostoevsky—originated in the non-identity of the ego with itself: not one of the brothers Karamazov is a "character." Stravinsky, as a product of the late bourgeoisie, has at his command such pre-subjectivity that he is finally able to validate the decline of the subject.

ful sound.[7] The images of mechanical music produce the shock of a modernity which is already past and degraded to a childish level. It becomes the gate to the most original and ancient past, as it is later to serve the Surrealists. The hand organ, once heard, functions—as an acoustical *déjà vu*—as remembrance. Suddenly—as upon the command of a magician—the *imago* of the shabby, fallen individual is to transform itself into a remedy against decay. The basic phenomenon in the spiritual movement perfected by Stravinsky is his substitution of the hand organ for the Bach organ. In so doing, the metaphysical joke is supported by the similarity of the two instruments. This joke actually concerns the price of life, which sound is forced to pay for its purification from intentions. All music—right down to the present day—has had to pay for the sound of collective responsibility with an act of violence against the subject with the enthronement of a mechanical factor as authority.

SACRE AND AFRICAN SCULPTURE

Le Sacre du printemps—Stravinsky's most famous work and, from the standpoint of material, his most progressive composition—was conceived, according to his autobiography, during his work on *Petrouchka*. This is scarcely coincidental. In spite of the stylistic contrast between *Petrouchka,* the masterpiece of almost culinary design, and the tumultuous ballet, both have a common nucleus: the anti-humanistic sacrifice to the collective—sacrifice without tragedy, made not in the name of a renewed image of man, but only in the blind affirmation of a situation recognized by the victim. This insight can find expres-

7. Technically, this piping is produced through a certain type of progression by octaves or sevenths in the contours of wood-wind melodies —clarinets, in particular—often at a wide range from each other. Stravinsky preserved this manner of instrumentation as a means of depicting death long after the grotesque intention had fallen victim to the verdict, as for example in the "Cercles Mystérieux des Adolescentes" ("Mystic Circle of the Adolescents") in *Sacre* (numbers 94ff.).

145

sion either through self-mockery or through self-annihilation. Such a motif, which completely determines the manner of conduct of the music, steps forth from the frivolous mask of Petrouchka and appears in sanguinary gravity in *Sacre*. This belongs to the years when wild men came to be called primitives, to the sphere of Frazer and Lévy-Bruhl, and further of Freud's *Totem and Taboo*.[8] This is by no means to say—and particularly not in France—that the primeval world is played off against civilization. It is much more a matter of "research"— in a positivistic detachment well suited to the distance maintained by Stravinsky's music from the atrocities on stage which this music accompanies without comment. Speaking of the prehistoric youthful generation of *Sacre,* Cocteau stated in somewhat condescending but well-intended tones of enlightenment: "These credulous men imagine that the sacrifice of a young girl, chosen above all others, is absolutely essential to the rebirth of Spring."[9] At first the music states: this is the situation as it was and the music is as far removed from assuming a position as was Flaubert in Madame Bovary. Atrocity is observed with a certain satisfaction, but it is not transformed. It is, rather, presented without mitigation. In the case of Schoenberg it has become, as a matter of principle, an accepted practice not to resolve dissonances. This determines the culturally bolshevistic aspect of the "Scenes from Pagan Russia" (as Stravinsky subtitled *Sacre*). When the avant-garde embraced African sculpture, the reactionary telos of the movement was totally concealed: this reaching out for primitive history seemed, rather, to serve the liberation of strangulated art rather than its regimentation. Still today, the difference between those culturally hostile manifestos of cultural fascism must be made clear if the dialectical double meaning of Stravinsky's experiment is not to be

8. Sir James Frazer (1854–1941), best-known for *The Golden Bough* (1911–1920). Of relevance to the thought complex referred to by Adorno are Frazer's *Taboo and the Perils of the Soul* (1911) and *Totemism and Exogamy* (1916). Lucien Lévy-Bruhl (1857–1939), a French psychologist, was the first to define the pre-logical character of the mentality of primitives. —Trans.

9. Cocteau, *op. cit.*

overlooked. This double meaning—as with Nietzsche—has its roots in liberalism. Cultural criticism presumes a certain substantiality in culture; it thrives under the protection of this substantiality and receives from it the right to ruthless pronouncement as a spiritual entity unto itself—even if, in the final analysis, it turns against this entity. Human sacrifice, in which the impending domination of the collective is proclaimed, is evoked out of the insufficiency of the individualistic condition in itself. The wild portrayal of the primitive—as the philistine reproachfully maintains—no longer only satisfies the romantically civilizing need for stimulus. It further gratifies the longing for the end of social illusion, the drive towards truth which lies beneath the bourgeois machinations and maskings of power. It is the very heritage of the bourgeois revolution which is present in such an attitude. Fascism, which literally sets out to liquidate liberal culture—along with its supporting critics—is for this very reason unable to bear up under the expression of barbarism. Not for nothing did Hitler and his cultural minister, Alfred Rosenberg, decide the cultural conflicts within their party against the nationally bolshevistic intellectual wing and in favor of the petty bourgeois dream of temple columns, noble simplicity, and quiet greatness. In the Third Reich—with its astronomical sacrifice of human beings—*Le Sacre du printemps* could never have been performed. Whoever dared to acknowledge the barbarism directly in practice within the ideology of the movement fell from grace. German barbarism—and this is perhaps an idea which Nietzsche had in mind—might thereby have eradicated barbarism without the lie of National Socialism. In spite of all this, the affinity is unmistakable between *Sacre* and the reproach of a Gauguin-like character. It recalls the sympathies of the man who—as Cocteau reports—shocked the gamblers at Monte Carlo by donning the jewelry of a negro king. It is not only that the work actually resounds with the noise of the impending war, but it further reveals its undisguised joy at the vulgar splendor of it all. Such joy, to be sure, was easily comprehended in the Paris of Ravel's *Valses Nobles et Sentimentales*. The force of hypostatized bourgeois culture

147

drives man to seek refuge in the phantasm of nature, which in the final analysis reveals itself as the herald of absolute suppression. The aesthetic nerves tremble with the desire to regress to the Stone Age.

TECHNICAL ELEMENTS IN SACRE

Le Sacre du printemps—as the virtuoso composition of regression—is an attempt to gain control over regression by offering an image thereof; the composition by no means intends to abandon itself to regression. This impulse to assume a position of command has played a large role in its indescribably vast effect on successive generations of musicians. Not only did it assert that the retrogression of musical language and its appropriate state of consciousness were up to date, but it further promised to hold its ground against the anticipated liquidation of the subject. This was accomplished by making such a threatened liquidation a concern of the music itself, or at least by registering it artistically from the vantage point of an impartial observer. The imitation of the primitive should serve as a miraculous, yet objective, magic means to avoid falling into the hands of the feared forces. During the early stages of such art— in *Petrouchka,* for example—the montage of various fragments is based upon wittily organizational procedure; in every instance it is achieved through technical trickery. In similar manner, Stravinsky manipulates every regression in his work, treating it as an image which does not lose sight of aesthetic self-control for a single moment. In *Sacre,* a ruthlessly applied artistic principle of selection and stylization achieves the effect of the primeval world.[10] Around 1910 the more sensitive artists

10. The concept of renunciation is basic for the total work of Stravinsky and actually determines the unity of all phrases. "Each new work . . . is an example of renunciation" (Cocteau, *op. cit.*). The ambiguity of the concept of renunciation is the vehicle of the total aesthetics of that sphere. It is used by Stravinsky's apologists in the sense of Paul Valéry's pronouncement that an artist is to be evaluated according to the quality of his refusal. As a formal generalization this need not be

must have rebelled against neo-Romantic melodizing, against the saccharin of Strauss's *Der Rosenkavalier*. Through such refutation, this kind of melody, and in particular lengthy, drawn-out melody, and eventually anything musical which developed subjectively, fell victim to taboo.[11] Thus in Impression-

---

disputed; it can be applied to the new Viennese school—to the implicit prohibition of consonance, symmetry, and uninterrupted upper-voice melody—equally as well as to the varying ascetics of the Western schools. Stravinsky's renunciation, however, is not merely renunciation as abstinence from worn-out and questionable means, but it is a denial as well. It is an exclusion, as a matter of principle, of all redemption or fulfillment of an element which appears in the immanent dynamics of musical material, as an expectation, or a demand. Speaking of Stravinsky, after his conversion to tonality, Webern said that "music had been withdrawn from him." Webern thus characterized the incessant process, which then distorts its self-chosen poverty into objective wretchedness. It is not sufficient to reproach Stravinsky's naïve technology for everything which he is lacking. Insofar as these lacks stem from the stylistic principle itself, such reproach would not differ essentially from that criticism of the Viennese school which complains about the predominance of "wrong sounds." The meaning of this denial for Stravinsky is to be defined by the standard of any self-made rule. It must be understood according to the idea involved, not just according to the omissions determined by it. It would be meaningless to reproach the artist for not doing what his principle does not indicate. The important factor is that the product of the will becomes entangled—permitting the surrounding landscape to wither away—and that it consequently loses its own validation.

11. Already before the First World War the audience lamented that composers no longer offered any "melody." In Strauss's compositions they were disturbed by the technique of permanent surprise, which interrupts melodic continuity, only to permit it occasionally in the crudest and most vulgar fashion, as a reward after turbulence. Reger causes the melodic profile to disappear behind unrelentingly mediated chords. In Debussy's mature works melodies are reduced to elementary tonal combinations, as materials in a laboratory are reduced to models. Mahler, finally, who clings to the traditional concept of melody more tenaciously than any other composer, made enemies in so doing. He is reproached for the banality of invention as well as for the forced aspects of his works—for those elements which do not proceed purely from the motivic driving force of elongated phrase structure. Mahler—parallel to Strauss in his role as the conciliator of opposing factions, and the life thereof as well—compensated exaggeratedly for the demise of Romantic melody as understood in the nineteenth century. In truth, his genius was necessary to recreate such exaggeration itself as a compositional means of representation, as the vehicle of musical meaning—the

149

ism the material is restricted to a rudimentary succession of tones. But the atomization of the motif—so typical of Debussy —is transformed from uninterrupted passages of continually merging color-splashes into a disintegration of the organic progress. All of the scattered infinitesimal remnants are intended to represent the heritage of the primeval age—now without a master and totally lacking in subject—in other words, phylogenetic traces of recollection—". . . little melodies out of the roots of centuries."[12] The melodic particles out of which any particular section of *Sacre* is constructed are for the most part diatonic in nature, their accent is folkloristic—or they are simply taken from the chromatic scale, as are the quintuplets of the final dance. These particles are never "atonal"—never a totally free succession of intervals without reference to a previously established scale. At times it is a matter of a limited selection of the twelve tones—as in the pentatonic scale—as if the other tones were taboo and not to be touched. In *Sacre*, it is possible to think of that deliriousness at a mere touch which

---

meaning, that is, of a desire conscious of the impossibility of any lasting fulfillment. It is by no means true that the melodic power of the individual composers was exhausted. Harmonic progression, however, historically speaking, moved more and more into the foreground of musical formulation and reception; this, in the final analysis, did not permit the melodic dimension to develop proportionally in homophonic thought. It was this melodic dimension which previously—particularly since early Romanticism—had made harmonic discoveries possible. This immediately explains the triviality of many Wagnerian motivic constructions, which Schumann criticized. It is as though chromatic harmony could no longer tolerate independent melody. If independent melody is the goal—as it was in Schoenberg's early compositions—then the tonal system itself fails as a result. Otherwise, only two possibilities remain for the composer: he can dilute melody to such an extent that it is transformed into a mere harmonic function; or, by sheer force, he can decree harmonic expansions which appear arbitrarily within the firmly defined harmonic scheme. Stravinsky drew the consequences of the first possibility—the one established by Debussy: fully aware of the weakness of melodic successions which in actuality are no longer such, he totally discards the concept of melody in favor of a truncated, primitivistic pattern. It was actually only Schoenberg who emancipated melos; in so doing, however, he liberated the harmonic dimension itself.

12. Cocteau, *op. cit.*

Freud traces back to the prohibition of incest. The most elementary principle of rhythmic variation—which is the basis of repetition—is that the motif be constructed in such a way that, if it immediately reappears, the accents of their own accord fall upon notes other than they had upon first appearance (for example, "Jeu de Rapt" in *Sacre*). Frequently, not only are accents shifted, but length and brevity are interchanged as well. In all cases, the differentiations derived from the motivic model appear to be the result of a simple game of chance. In this perspective, the melodic cells seems to be under a spell: they are not condensed, rather they are thwarted in their development. For this reason, even in those works of Stravinsky which are most radical from the standpoint of surface sound, there is a contradiction between the moderated horizontal and the insolent vertical. Such a contradiction already implies the conditions for a re-employment of tonality as a system of relationships, whose structure is better suited to the melismata than are chords constructed of several sounds. Such chords function coloristically, not constructively. In Schoenberg, on the other hand, the emancipation of harmony, from the very beginning, affected melody as well. In the latter's melodic structures, the major seventh and the minor ninth are treated as equals with the customary intervals. However, *Sacre* shows no lack of tonal infusion, particularly in its harmonic make-up. One such example is the antiquated modal entrance of the brass in the "Danse des Adolescentes." On the whole, harmony as such is most closely related to what the group The Six after the First World War called polytonality.[13] The Impressionistic model of polytonality consists of the interlaced sounds of varying and spacially separated musics, as at a fair. This concept is common to Stravinsky and Debussy: in French music around 1910 it plays a role similar to that of the mandolin and the guitar in

13. The Six: *"les Six"*—a name applied in 1920 to a group of six French composers—Louis Durey, Arthur Honegger, Darius Milhaud, Germaine Tailleferre, Georges Auric, and Francis Poulenc—who around 1916 formed a loose association based on their acceptance of the aesthetic ideas of Eric Satie. They found an eloquent advocate in Jean Cocteau. (Cf. *Harvard Dictionary*, 779.) —Trans.

Cubism. At the same time, it belongs to the treasure of Russian motifs: one of Mussorgsky's operas even has a fair as its setting. Fairs continue to exist apocryphally in the midst of cultural order, recalling a vagrant way of life—not a fixed, stationary form of existence, but rather a pre-bourgeois state, the rudiments of which now serve economic exchange. In Impressionism this becomes the penetration of the uncomprehended into bourgeois civilization—its very "life." Later, however, this factor is reinterpreted as archaic impulses which threaten the very life of the bourgeois principle of individuation. Such a functional shift takes place in Stravinsky, but not in Debussy. The passage in *Sacre* which is harmonically most frightening— the dissonant transformation of the modal theme in the winds in the "Rondes Printanières," measures 53–54—is an hysterically intensified fair effect and offers no liberation of the "basic drives of the sounds." Consequently, harmonic progression disappears along with harmonic development. Pedal points had already played a major role in *Petrouchka* as a means of representing a somewhat timelessly hovering roar. They are now dissolved throughout into ostinato rhythms and become the exclusive principle of harmony. The cohesive force of harmonic-rhythmic ostinato makes it possible, from the very beginning, to follow the music easily, in spite of all raw dissonance. In the final analysis, this is the source of the boredom which has become the norm for music performed at typical music festivals since the First World War—insofar as such music even feigns modernity. The specialist has always lacked any meaningful interest in counterpoint; it is sufficiently characteristic that the few modest combinations of themes in *Petrouchka* are composed in such a way that they can hardly be detected. Now it assaults all polyphony—except for multi-toned chords as such. Contrapuntal statements are encountered only seldom and then, for the most part, with oblique overlappings of thematic fragments. Questions of form as progressive totality are completely absent and the construction of the whole reveals little concern for the structure. Consequently, the three rapid movements— "Jeu du Rapt," "Danse de la Terre," and "Glorification d l'Élue"

with the fragmentary principal voices in the high woodwinds—
are all awkwardly similar. The concept of speciality finds its
musical formula: of all the elements of music, only two are still
permissible: first, the accentuating articulation of succession
which is acceptable only in a highly specialized sense: The second is instrumental color, either as an expansive or resounding
tutti, or as a special coloristic effect. One among many possible
compositional procedures—the joining together of complexes
defined by a pattern—is elevated hereafter to the level of
exclusiveness.

"RHYTHM"

Stravinsky's imitators remained far behind their model, because
they did not possess his power of renunciation, that perverse
joy in self-denial. The modern aspect in Stravinsky is that element which he himself can no longer bear: his aversion,
actually, to the total syntax of music. All of his followers—
with the possible exception of Edgar Varèse—are completely
void of this sensitivity. The greater breadth of musical means in
which they indulge—harmless as this might be in origin—deprives them of that very air of authenticity, for the sake of
which they chose Stravinsky as their model. The comparison of
an imitation of *Sacre*—such as Claude Devincourt's *Offrande
à Shiva*—with the original might be instructive. The Impressionistic tonal voluptuousness of the work functions as a caustic
into which the victim is placed in order that his sense of taste
be destroyed. An analogous relationship, incidentally, existed
earlier between Debussy and his adept followers, such as Dukas.
To a very large degree taste coincides with the ability to refrain
from tempting artistic means. The truth of taste as the truth of
historical innervation is based upon this negativity, which, however, manifests at the same time an element of finality as a
private concern.[14] The tradition of German music—as it in-

14. "Profundity of this kind demands not merely sensitive reception
and abstract thought, but the reason is its concrete grasp and the most

cludes Schoenberg—has been characterized since Beethoven, both in the positive and the negative sense, by the absence of taste. In Stravinsky the primacy of taste collides with the "thing." The archaic effect of *Sacre* is a product of musical censorship, a self-denial of all impulses which do not agree with the basic stylistic principle. Artistically produced regression then leads, however, to the regression of composition itself—to the progressive deterioration of compositional procedures, to the ruin of technique. Stravinsky's admirers have grown accustomed to living with the resulting discomfort, by declaring him a rhythmist and testifying that he has restored the rhythmic dimension of music—which had been overgrown by melodic-harmonic thinking—again to honor. In so doing, they assert, he has excavated the buried origins of music; as, for example, the events of *Sacre* might well evoke the simultaneously complex and, at the same time, strictly disciplined rhythms of primitive rites. In contrast it has been rightly asserted by the Schoenberg school that the rhythmic concept—for the most part manipulated much too abstractly—is constricted even in Stravinsky. Rhythmic structure is, to be sure, blatantly prominent, but this is achieved at the expense of all other aspects of rhythmic organization. Not only is any subjectively expressive flexibility of the beat absent—which is always rigidly carried out in Stravinsky from *Sacre* on—but furthermore all rhythmic relations associated with the construction, and the internal compositional organization—the "rhythm of the whole"—are absent as well. Rhythm is underscored, but split off from musical content.[15] This results not in more, but rather in less rhythm

---

sterling qualities of soul-life. Taste on the contrary is merely directed to the outside surfaces, which are the playground of the feelings, and upon which one-sided principles may very well pass as currency. But for this very reason our so-called good taste is scared by every kind of profounder artistic effect, and is dumb where the ideal significance is in question, and all mere externalities and accessories vanish" (Hegel, *Fine Art,* Vol. I, 46). The coincidental nature of "one-sided principles," the hypostatized sensual sensitivity, idiosyncrasies as rules, and the dictate of taste are various aspects of the same basic state of affairs.

15. The formal analogy between twelve-tone constructivism and Stra-

than in compositions in which there is no fetish made of rhythm; in other words, there are only fluctuations of something always constant and totally static—a stepping aside—in which the irregularity of recurrence replaces the new. This is evident in the final dance of the chosen victim—in the "sacrificial dance," where the most complicated rhythmic patterns restrain the conductor to puppet-like motions.[16] Such rhythmic patterns alternate in the smallest possible units of beat for the sole purpose of impressing upon the ballerina and the listeners the immutable rigidity of convulsive blows and shocks for which they are not prepared through any anticipation of anxiety. The concept of shock is one aspect of the unifying principle of the epoch. It

---

vinsky's procedures extends to rhythm as well; in Schoenberg and Berg, rhythm occasionally makes itself independent from the intervallic-melodic substance and assumes the role of the theme. The difference between these composers is, however, far more important: even in those cases where the Schoenberg school operates with such rhythms, they are for the moment charged with melodic and contrapuntal content, while the rhythmic proportions which in Stravinsky dominate the musical foreground are employed solely in the sense of shock effects. They refer to decorative melismata, and in that they appear as an end in themselves, and not, for example, as the articulation of lines.

16. The polemics of Stravinsky's followers against the atonality of the central European countries tends towards an accusation of anarchy. With regard to this situation, the following insights into Stravinsky the "rhythmist" are by no means superfluous: he designs the picture of immutable objectivity through the equality of all rhythmic unities within a given complex; further, the modifications of accents in which the dynamic markings stand are in no prudent relationship to the construction; in all cases they could just as well be fixed in another way; and, finally, beneath the rhythmic shocks there is concealed what Viennese atonality is continually accused of: arbitrariness. Modifications have the effect of abstract irregularities as such—not of specific rhythmic events. The last admission which the outward appearance of music would be inclined to make is that shocks are effects which can be controlled only by taste. The subjective moment lives on in pure negation—the irrational tremor, which is the response to stimulus. The assembled rhythmic patterns of exotic dances are imitated, but they remain on the level of free invention, void of all traditional meaning. They are an arbitrary game, and, to be sure, their arbitrariness is deeply related to the habit of authenticity throughout Stravinsky's music. *Sacre* already contains those elements which later undermine any claim to authenticity and revert music —because it aspires to power—to impotence.

155

belongs to the fundamental level of all modern music, even of that which stands at extremes: the significance of this concept for Schoenberg in his Expressionist phase was discussed earlier. The social origin of shock can be presumed in the overpoweringly intensified disproportion in modern industrialism between the body of the individual and the things and forces in technical civilization over which shock has power. The sensory capacity —the possibility for experience—present in shock, however, was in no way the equal of the unchained excesses of such disparity so long as the individualistic form of social organization excluded collective relationships—which perhaps might have been a match for the objectively technical forces of production. Through such shocks the individual becomes conscious of his nothingness in the face of the gigantic machine of the entire system. Since the nineteenth century, shock has left its traces in works of art; in music Berlioz may well have been the first for whose work they were of particular essence.[17] However, everything depends upon the manner in which music deals with the experience of shock. The works of Schoenberg's middle years take up a defensive position by portraying such experiences. In *Erwartung*—which can be traced from "Lockung" [*opus* 6] all the way to the second of the *Five Pieces for Piano* [*opus* 23]—the gesticulation recalls a man gripped by wild anxiety. Psychologically speaking, however, the man is saved by his anticipation of anxiety: while shock overcomes him, dissociating the continuous duration of traditional style, he retains his self-control. He remains the subject and, consequently, is able to assert his own constant life above the consequence of shock experiences which he heroically reshapes as elements of his own language. In Stravinsky, there is neither the anticipation of anxiety nor the resisting ego; it is rather simply assumed that shock cannot be appropriated by the individual for himself. The musical subject makes no attempt to assert itself, and contents itself with the reflexive absorption of the blows. The subject behaves literally like a critically injured victim of an accident

17. Cf. Walter Benjamin, *Schriften* I, 426ff., where several of Baudelaire's motives are treated.

which he cannot absorb and which, therefore, he repeats in the hopeless tension of dreams.What appears as the complete absorption of shock—the submission of music to the rhythmic blows dealt it from an external source—is in truth the obvious sign that the attempt at absorption has failed. This is the innermost deception of objectivism: the destruction of the subject through shock is transformed into the victory of the subject in the aesthetic complexion of the work; at the same time this destruction results in the overcoming of the subject by being-in-itself.

IDENTIFICATION WITH THE COLLECTIVE

The choreographic idea of sacrifice determines the musical invoice itself. What distinguishes the individualized from the collective is already eliminated in the idea—not only upon the stage. Stravinsky's polemic force has become more intense with the increasing refinement of his style. In *Petrouchka,* the element of individuation appeared under the form of the grotesque and was condemned by it.[18] In *Sacre,* there is no longer

18. From society's perspective the grotesque is generally the form employed to make alien and progressive factors acceptable. The bourgeois is willing to become involved in modern art if—by means of its form—it assures him that it is not meant to be taken seriously. The most obvious example thereof is the popular success of Christian Morgenstern's lyric poetry. *Petrouchka* manifests clear traits of such conciliation, reminiscent of the master of ceremonies, who tells jokes to reconcile his audience with whatever else strikes them squarely and directly. The pre-history of this function of humor is to be found in music. Not only Strauss and the conception of Beckmesser in *Meistersinger* come to mind, but Mozart as well. If it is insinuated that a composer were attracted by dissonance long before the turn of the twentieth century and were to resist it only through the convention regarding the sounds of subjective suffering, then Mozart's rustic sextet *Der Musicalische Spass* ("The Musical Joke") assumes far greater importance than that of eccentric frivolity. Precisely in Mozart the irresistible inclination to dissonance is to be found; this is present not only at the beginning of the *C-Major Quartet,* but also in various late piano pieces. Because of his lavish use of dissonance, Mozart's style was distasteful to his contemporaries. The emancipation of dissonance is per-

157

any basis for laughter. There is perhaps no single factor which demonstrates so clearly the extent to which modernism and archaism are two facets of the same thing in Stravinsky. With the elimination of the harmlessly grotesque, the work takes the side of the avant-garde—particularly of Cubism. This modernity, however, is achieved by means of an archaism of a totally different type from that pseudo-archaism which was so popular at the same time in Max Reger, for example—the beloved archaism of his "Im Alten Stil".[19] The interweaving of music and civilization is to be rent apart. Music, however, provokingly designs itself as a parable of a condition which is enjoyed precisely in the stimulus it provides as a contradiction to civilization. By means of its totemistic bearing, it offers the pretense of an undivided phylogenetically determined unity of man and nature. At the same time, however, the system reveals its central principle—the principle of sacrifice—as a system of domination, a system again consequently rent by inner antagonisms. The denial of antagonisms, however, is the ideological trick upon which *Sacre* is based. Just as the magician on the stage of the vaudeville theater causes the beautiful girl to disappear, so the subject in *Sacre* vanishes—the subject which has to bear the burden of the religion of nature. In other words, there is no development of an aesthetic antithesis between the sacrificial victims and the tribe. Yet their dance completes the unopposed,

---

haps not at all the result of the late-Romantic post-Wagnerian development—as the official history of music teaches—but rather the desire for it underlying all bourgeois music since Gesualdo and Bach—somewhat comparable to the role which the concept of the unconscious secretly plays in the history of bourgeois rationality. This is not simply a matter of analogy; the dissonance has been, rather, since the very beginning, the vehicle of meaning for all those factors which have fallen victim to the taboo of order. Dissonance is responsible for the censured sex drive. As tension it further contains a libidinal moment—the lament over denial. This would explain the rage which characterizes the rather universal reaction to manifest dissonance. Mozart's *Musical Joke* is an early anticipation of that factor in Stravinsky which entered into common consciousness.

19. *Konzert im alten Stil* (*Concerto in the Old Style*), for orchestra, *opus* 123. —Trans.

direct identification with the tribe. The subject is as far removed from exposing a conflict as is the structure of the music in presenting it. The chosen girl dances herself to death, in somewhat the same way as—according to reports of anthropologists—primitives who have unknowingly violated a taboo actually die away thereafter. As an individual, she reflects nothing but the unconscious and coincidental reflex of pain: her solo dance—like all the others, in its inner organization a collective dance, a round dance—is void of any dialectics of the general and the specific. Authenticity is gained surreptitiously through the denial of the subjective pole. The collective standpoint is suddenly seized as though by attack; this results in the renunciation of comfortable conformity with individualistic society. But at the very point where this is achieved, a secondary and, to be sure, highly uncomfortable conformity results: the conformity of a blind and integral society—a society, as it were, of eunuchs and headless men. The individual stimulus, activated by such art, permits the survival only of self-negation and the destruction of individuation; this indeed was the secret goal of the humor in *Petrouchka*—actually of all bourgeois humor in general—but now this obscure drive becomes a shattering fanfare. The pleasure in a condition that is void of subject and harnessed by music is sado-masochistic. If the liquidation of the young girl is not simplistically enjoyed by the individual in the audience, he feels his way into the collective, thinking (as the potential victim of the collective) to participate thereby in collective power in a state of magic regression. The sado-masochistic element accompanies Stravinsky's music through all its phases. *Sacre,* by unique contrast to this pleasure, has a certain gloomy melancholy in its total coloration as well as in its individual musical figures. However, this is intended less as an expression of mourning for the ritual of murder, which is in truth insane, than as the expression of the mood of the enchained and the unfree—the outcry of creatural incarceration. This tone of objective mourning in *Sacre* is achieved technically through the predominance of dissonance, but often by means of con-

159

densed orchestral technique. The tone portrays the only counter-instant against the cultic gesture, which the horrible act of violence by the mysterious medicine man—along with the round dance of the young girls—would like to consecrate as a holy morning.[20] At the same time, however, it is the tone which imprints a type of dull and ill-humored submissiveness upon this monstrosity of shocks which nonetheless remains weak in contrast, in spite of all the color lavished upon it. This sub-missiveness, in the final analysis, consigns what was previously sensational to a boredom which is in no way greatly different from the boredom which Stravinsky later methodically developed. But this very fact, at such an early point, makes it difficult to understand the desire for imitation which *Sacre* once inspired. The primitivism of yesterday is the naïveté of today.

ARCHAISM, MODERNISM, INFANTILISM

However, it was by no means the insufficiency of his highly stylized impoverishment which drove the Stravinsky of *Sacre* further. He must rather have become aware of a Romantic-historical element in anti-Romantic pre-history—of the domesticated desire, that is, for an objective state of the spirit, which can be evoked here and now only through costume. The aboriginal Russians bear an uncanny resemblance to Wagner's ancient Germanic figures—the stage settings for *Sacre* recall the rocks of the Valkyries. The configuration of the mythically monumental, as well as the nervous tension of the ballet, are also Wagnerian, as Thomas Mann emphasized in his essay in 1933,

20. There is already a counterpart in *Petrouchka* to the figure of the Wise Elder in *Sacre:* the Showman who commands the marionettes to life. He is a charlatan. It would be a simple matter to see the meaning of Stravinsky's vaudeville act as the transfiguration of the charlatan into the all-mighty magician. His principle of domination—the musical principle of authenticity—emerged out of play—from deception and suggestion. It is as though contrived authenticity recognized its own untruth in such an origin. In Stravinsky's later works, charlatans and medicine men no longer appear.

"The Sufferings and Greatness of Richard Wagner."[21] The sound of the work in particular—the idea, for example, of suggesting obsolete wind instruments through the unique coloration of the modern orchestra, is of Romantic origin. Examples of this are the basoon, which offers an effect of "depth" in its high register; the rasping English horn and the reed-like alto flute; and the exposed tubas of the medicine man. Such effects are as much a manifestation of musical exoticism as is the pentatonic in a work stylistically so opposed to it as was Mahler's *Das Lied von der Erde*. The tutti sound of the orchestra also has at times a touch of Strauss-like excessive luxury, an element totally detached from the compositional substance. The style of accompanying design, conceived purely in color, against which repeated melodic fragments appear, is directly rooted in Debussy, in spite of the difference in sound itself and in the harmonic inventory. Regardless of all theoretical anti-subjectivism, the effect of the whole work is largely a matter of mood, of anxious excitement. Often the music itself seems psychologically excited, in the "Danses des Adolescentes," from measure 30, for example, or in the "Cercles Mystérieux" of the second scene, from measure 193. With this almost historicizing evocation of primeval times—from which he basically, nevertheless, keeps a playful distance—Stravinsky soon finds himself unable to satisfy the most objective drive. His attempt to evoke the spiritual landscape of Strauss's *Elektra* fails. He designs the tension of the archaic and the modern in such a way that, for the sake of the authenticity of the archaic, he rejects the primeval world as a stylistic principle. *Les Noces* is the only one of his later major works which concerns itself with formulations which are far more unrelenting than those in *Sacre*. Stravinsky searches for authenticity in the organization and decline of the world of imagery in modernity. Freud defined the similarity between the spiritual life of primitives and neurotics. The composer now despises the primitives and clings to that upon which the experience of the modern can rely: to that archaism which de-

21. *Essays of Three Decades*, trans. H. T. Lowe-Porter, New York, 1968, 307–352.

termines the basic stratum of the individual and which reappears directly and without disguise in the decomposition of the individual. The works between *Sacre* and the turn to neo-classicism imitate the gesture of regression, as it belongs to the dissolution of individual identity. Through this attitude, these works would appear to achieve collective authenticity. The thoroughly close relationship between this ambition and the theories of Carl Gustav Jung, with which Stravinsky could hardly have been familiar, is as striking as is the reactionary potential indicated by it. The search for musical equivalents of the "collective unconscious" prepares the transition to the installation of a regressive collective as a positive accomplishment. At first, however, this appears audaciously avant-garde. The compositions grouped around *Histoire du Soldat* and belonging to the period of the First World War could easily be labeled infantile; traces of this development, incidentally, go all the way back to *Petrouchka*. Stravinsky was always prone to exploit children's songs as messengers of the primeval to the individual. In an article on *Renard,* published in 1926, Else Kolliner—who otherwise hardly wrote about music—offers the first critical evaluation of such infantilism; though it was also, to be sure, thoroughly apologetical.[22] Miss Kolliner states that Stravinsky moved "in a new realm of phantasy. . . , which every individual once in his childhood enters with closed eyes." The composer does not portray this moment with idyllic praise, nor does he design it episodically as did Mussorgsky, "but as the only scene which for the duration of the performance is totally closed off from all other real or unreal worlds." Stravinsky creates an inner stage which to a certain degree is hermetically sealed off from the conscious ego. This stage is the scene of pre-individual experiences which are common to all and now through shock again become accessible. The establishment of this scene of action results in a "collective phantasy" which reveals itself through "an understanding with the audience which is accomplished with lightning speed"—in the anamnesis of

22. *Anbruch* (1926), 8:5, 214ff.

rites as they survive in play. "The continual change of beat; the stubborn repetition of individual motives—as well as the disassembling and totally new recomposition of their elements; this pantomimic character, strikingly expressed in the passages of sevenths which are then expanded into ninths; the ninths which then contract into sevenths; the drum rolls as the most precise form of the frenzy of the rooster—all of these factors are instrumentally accurate translations of child-like gestures of play into music." The exciting aspect is that the listener—due to the unfixed fluctuation of the repetitions—"thinks to see the process of origination before his very eyes." In other words, he experiences this because the musical gesture avoids every singularity of meaning, thereby designing a non-alienated state, the roots of which stem from childhood. The process of genesis which is thus envisioned has nothing to do with musical dynamics, and even less to do with the origin of large, continually progressing musical forms out of nothingness. This latter concept conditioned one of Beethoven's fundamental ideas all the way to the first movement of the *Ninth Symphony*. Through misunderstanding, this idea has more recently been attributed to Stravinsky. Behind this idea lies the conviction that clearly defined musical models—motives which have been set down once and for all—do not yet exist; but rather that there is a latent, implied motivic nucleus around which the work hovers. This is the case in all of Stravinsky's compositions and it explains their metrical irregularities. He has not, however, arrived at a conclusive definition. In Beethoven the motives are definitive and reveal a specific identity, even if they are in themselves no more than meaningless formulae of basic tonal relationships. Stravinsky's technique of archaic-musical images views the circumvention of such identity as one of its primary concerns. Nevertheless, precisely because the motif itself is not yet "there," the displaced complexes are continually repeated, instead of drawing the consequences, as Schoenberg's terminology so designates. The concept of dynamic musical form which dominates Western music from the Mannheim school down to the present Viennese school assumes this motif as a prerequisite in a firmly

163

defined identity, even if it is minutely small. The dissolution
and variation of the motif is possible only if it is firmly preserved in the memory of its original identity. Music permits
only that degree of development which any firmly constituted
element allows. Stravinsky's regression, reaching back beyond
this, for this very reason replaces progress with repetition.
Philosophically, this leads to the very core of music. In music,
generally speaking—or prototypically according to Kant's epistemological theory—subjective dynamics and hypostatization
beyond together as poles of the same total attitude. The subjectification and objectification of music are the same thing. This
aspect is perfected in twelve-tone technique. Stravinsky is distinguished from the subjectively dynamic principle of the variation of an element unequivocally determined by a technique of
permanent beginnings which reach out in vain, as it were, for
what in truth they can neither reach nor retain. His music is
devoid of recollection and consequently lacking in any time
continuum of permanence. Its course lies in reflexes. The fateful
error of his apologists is their interpretation of the absence of
anything firmly defined in his music as their guarantee of life.
This lack in Stravinsky's music is, in the narrowest sense, a
lack of thematic material, a lack which actually excludes the
breath of form, the continuity of the process—indeed, it excludes "life" itself from his music. The amorphous is totally
without freedom, but comes to resemble the coercive force of
mere nature: there is nothing more rigid than the "process of
genesis." This process, however, is glorified as that which is
not alienated. Stravinsky's admirers state that individual identity
is suspended, by and large, through the principle of the ego.
They find his aesthetic game similar to play "as the child experiences it." It has no need of effective invisibility; it moves
figures in its imagination back and forth between reality and
unreality without rational inhibition. (It lies, according to ed-
ucators.) Children dissimulate in self-invented games; they love
to eradicate all traces—they slip into masks and unexpectedly
out of them again; they assign several roles to one player with
no rebellion of logic; and—once in the game—they recognize

no other logic other than keeping their movement continually fluid. In like manner, Stravinsky separates portrayal and song; he does not bind the figure to a specific voice, nor the voices to a specific figure. In *Renard,* there is singing from the orchestra pit which accompanies the action on the stage.

PERMANENT REGRESSION AND MUSICAL FORM

Regarding a Berlin performance of *Renard,* a critic raises the objection that "it takes a primitive fable and dresses it up as a circus act." This objection was based upon Stravinsky's concept of "folk" as a "collectively experiencing community related by clan—the primeval womb of all symbols and myths, the metaphysical forces of which religion is constructed." This interpretation, the tone of which later appeared in Germany in a sinister context, is far too loyal to Stravinsky and, at the same time, does him an injustice. It interprets modern archaism in a literal sense, as though only the artistically redeeming word were needed to reconstruct, directly and happily, the desired primeval world—a world filled with terror in its own age—as though the heedful recollection of the musician could cancel out history. However, this is the manner in which an affirmative ideology is read into Stravinsky's infantilism. The absence of any such ideology designates the substance of truth in every phase of his work. Psychology has proven that the individual passes through archaic stages of development in early childhood. In like manner, Stravinsky's anti-psychological rage, on the whole, cannot possibly be separated from the psychological conception of the unconscious as a principal prerequisite of individuation. His effort to fashion an organ of the pre-ego out of the non-conceptual language of music falls into the very same tradition proscribed by him as a stylistic technician and cultural politician —the tradition, that is, of Schopenhauer and Wagner. There is an historical solution to the paradox. It has often been pointed out that Debussy, the first productive exponent of hostility

165

towards Wagner in the West, is inconceivable without Wagner: in short, *Pelléas et Melisande* is a music drama. Wagner, whose music reveals a close relationship to German philosophy of the early nineteenth century, in more than a mere literary sense, had in mind a dialectics between the archaic—that is, the "will"—and the individualized. In Wagner, however, this dialectics—from every perspective—pursues a course which is detrimental to the principle of individuation; indeed, from the very beginning it takes a position against individuation in musical and poetic structure. In Wagner, the musical vehicles, intended to convey the meaning of the individual, reveal an impotent, feeble character, as though they were already historically condemned. His work disintegrates into fragments as soon as individuated moments appear in substantial form, while the moments themselves are already decadent clichés. Stravinsky takes this into account: his music, as permanent regression, gives answer to the situation in which the principle of individuation degenerated into an ideology. According to the philosophy implied, he belongs to the positivism of Ernst Mach: "The ego is not to be saved." According to his attitude, he belongs to a type of Western art the highest summit of which lies in the work of Baudelaire, in which the individual—through the force of emotional sensation—enjoys his own annihilation. Therefore, the mythologizing tendency of *Sacre* continues where Wagner left off, negating the tendency at the same time. Stravinsky's positivism clings to the primeval world as though it were a matter of proven actuality. He constructs an imaginary ethnological model of the pre-individualized, which he would like to distill with precision in his works. In Wagner, the myth is intended as a symbolic presentation of general human relationships, in which the subject is reflected; for these relationships are the unique concern of the subject. Stravinsky's pre-history—in its scholarly representation—seems by comparison much older than that of Wagner's which, in spite of all the archaic drives and impulses which it expresses, does not extend beyond bourgeois formal bases. The more modern this pre-history is made, the earlier are the stages to which it regresses. Early Romanticism became deeply involved in the Middle Ages; Wagner with Germanic polytheism; and Stravinsky with the totem clan. However, there are for Stravinsky no communicative symbols for that abyss between the regressive impulse and its musical materialization; for this reason he is no less dependent upon psychology than is Wagner—indeed, his dependence is perhaps even greater. The outspoken sado-masochistic pleasure in self-annihilation—an element so clearly perceptible in his anti-psychologism—is determined by the dynamics of the basic drives and not by the demands of musical objectivity. This characterizes the type of human being whose external measurements are taken by Stravinsky's works; he is to tolerate no introspection or self-contemplation. The obstinate health, which clings to the external and denies the spiritual—as though this were already an illness of the soul—is the product of defense mechanisms in the Freudian sense. Convulsive stubbornness, along with the exclusion of any inspiration from music, betrays the unconscious presentiment of something incurable which otherwise would manifest itself disastrously. Music resigns itself all the less willfully to the conflict of psychic forces the more obstinately it withholds itself from the manifestations of the conflict. Musical form is eventually crippled by all of this. By virtue of his willingness to engage in psychological case studies, Schoenberg hit upon objectively musical validities. In Stravinsky—whose works are in no sense to be understood as the organ of an inner force —the immanently musical validity is, as a consequence, almost impotent: the structure is externally superimposed by the composer's will which determines the nature of his formulations and, further, those elements which they are expected to renounce.

THE PSYCHOTIC ASPECT

As a result of all of this, however, that easy road back to the origins—which Else Kolliner perceived in works such as *Renard* —is out of the question. In this regard, psychology teaches

167

that, between the archaic level in the individual and his ego there are walls erected which can be broken down only by the most powerfully explosive forces. The belief that the archaic simply lies at the aesthetic disposal of the ego—in order that the ego might regenerate itself through it—is superficial; it is nothing more than a wish fantasy. The force of the historical process, which has crystallized the firm contours of the ego, has objectified itself in the individual, holding him together and separating him from the primeval world contained within him. Obvious archaic impulses cannot be reconciled with civilization. The painful operation of psychoanalysis—as it was originally conceived—had, among its primary tasks and difficulties, the break-through of this wall. The archaic can be revealed without censorship only through the explosion to which the ego has succumbed: this takes place in the disintegration of the integral individual being. Stravinsky's infantilism is well aware of the price to be paid. He scorns the sentimental illusion of the Brahmsian "O, if I could only turn back" and constructs a perspective of mental illness in order to manifest the primeval world as it permeates the present.[23] The bourgeois accuse Schoenberg's school of insanity because it does not engage in their games. At the same time they find Stravinsky clever and normal. In truth, however, the make-up of his music is an aping of obsession and, even more so, of schizophrenia—the psychotic intensification of obsession. It appears as a strict system which is ceremonially invulnerable, without the pretended regularity being transparent or rational in itself by force of any inherent logic. This is the attire of an illusory system. At the same time, it makes it possible to encounter anything which is not caught up in the system in an authoritarian manner. Thus the archaic is transformed into modernity. Musical infantilism belongs to a movement which designed schizophrenic models everywhere as a mimetic defense against the insanity of war: around 1918, Stravinsky was attacked as a Dadaist, for the

23. Adorno refers to the Brahms song "O wüsst ich doch den Weg zurück" [opus 63, number 8]. —Trans.

Histoire du Soldat and *Renard* shattered all individual unity in order to startle the bourgeois philistines.[24]

RITUAL

Stravinsky's fundamental impulse was to develop a disciplined command over regression; this impulse determines his infantile phase perhaps more decisively than any other phase of his work. To prescribe physical gestures and—beyond these—even attitudes lies in the nature of ballet music. Stravinsky's infantilism remains true to this nature. It is not that schizophrenia is directly expressed therein, but the music imprints upon itself an attitude similar to that of the mentally ill. The individual brings about his own disintegration. From such imitation he promises himself a chance to survive his own demise. He imagines the fulfillment of the promise through magic, but nonetheless within the realm of immediate actuality. This bespeaks an effect which can hardly be explained in specifically musical terms, but only anthropologically. Stravinsky designed schemata of human forms of reaction, which then became inescapable under the pressure of late industrial society. The concern was everything which—according to its own drives and by its own nature—wanted to pursue the course along which society forced its defenseless members: self-elimination, unconscious dexterity, and adjustment to the blind totality. The sacrifice of the self, expected of every individual by the new form of organization, attracts as a residue of the primeval past, and at the same time

24. There is no stage of Schoenberg's work which is characterized by any aspect of startling; his work rather reveals an aspect of credulous confidence in the objectively compositional accomplishment—a confidence which refuses to understand that the products of Brahms or Wagner were of a quality different from his own. In unshakable faith in tradition, the tradition is dissolved by its own consequence. In the startling moment, on the other hand, the thought of effect is always present, even if the effect is one of alienation. There is scarcely a work of Western art which has totally freed itself from effect. For this reason it is, in the end, so much easier for those who startle to reach an understanding with the existing order.

is filled with horror before a future in which the individual must cast aside everything which made him and for whose sake, after all, the machinery of adjustment is meant to function. Reflection in the aesthetic image assuages this anxiety and strengthens the attraction. Every moment of soothing comfort, of the harmonious, of the displacement of horror in art—the aesthetic heir of the magic practice, against which all Expressionism, down to the revolutionary works of Schoenberg, protested—this harmoniousness triumphs in Stravinsky's scornful and cutting tone as the herald of the Iron Age. He is the yea-sayer of music. Such sentences by Brecht as "It can be done otherwise, but it can be done this way too" or "I don't even want to be human" might serve as the motto of the soldier's story or of the animal opera *Renard*. The composer insisted that the *Concertino for String Quartet* should hum along like a sewing maching. This he demanded of that combination of instruments once more purely suited to musical humanism, to the absolute spiritual penetration of the instrumental. The *Piano Rag Music* evokes the sound of a player piano. Anxiety before dehumanization is recast into the joys of revealing such dehumanization and, in the final analysis, into the pleasures of that same death wish whose symbolism was prepared by the much-hated Tristan. Sensitivity to the exhaustion of expressive characters, intensified to an aversion towards all unrefined expression (the only type of expression suited to the entire streamlined epoch of civilization) admits its pride in the negation of the concept of the human being through agreement with the dehumanized system. The supreme irony is that this could be accomplished without the actual death of the system. The schizophrenic demeanor of Stravinsky's music is a ritual which attempts to overcome the coldness of the world. His work goes vehemently to battle against the insanity of the objective spirit. By expressing the insanity which kills all expression, such sanity is not only reduced by provoking reaction—as psychology views the process—but the insanity itself is subjected to the organizing force of reason.[25]

25. The close relationship of this stage of the ritualistic in Stravinsky's music to jazz—which became internationally popular at exactly the same

ALIENATION AS OBJECTIVITY

Nothing would be more false than to interpret Stravinsky's music analogously to what a German fascist once called the sculpting of the mentally ill. Rather its concern is to dominate schizophrenic traits through the aesthetic consciousness. In so doing, it would hope to vindicate insanity as true health. A certain aspect of this idea has always been present in the bourgeois concepts of normality. This concept demands feats of self-preservation to the point of absurdity, to the very disintegration of the subject; for the sake of the unlimited justice of reality, which permits self-preservation only by victimizing that which is preserved. There is also a corresponding illusory realism: on the one hand, the principle of reality alone is decisive; on the other,

---

time—is evident. The comparison is valid in technical details such as the simultaneity of rigid tempi and irregular syncopated accents. Stravinsky experimented with jazz forms precisely in his infantile phase. The *Ragtime for Eleven Instruments,* the *Piano Rag Music,* and also the "Tango" and "Ragtime" from *L'Histoire du Soldat,* are among his most successful pieces. Unlike the numerous composers who thought to benefit their own "vitality"—whatever that might mean musically— through tactless familiarity with jazz, Stravinsky reveals, by means of distortion, the shabby and worn-out aspects of a dance music which has held sway for thirty years and has now given in completely to the demands of the market. In a certain respect he forces the flaws of this music to speak, and transforms the standardized elements of it into stylized ciphers of decay. In so doing he eliminates all traits of false individuality and sentimental expression, which irrevocably belong to naïve jazz, and converts such traces of the human—insofar as they might survive in the artful fragmentation of the formulae which he has put together—into ferments of dehumanization, with glaring mockery. His compositions are pieced together out of scraps of commercial goods just as many pictures or sculptures of the same time were composed of hair, razor blades, and tinfoil. This defines its difference in *niveau* from commercial trash. At the same time, his jazz pastiches appear to absorb the threatening attraction of that which has been abandoned to the masses, enchaining the danger thereof by giving in to it. Compared to these practices, every other interest of composers in jazz was a modest effort to gain an audience—a simple matter of selling-out. Stravinsky, however, thoroughly ritualized the selling-out itself, indeed even the relationship to consumer goods. He performs a *danse macabre* around its fetish character.

171

this reality grows empty for him who unconditionally follows it. In terms of its own substance, such reality is unattainable and removed from the striving individual through an abyss of meaning. Stravinsky's objectivity rings with such illusory realism. The totally shrewd and illusionless ego elevates the non-ego to the level of an idol, but in its eagerness it severs the threads that connect subject and object. The shell of the objective—now abandoned with no relationship whatsoever—is now offered as truth, as a super-subjective objectivity, all for the sake of such externalization. This is the formula not only for Stravinsky's metaphysical maneuver, but for his double social character as well. The physiognomy of his work combines that of the clown with the physiognomy of an upper-level civil servant. His work plays the fool, thus offering its own grimace for practical purposes. It bows mischievously before the audience, removes the mask, and shows that there is no face under it, but only an amorphous knob. The conceited dandy of aestheticism from the good old days, who has now had his fill of emotions, turns out to be a tailor's dummy: the pathological outsider as the model of innumerable normal men, all of whom resemble each other. The challenging shock of dehumanization by its own will and effort becomes the original phenomenon of standardization. The macabre elegance and courtesy of the eccentric, who places his hand where his heart once was, in so doing expresses the gesture of capitulation—the recommendation of that which is without subject to omnipotent macabre existence, which he had only recently mocked.

FETISHISM OF THE MEANS

The realism of the façade manifests itself musically in the overrated effort to orient oneself according to established media. In his technique, Stravinsky does justice to reality. The primacy of speciality over intention, the cult of the clever feat, the joy in agile manipulations such as those of the percussion in *L'Histoire du Soldat*—all these play off the means against the end. The means in the most literal sense—namely, the instrument—is hypostatized: it takes precedence over the music. The composition expresses only one fundamental concern: to find the sounds which will best suit its particular nature and result in the most overwhelming effect. There is no longer any interest in instrumental values per se which will—as Mahler demanded—serve the clarification of continuity or the revelation of purely musical structures. This has brought to Stravinsky the fame of a man who knows his material—of the unerring craftsman—and the admiration of all those listeners who worship mere skill. In so doing he perfects an old tendency. The intensification of "effect" had always been associated with the progressive differentiation of musical means for the sake of expression: Wagner is not only the composer who knew how to manipulate the impulses of the psyche by finding for them the most penetrating technical correlates, but further he is the heir of Meyerbeer, the showman of opera. In Stravinsky, finally, what had reached priority in Strauss has now become independent. The goal of musical effects is no longer stimulation, but rather the "doing" per se. This is carried out, as it were, in abstraction and enjoyed as a *salto mortale*—a fatal leap—totally without aesthetic purpose. In the emancipation from the meaning of the whole, the effects assume a physically material character, becoming evident and almost athletic. The animosity against the anima, which runs throughout Stravinsky's work, is of the same essence as is the desexualized relationship of his music to the body. The body is treated by this music as a means—an object which reacts precisely, it drives the body to its highest attainments, as manifested drastically on the stage in the robbery and in the competition of the tribes in *Sacre*. The rigidity of *Sacre* makes it insensitive to all subjective impulses, as does ritual against pain in initiations and sacrifices. At the same time, this rigidity is the commanding force which trains the body—forbidding it the expression of pain through its permanent threat—for the impossible, just as it conditions the body for ballet, the most important traditional element in Stravinsky. Such rigidity—the ritual exorcising of spirits—contributes to the impression that the product is

173

nothing subjectively produced, thus reflecting the human being, but rather something which exists per se. In an interview for which he was later taken to task because of his supposed arrogance, but which nevertheless accurately characterizes his driving force, Stravinsky said of one of his later works that it was unnecessary to discuss its quality, for it was simply there— one aspect among all others. The air of the authentic is attained with emphatic lifelessness. Its sole concern is its mere existence, and the concealing of the role of the subject beneath its emphatic muteness. In so doing, it promises the subject an ontological footing, which it had lost through the same alienation chosen by music as a stylistic principle. The lack of relationship between subject and object is driven to an extreme, which is substituted for the relationship. It is precisely the insanity and obsession of this process—the crass contrast to the work of art organized from within itself—which has undoubtedly attracted countless composers.

DEPERSONALIZATION

The relative value of the schizophrenic elements in Stravinsky's music are defined within this system. During his infantile phase, schizophrenia assumes near thematic character. *L'Histoire du Soldat* ruthlessly weaves psychotic attitudes and behavior into musical configurations. The organic-aesthetic unity is dissociated. The narrator, the events on stage, and the visible chamber orchestra are juxtaposed; this challenges the identity of the supporting aesthetic subject itself. The anorganic aspect blocks every empathy and identification. The score itself formulates this aspect. The score arouses an impression of consternation, which has been formulated with the utmost mastery: in particular, through the sound which blasts the usual proportions of balance, placing immoderate demands upon the trombone, percussion, and contrabass. The result is a one-sided sound bereft of acoustic balance, comparable to the perspective of a small child to whom the trouser legs of a man seem huge and powerful and his head, by comparison, minute. The melodic-harmonic inventory is distinguished by a duplicity of error and unyielding control, which grants the external arbitrariness an aspect of determination—an element of inescapable, irrepressible logic of defect. This logic displaces the logic of the matter per se. It is as though decomposition were completely in charge of designing its own composition. *L'Histoire* is Stravinsky's pivotal work, but at the same time it scorns the concept of a *chef d'oeuvre* as *Sacre* still had hopes of being. *L'Histoire* sheds light upon Stravinsky's total production. There is hardly a schizophrenic mechanism—as defined in psychoanalysis by Otto Fenichel, for example[26]—which does not find therein a highly valid equivalent. The negative objectivity of the work of art recalls in itself the phenomenon of regression. In the psychiatric theory of schizophrenia, this is known as "depersonalization" according to Fenichel, it is a defensive reaction against the omnipotence of narcissism.[27] The alienation of music from the subject and, at the same time, its relationship to physical sensations find a pathological analogy in the illusory physical sensations of those who are conscious of their own body as an alien object. The division of Stravinsky's production into ballet and objectivistic music might well document physical sensations which are at the same time pathologically intensified and alienated from the subject. The physical feeling of the ego would then be a projection upon a medium which in reality is alien to the ego, namely, upon the dancers. In themselves, the dancers inhabit a sphere "unique to the ego" and totally dominated by it. The music, however, remains alienated; it stands in contrast to the subject as being-in-itself. The schizoid dispersion of aesthetic functions in *L'Histoire* might well have been formally anticipated in the ballet music which was without expression but at the same time found a continuity of meaning in a transcendent factor. This factor was, in turn, relegated to the world of the physical. Even in Stravinsky's earlier ballets there is no lack of passages in which

26. Otto Fenichel, *The Psychoanalytic Theory of Neurosis,* New York, 1945.
27. Fenichel, 419.

the "melody" is by-passed, in order that it might appear in the actual leading voice—in bodily movement on the stage.[28]

HEBEPHRENIA

The rejection of expression—the most conspicuous moment of depersonalization in Stravinsky—has in schizophrenia, its clinical counterpart in hebephrenia, or the indifference of the sick individual towards the external. Frigidity of feeling and emotional "shallowness"—as they are observed by and large in schizophrenics—are not in themselves the impoverishment of alleged inwardness. This impoverishment results from the lack of a libidinal possession of the objective world—in alienation itself—which hinders the development of the inner resources. It rather externalizes the realm of the psyche in rigidity and immobility. Stravinsky's music converts this to its advantage: expression, which has always proceeded from the suffering of the subject and the object, is scorned because a contact is no longer established. The impassibility of the aesthetic program is a stratagem of reason over hebephrenia. Hebephrenia is now recast as superiority and artistic purity. It can no longer be disturbed by impulses, but behaves as though it were operating in the realm of ideas. Truth and untruth therein, however, mutually condition each other. The negation of expression is not—as might suit the more naïve variety of humanism—simply regression into evil inhumanity. Expression reaps what it has earned. It is not only that the civilizing taboos are perfected beyond expression in the music which, up to now, as a medium of expression has remained far behind civilization.[29] At the same time,

29. Horkheimer and Adorno, *Dialektik der Aufklärung,* 212ff.
28. The inner-aesthetic tendency towards dissociation, which asserts itself here, stands in a remarkably pre-established harmony with the harmony of the film. Here the harmony can be explained only out of the unity of society as a totality; in the film it is technologically determined, representing the decisive medium of contemporary cultural industry. In the film, picture, word, and sound are disparate. Film music obeys laws similar to those of the ballet.

an account is given indicating that the substratum of expression —the individual—is socially condemned, because this very substratum gave rise to the destructive basic principle of that society, which today threatens to perish as a result of its own antagonistic nature. Busoni, in his day, accused the Expressionistic Schoenberg school of new sentimentalism; in so doing, however, he did not offer the modernistic excuse of a person who had not been able to keep up with musical development. Rather he felt that in expression itself there remained a residue of the injustice of bourgeois individualism—something of that lie which is, in reality, nothing more than a social agent although it would pretend to being-in-and-for-itself. Busoni intones the meaningless lament that the world has been overtaken by the principle of self-preservation, which had only recently been represented as individuation itself and reflected as such in expression. All responsible music today has in common a critical relationship to expression. The Schoenberg school and Stravinsky have attained to it by diverging courses, although Schoenberg and his disciples did not dogmatize it, even after the introduction of twelve-tone technique. There are passages in Stravinsky which, in their melancholy indifference or unrelenting harshness, do more honor to expression and its vanishing subject than do those moments of exuberance in his music in which the subject simply overflows. This it can do only because it does not realize that it is already dead: in such an attitude, Stravinsky actually concludes the lawsuit of Nietzsche contra Wagner.[30] The empty eyes of his music have at times more expression than does expression itself. The denial of expression becomes untrue and reactionary only when the force exerted thereby upon the individual appears directly as the overcoming of individualism, the atomization and levelling of human society. Stravinsky's hostility towards expression coquets with this process in all its various stages. Hebephrenia is finally revealed from a musical perspective to be what the

30. This is historically mediated by Cocteau's *Cock and the Harlequin*, a work opposing the theatrical element in German music. It coincides with the expressive: musical theatrics are nothing but the prevalence of command over expression. Cocteau draws heavily upon Nietzsche's polemics. Stravinsky's aesthetic is derived from the same source.

177

psychiatrists claim it to be. The "indifference towards the world" results in the removal of all emotional affect from the non-ego and, further, in narcissistic indifference towards the lot of man. This indifference is celebrated aesthetically as the meaning of this lot.

CATATONIA

Even in cases where Stravinsky's music evidences frenetic activity, there is passivity in the hebephrenetic indifference which does not succumb to expression. His rhythmic procedures closely resemble the schema of catatonic conditions. In certain schizophrenics, the process by which the motor apparatus becomes independent leads to the infinite repetition of gestures or words, following the decay of the ego. Similar behavior is familiar in patients who have been overwhelmed by shock. Thus Stravinsky's shock music stands under the pressure of repetition which thereby further injures the repeated material. The conquest of regions previously unexplored by music, such as the animalized insensitivity in L'Histoire, is due to the catatonic impact. This not only supports the intention of characterization, but affects the course of the music itself. The school rooted in Stravinsky has been called motoric. The concentration of music upon accents and time relationships produces an illusion of bodily movement. This movement, however, consists of the varied recurrence of the same: of the same melodic forms, of the same harmonies, indeed of the very same rhythmic patterns. Motility—Hindemith named one of his works Das Unaufhörliche—is actually incapable of any kind of forward motion.[31] Consequently, insistency—the pretension of power—falls victim to a weakness and uselessness of the same type as the gesticulatory schemata of the schizophrenic. The total energy exerted is placed in the service of blind and aimless obedience according to blind rules; this energy is devoted to

31. Das Unaufhörliche, oratorio in three parts after a text by Gottfried Benn, for solos and mixed chorus, boy's choir and orchestra. —Trans.

Sisyphus-like tasks. The best of the infantile compositions exhibit the delirious and confining gesture of chasing-one's-tail. This provides the alienated effect of not being able to escape one's own grasp. Catatonic actions are at the same time rigid and bizarre; thus the repetitions unite Stravinsky's conventionalism with his damaging machinations. The former recalls the mask-like, ceremonial politeness of many schizophrenics. Once this music has successfully exorcized the spirits, it is faced by the empty abodes of those once animated by these spirits which remain behind. At the same time, such conventionalism functions as a "phenomenon of restitution"—as a bridge back to the "normal." (It was out of this conventionalism that the neoclassic ideal proceeded; in the process, of course, there was a slight shift of emphasis.) In *Petrouchka* conventional recollections—the banality of the hand-organ and children's rhymes—appeared as stimuli. *Le Sacre du Printemps* by and large cast them aside: with its many dissonances and all the prohibitions stylistically dictated therein, it strikes conventions squarely in the face and has been, consequently, understood in all quarters as a revolutionary work in the culturally hostile sense of the word.[32] All this changes with *L'Histoire du Soldat*. The factors

32. Even *Sacre* is not unconditionally anti-conventional. Thus the passage of jousting which prepares for the entrance of the Medicine Man (from number 62 on; page 51 of the miniature score) is the stylization of a gesture of operatic convention, as opera might well provide the background for the excitement of the masses of common people; formally, it is repetition composed to death. Grand opera has contained such moments since Auber's *La Mouette de Portici*. Stravinsky's entire work exhibits a tendency not so much to eradicate all conventions as to work out their essence. Several of his last works—such as the *Danses Concertantes* and the *Scènes de Ballet*—have almost converted this tendency into theory. Such an inclination does not belong to Stravinsky alone, but rather to an entire epoch. The more musical nominalism increases and traditional forms lose their cohesiveness, the less important it becomes to add one more special case of a type to its already existing representatives. Wherever composers are not willing to renounce every established generality of form, they must attempt to formulate purely the essence of form with which they are involved, as though it were the Platonic idea thereof. Schoenberg's *Woodwind Quintet* is a sonata in the same sense that Goethe's *Märchen* embodies the idea of *Märchen*. (Cf. T. W. Adorno, "Schönbergs Bläserquintett," in *Pult*

179

of degradation and insult, the triviality—which in *Petrouchka* functioned as a joke in the midst of the sound—now becomes the sole material and is made the agent of shock. Thus began the renaissance of tonality. The melodic nuclei are now totally devaluated—following the example of *Sacre* and, to some extent, the three compositions for quartet. These nuclei now bear traces of commonplace music—the march, the idiotic fiddle, the anti-quated waltz, indeed even of the current dances such as tango and ragtime.[33] The thematic models can be detected not in artistic musical composition, but rather in various standard-ized commercial pieces. Such music—degraded by the market—needs, to be sure, only be made transparent by compositional virtuosos and their rattling skeleton is revealed. Through its affinity to this musical sphere, infantilism gains its "realistic" hold—no matter how negative it might be—on the customary and traditional; this is revealed, above all, in the manner in which it conveys shock. Infantilism does this by bringing popular music, well known to people, so close to them that they are shocked, as though the music were something from the market place, yet objective and from very far away. Convention collapses: it is only through convention that music accomplishes alienation. Convention has discovered the latent horror of com-monplace music in the failures of its interpretation and in its construction out of disorganized particles as well; out of this general disorganization, convention forms its principle of organi-zation. Infantilism is the style of the wornout and ruined. Its sound resembles the appearance of pictures pasted together out

---

und Taktstock (1928), 5, 45ff. Regarding the "destillation" of figures of expression, cf. Thomas Mann, *Doctor Faustus,* trans. H. T. Lowe-Porter, New York, 1965, 488ff.)

33. Therewith the danger of the unendangered becomes acute, the parody of that which is already so despised that it is no longer in need of parody. The superior imitation of this situation provides the cultural bourgeois with a certain melancholy joy. Shock is absorbed by laughter in the outspokenly charming four-handed piano pieces, which were later orchestrated in such a virtuoso manner as the *Suite No. 1 for Small Orchestra.* Nothing can be noticed of the schizoid alienation of *L'His-toire,* and the pieces have become concert favorites in the ever-present cabaret tradition.

of postage stamps—disjunct—but on the other hand a montage which has been constructed with labyrinthine density. It is as threatening as the worst nightmares. Its pathogenic arrangement, which is at the same time hoveringly hermetic and disintegrated, leaves the listener breathless. In this work the decisive anthropological condition of the era at whose beginning it stands is musically indicated; it is characterized by the impossibility of experience. Walter Benjamin characterizes Franz Kafka's narratives as the illness of healthy common sense; by analogy the defective conventions of *L'Histoire* are scars resulting from the wounds of everything which was viewed as common sense in music throughout the bourgeois epoch. They reveal the irreconcilable break between the subject and that which musically stood in contrast to it as an objective factor—the idiom. The former has decayed to the same level of impotence as the latter. Music must give up the attempt to design itself as a picture of the good and virtuous, even if the picture is tragic. Instead it is to embody the idea that there no longer is any life.

MUSIC ABOUT MUSIC

The decisive contradiction in Stravinsky's music is thereby explained. It is the counter-blow to every "literary" aspect of music, not only in program music but in the poetic aspirations of Impressionism as well. Even Satie, who was close to Stravinsky intellectually—even if he was inadequate as a composer—poked fun at such aspirations. However, Stravinsky's music does not appear upon the scene as a direct life process, but rather as absolute indirectness. In its own material, his music registers the disintegration of life and, simultaneously, the alienated state of the consciousness of the subject. In so doing, this music becomes literary in a wholly different sense, thus revealing the ideology of proximity to its original roots as a lie. This is, of course, the ideology which it would like to claim as its own. Compositional spontaneity itself is overwhelmed by the prohibition placed upon pathos in expression: the subject, which is

181

no longer permitted to state anything about itself, thus actually ceases to engage in "production" and must content itself with the hollow echo of objective musical language, which is no longer its own. In the words of Rudolf Kolisch,[34] Stravinsky's work is music about music; this is most evident during his infantilistic phase, but it is actually true throughout his career.[35]

34. Rudolf Kolisch, Austrian violinist, born 1896; brother-in-law of Schoenberg; founded his own string quartet which was renowned for its extensive repertory of modern works. —Trans.

35. The inclination to write music about music was widespread at the beginning of the twentieth century. This may be traced back to Spohr, if indeed the blame is not to be placed upon Mozart and his imitations of Händel (*Overture in the Style of Händel*, K. 399. —Trans.). Even Mahler's themes, however—free as they are of such ambitions—are childhood memories from the Golden Book of Music which have been displaced through blissful desire. Strauss has found pleasure in innumerable allusions and pastiches. The model for all this is in Wagner's *Meistersinger.* It would be superficial to condemn this inclination as Alexandrian and civilizing in Spengler's sense, as though the composition no longer had anything of its own to say and therefore had attached itself parasitically to something already lost. Such concepts of originality are derived from the concept of bourgeois property: unmusical judges condemn musical thieves. The basis of the tendency is technical in nature. The possibilities of "invention" or "discovery," which seemed unlimited to aestheticians in the age of competition, are limited in the scheme of tonality: on the one hand they are defined, to a large extent, by the dissected triad, on the other by the diatonic succession of seconds. At the time of Viennese classicism, when the formal totality was of greater importance than melodic "inspiration," the restrictive narrowness of that which lay at the disposal of the composer had not yet been felt. With the emancipation of the subjective melos of the *Lied,* however, the barriers became evermore perceptible: composers were forced to rely upon "inspiration"— as in the cases of Schubert or Schumann. The scant material, however, was so totally exhausted that no further inspiration could come forth which had not been present previously. They therefore absorbed the depletion of this supply into a subjective relationship and then constructed their thematic motives—more or less openly—as "quotations" with the effect of the recurrence of the familiar. In Stravinsky this principle becomes absolute: the only procedure which can be contrasted with it is that which departs from the harmonic-melodic circle, as in the case of Schoenberg. Among the impulses towards atonality, the desire to escape into freedom was certainly not the least important. It was the impulse to flee from a material which was exhausted not only in terms of its own configurations, but of its symbolism as well. The relationship between the historical aspect of writing music about music and the collapse of what was once commonly known as "melody" is unmistakable.

He could not conform to the dictate of his aesthetician: *ne faites pas l'art après l'art*. The concept of mutilated tonality itself, upon which all Stravinsky's works since *L'Histoire* are more or less based, presumes "literarily" established subject matter for music. Such material exists outside the immanent formal validity of the work and it is determined through a consciousness which exerts itself also from outside the work. The composition concerns itself with such subject matter. The composition feeds upon the difference between its models and the use which it makes of them. The concept of a musical material contained within the work itself—a central idea for Schoenberg's school—can hardly be applied to Stravinsky in any narrow sense. His music continually directs its gaze towards other materials, which it then "consumes" through the over-exposure of its rigid and mechanical characteristics. Out of the externalized language of music, which has been reduced to rubble, *L'Histoire* constructs a second language of dream-like regression; this it does by means of consequent manipulation. This new language would be comparable to the dream montages which the Surrealists constructed out of the residue of the wakeful day. It might well be in this way that the interior monologue is constructed which music, deluged upon city dwellers from radio and juke boxes, carries in its relaxed consciousness. This second language of music is synthetic and primitive; it bears the markings of technology. Stravinsky's attempt to achieve such a language recalls that of Joyce: nowhere does he come closer to his basic desire to construct what Benjamin called the primitive history of the modern. He did not remain at this extreme, however: even compositions such as the two ragtimes do not actually alienate the tonal language of music itself, to any great degree, through the dream-process of remembrance; they rather recast individual, clearly separable models from the commercial sphere into structures of absolute music. A marginal notation could be made as to how they might "correctly" sound: polkas, galops, and the vulgar salon hits of the nineteenth century. The damaging action is diverted from the idiom, as such, to the remains: it is the first significant turning point. According to psychology, the "authoritarian personality" expresses an ambivalent attitude towards authority. Stravinsky's music thus turns up its nose at the music of our fathers.[36] Respect for authority—which is thus rudely treated—rather than absorbing authority in the critical effort of personal production, combines with the furor over renunciation, an emotion otherwise well suppressed in Stravinsky's music. This attitude strikes the new authoritarian public in mid-course. The ridiculousness of the polka flatters the jazz fanatic; the abstract triumph over time—over everything which is presented as obsolete because of the change in fashion—is the substitute for revolutionary impulse, which is still able to find affirmation only in those instances where it can rely upon protection by great forces. Nevertheless, Stravinsky's literary character prohibits any possibility of scandal. His imitators further differentiated themselves from him in that, less assailed by the spirit, they quickly overcame the temptation to compose music about music. Hindemith, in particular, adopted from Stravinsky a claim to New Objectivity, but he translated its broken musical language—after a few short-lived excesses—into a literary and sound-medium. He further promoted a retrogressive relationship between the masks and hollow sculptures on the one side, and the "absolute" musical ideal of German academicism on the other. The short circuit which led from the aesthetics of Apollinaire and Cocteau to the popular music movement and the youth music movement—as well as to similar Philistine undertakings—would easily be one of the most unusual examples of the decline of the cultural heritage, if it did not have its counterpart in the fascination which German cultural fascism exercised internationally upon those intellectuals whose innovations were at one and the same time perverted and annulled by Hitler-style regimentation..

36. This ambivalence is so strong that it repeatedly manifests itself—even during the neo-classic phase, where it was posed in the incessant affirmation of authority. The most recent example thereof is the circus polka with the minor caricature towards the end of Schubert's *Marche Militaire.*

DENATURATION AND SIMPLIFICATION

Stravinsky's music about music-making disavowed the provincialism of the good German musician, which paid for the consequences of craftsmanship with cultural retardation. In Stravinsky there is no musical event which lays claim to being "nature" in itself; in so doing he has emphatically renounced the figure of the man of letters in music. He is able, consequently, to defend his position to the same degree that the man of letters can defend himself against the claim of the poet in his cherished image of himself as the lonely inspired creator in the forest in the midst of the late industrial commercial world. The schizoid isolation from nature which his work has fashioned for itself becomes a corrective against an attitude in art which covers up alienation rather than stands up to it. In Western music the man of letters has his early history in the ideal of moderation. The finite is that which is well executed. Only that which lays metaphysical claim to infinity attempts thereby to eliminate the character of the well executed as all too limiting, thus establishing itself as an absolute. Debussy and Ravel were similar to men of letters not only because they wrote good poems. Particularly Ravel's aesthetics of the well-turned-out toy—of the "bettor" or one who wagers or the *tour de force*—submitted to the verdict of the Baudelaire of *Les Paradis Artificiels,* whose production of natural lyric broke off at this time. No music which plays a role in technological enlightenment is any longer able to evade this verdict. In the works of Wagner the technical, sovereign fabrication already came to dominate, in every sense, over inspiration—the self-abandonment of the artist to the unmastered material. German ideology demands, however, that this precise moment of inspiration be concealed: it is the domination of the artist over nature which is to appear as nature itself. Wagner's vicious irrationalism and his rationalism, in the conscious disposition over the means, are two sides of the same state of affairs. The Schoenberg school has not advanced beyond

185

this point; it is blind to those historical changes in that process of aesthetic production which abrogates completely the category of the gifted singer. In twelve-tone technique, a childlike belief in genius runs parallel to the total rationalization of material; this belief culminates, finally, in ludicrous priority conflicts or possessive claims to originality. Such blindness—perhaps the necessary condition for the strict and total formation of things—refers not only to the attitude of the composers, which as such is a matter of indifference. This blindness further renders the composers helpless in all questions of the spiritual function of their music. Viennese music, striving for the most extreme autarky possible, innocently insists upon doubling literary accusations according to the scheme of music-drama, instead of distancing itself from them or treating them antithetically. This atmosphere has withdrawn into Stravinsky's work. Once the artificial moment of music—the "fabrication"—has become conscious of itself and recognized this dilemma, it loses the sting of the lie involved in thinking of itself as the pure sound of the soul, as a matter of primacy, as unconditional. This is the gain in truth, attained through the exorcism of the subject. An artful *"mal fait"* replaces the French *"bien fait"*: music about music insists that it is not a microcosm fulfilled within itself, but rather the reflection of shattered depletion. Its calculated errors are related to the open contours of legitimate contemporary painting—such as that of Picasso; such painting dismantles every hermetic aspect of the depicted figure. Parody, the basic form of music about music, implies the imitation of something and its resulting degradation through this imitation. This attitude—which the bourgeois regarded suspiciously as the attitude of the intellectual music-maker—adapts to regression with ease. Infantile music treats its model in a manner much like that of the child who takes apart his toys and puts them together again incorrectly. In this unnaturalness there is an element which is not entirely domesticated, an undisciplined mimetic factor—indeed, something of true nature itself. This might well be the way in which primitives would portray a missionary through dance, before they devour him. The impulse in this direction, however, has

186

proceeded from civilizing forces, which scorn affectionate imitation and tolerate it only as a mutilating force. This—not the
alleged Alexandrianism—is the subject of criticism. The evil
glance at the model casts a spell of bondage upon music about
music. It atrophies through its dependence upon heteronomy. It
is as though it could expect of its compositional content nothing
more than that which is present in the shabbiness of that music,
the reverse reflection which determines fortune. The danger of
the musical man of letters with his various reaction patterns, the
justification of the music hall against Wagner's *Parsifal,* of the
player piano against the intoxication of string instruments, of a
romantic dream-America against the childlike horrors of German Romanticism—all of this is not an excess of cognizance,
exhaustion, and differentiation, but rather of half-wittedness. It
becomes evident as soon as music about music conceals the
quotation marks.

DISSOCIATION OF TIME

The remnants of the memory are joined together; direct musical
material is not developed out of its own driving force. The
composition is realized not through development, but through the
faults which permeate its structure. These assume the role which
earlier was the province of expression: this recalls the statement
which Eisenstein once made about film montage; he explained
that the "general concept"—the meaning, that is, or the synthesis of partial elements of the theme—proceeded precisely
out of their juxtaposition as separated, isolated elements.[37] This
results, however, in the dissociation of the musical time continuum itself. Stravinsky's music remains a peripheral phenomenon in spite of the extension of its style over the entire younger
generation, because it avoids the dialectical confrontation with
the musical progress of time. This, in turn, is the basis of all
great music since Bach. The eradication of time, however, which
is accomplished by rhythmic tricks, is no sudden achievement

37. Sergei Eisenstein, *The Film Sense,* New York, 1942, 30.

187

of Stravinsky. Ever since *Sacre* he had been proclaimed as the anti-pope to Impressionism; from Impressionism he learned musical "timelessness." Anyone who has been schooled in German and Austrian music and who has listened to Debussy will be familiar with the experience of frustrated expectation. Throughout any one of his compositions, the naïve ear listens tensely, asking whether "it is coming"; everything appears to be a prelude, the overture to musical fulfillment, to the organic resolution of the *Abgesang*—which, however, never arrives. The ear must be re-educated if it is to understand Debussy correctly, seeking not a process of obstruction and release, but perceiving a juxtaposition of colors and surfaces such as are to be found in a painting. The succession simply expounds what is simultaneous for sensory perception: this is the way the eye wanders over the canvas. Technically, this is accomplished at first by "functionless" harmony—to use the expression of Kurt Westphal. The tensions of step-progression are not executed within the key or by modulations; instead harmonic complexes relieve each other. These complexes can be either static or exchangeable in time. The harmonic play of forces is replaced through the exchange of forces; conceptually, this is not dissimilar to the complimentary harmony of twelve-tone technique. Everything else proceeds out of the harmonic thought peculiar to Impressionism: the suspended treatment of form—a treatment which actually excludes "development"; the predominance of a type of character piece, which originated in the salon—it acquires its dominance at the expense of actual symphonic structure even in lengthier compositions; the absence of counterpoint; and finally a superior coloration, allotted to harmonic complexes. There is no "end"; the composition ceases as does the picture, upon which the viewer turns his back. In Debussy this tendency became gradually intensified up to the second volume of the *Preludes* and the ballet *Jeux;* in his works it is characterized by a growing atomization of thematic substance. His radicalism in this regard cost several of his most masterly compositions their popularity. Debussy's late style is, therefore, a reaction against the attempt to indicate once more something

188

approximating a musical course in time without sacrificing the ideal of suspension for the sake of it. Ravel's work, to a large degree, took a reverse course. The early *Jeux d'eau,* in spite of its sonata-like disposition, is one of the most non-developmental compositions of the entire school; it is further characterized by the absence of dynamics. Following this, however, Ravel strove to strengthen his consciousness of progression. This explains the unique role of modality in his work; it plays there a role different from, for example, that in Brahms. The church modes provide a substitute for tonal progressions. These, however, lose their dynamic quality through the lessening of emphasis upon the function of the cadence—a function not inherent in modality. The archaism of *organum-* and *faux bourdon*-effects helps to produce a type of step progression, yet retains the feeling of static juxtaposition.[38] The undynamic nature of French music might well be traced back to its arch-enemy Wagner, who was accused of an insatiable appetite for dynamics. In Wagner's works progression is, in many places, actually mere displacement. Debussy's motivic technique is derived from this source; it consists of an undeveloped repetition of the simple tonal successions. Stravinsky's calculated and sterile melismata are the direct descendants of Debussy; they are almost physical. They allegedly signify "nature"—as do many of the Wagnerian melismata—and Stravinsky remained faithful to his belief in such primeval phenomena, even if he hoped to achieve this precisely by avoiding the expression of them. In Wagner's untiring dynamics which, without exception, actually annul themselves, there is indeed something illusory and futile. "Every peaceful beginning was followed by a rapid upward drive. Wagner—insatiable, but not inexhaustible in this procedure—hit of necessity upon the alternative of another soft beginning after reaching such climaxes, only to expand again anew."[39] In other words, the intensification actually does not lead further; rather

38. *Fauxbourdon* effect: the parallel progression of first-inversion triads common in the fifteenth century. —Trans.

39. Feruccio Busoni, *Sketch of a New Esthetic of Music,* in *Three Classics in the Aesthetics of Music,* New York, 1962.

the same thing is simply repeated. Correspondingly—in the second act of *Tristan,* for example—the musical content of the motivic models upon which the passages of intensification are based is hardly anywhere affected by sequential progressions. The mechanical is joined to the dynamic. The old, narrow reproach upon Wagner of formlessness might well refer to this. The music drama resembles a gigantic container, offering the first indication of that substitution of a spatial aspect for progress in time, of the disparate co-existence in time which later was to become predominant among the Impressionists and in Stravinsky, resulting in the phantasm of form. Wagner's philosophical theory, which is amazingly homogeneous with his compositional theory, is really unfamiliar with history and recognizes only permanent revocation in nature. Such suspension of musical time consciousness corresponds to the total consciousness of a bourgeoisie which—in that it no longer sees anything before it—denies the time process itself and finds its utopia in the withdrawals of time into space. The sensual melancholy of Impressionism is the heir to Wagner's philosophical pessimism. In no case does sound go beyond itself in time; it rather vanishes in space. In Wagner, renunciation—the negation of the will to life—was the sustaining metaphysical category; French music, which renounced all metaphysics—even the metaphysics of pessimism—emphasized such renunciation all the more strongly the more it contented itself with a fortune which—as a mere here and now, as absolute transitoriness—is no longer fortune. Such steps of resignation are the pre-forms for the liquidation of the individual that are celebrated by Stravinsky's music. With some exaggeration, he might be called a Wagner who has regained consciousness as a composer abandoning himself, as a matter of principle, to the pressure of repetition—indeed, even to the "music-drama" vacuity of musical progress, while no longer concealing the regressive impulse through the bourgeois ideals of subjectivity and development. Earlier Wagnerian criticism—Nietzsche, in particular—raised the objection that Wagner's motivic technique wanted to pound his thoughts into the heads of the musically illiterate, whose characteristics were determined by industrial mass culture. Accordingly, in Stravinsky—the master of all percussion—this pounding becomes the admitted principle not only of technique but of effect as well: authenticity becomes its own propaganda.

MUSIC—A PSEUDOMORPHISM
OF PAINTING

The analogy which has been noted repeatedly between the transition from Debussy to Stravinsky in music, and the development from Impressionistic painting to Cubism, demonstrates more than a vague common denominator of cultural history, according to which music limped along behind literature and painting at the customary distance. The development of a spatial perspective in music is much rather a testimony of a pseudomorphism of painting in music. At its innermost core, it is the abdication of music. This might at first be explained with regard to the unique situation in France, where the development of productive forces in painting was so far superior to those in music that musicians involuntarily sought support in great painting. But the victory of genius in painting over genius in music submits to the positivistic trend of the entire age. All painting—even abstract—has its pathos in that which is; all music purports a becoming. This, however, is exactly what, in Stravinsky, music attempts to evade through the fiction of its mere existence.[40] In

40. The bourgeois idea of the pantheon would like to join painting and music in a peaceful relationship. Their relationship, however—in spite of synaesthetic double talents—is contradictory to the point of incompatibility. This became obvious precisely at that point where their union was proclaimed in cultural philosophy, that is, in Wagner's concept of the composite work of art—the *Gesamtkunstwerk*. The plastic aspect of this idea was from the outset so rudimentary that it is hardly amazing that Bayreuth performances, representing the absolute height of musical perfections, were presented with hopelessly outmoded stage settings. Thomas Mann has pointed out the "dilettante" aspect involved in the concept of unification of the arts. He defines this dilettantism as an essentially unartistic relationship to painting. From Rome and from Paris, Wagner wrote to Mathilde Wesendonk: ". . . my eyes are not enough

Debussy the individual color complexes were still related to each other and mediated as in the tradition of Wagner's "art of transition": sound is not devaluated, but soars for the moment beyond its boundaries. A perspective of sensory infinity is attained by means of such confluence. In Impressionistic paintings, whose technique absorbed music, dynamic effects and light impressions are produced according to the same procedures through the juxtaposition of spots of color. That sensory infinity was the poetic-aural nature of Impressionism in its age; the artistic rebellion shortly before the First World War was directed against it. Stravinsky directly adopted the conception of music involving spaciousness and surface expanse from Debussy; and his technique of complexes as well as the make-up of his atomized melodic models also illustrate Debussy's influence. The innovation actually consists only in the severance of the connecting threads and the demolition of remnants of the differential-dynamic procedure. The partial spatial complexes stand in harsh contrast to one another. The polemic negation of the gentle reverberation is fashioned into the proof of force, and the disconnected end-product of dynamics is stratified like blocks of marble. What earlier had sounded congruent unto itself now establishes its independence as an anorganic chord. The spatial dimension becomes absolute: the aspect of atmosphere, in which all Impressionistic music retains something of the subjective experience of time, is eradicated.

---

for me to use to take in the world," and ". . . Raphael never touches me." He continued: "See everything for me" (Thomas Mann, "The Sufferings and Greatness of Richard Wagner," *Essays of Three Decades,* trans. H. T. Lowe-Porter, New York, 1948, 316–317). For this reason Wagner calls himself a "vandal." He was guided by the presentiment that music contains an element not grasped by the process of civilization —which has not been fully subjugated to objectified reason—while the art of the eye, which holds to the deigned objects—to the objective practical world—reveals itself to be intimately related to the spirit of technological progress. The pseudomorphism of music with the technique of painting capitulates before the superior power of rational technology in that very sphere of art which had its essence in protest against such domination and which nevertheless became the victim of progressive rational domination of nature.

THEORY OF BALLET MUSIC

Stravinsky and his school bring about the end of musical Berg-sonianism. They play off *le temps espace* against *le temps durée*. The procedural method originally inspired by irrationalistic philosophy establishes itself as the advocate of rationalization in the sense of that which can be measured and counted without memory.[41] Music, which has become the victim of its own

41. The *Histoire du Soldat* further reveals itself as the true focal point of Stravinsky's work in that, in the composition of the Ramuz text, the score leads to the very threshold of consciousness of the state of affairs expressed in the text. The hero—a prototype of that generation after the First World War, out of which fascism recruited the hordes who were ready to march to the battlefields—perishes because he transgresses against the commandment of the unemployed: to live only for the moment. The continuity of experience in his memory is the mortal enemy of self-preservation which can be gained only through self-annihilation. In the English text the narrator warns the soldier:

> "One can't add what one had to what one has
> Nor to the thing one is, the thing one was.
> No one has a right to have everything—
> It is forbidden.
> A single happiness is complete happiness
> To add to it is to destroy it. . . ."

This is the anxiety-ridden, irrefutable maxim of positivism, the proscription of the recurrence of everything past, which would threaten regression into myth—it would represent deliverance to forces which in the composition are embodied by the devil. The princess complains that she has never heard the soldier speak about his earlier life; thereupon he vaguely mentions the city where his mother lived. His sin—the transgression of the narrow boundaries of the kingdom—can hardly be understood as anything but a visit to that city: as a sacrifice to the past. "La recherche du temps perdu est interdite"—this is of greater validity for no other art form than that for which the innermost law is regression. The regressive transformation of the subject into its pre-worldly being is made possible by cutting him off from the means by which he might become aware of himself. The soldier remains under the spell of the mere present; this fact unravels the taboo which prevails throughout Stravinsky's music. The jerky, blatantly present repetitions in the music should be understood as the means by which permanence can be given a dimension in memory while remaining static. These repetitions further

confusion, fears—in the face of the expansion of technology in the late stage of capitalism—that it might regressively fall victim to the contradiction between itself and technology. Music escapes this momentarily by means of a ballet-like leap, but in so doing it becomes all the more deeply enmeshed in the dilemma. Stravinsky, to be sure, hardly ever concerned himself with machine art in the sense of the ominous "tempos of the time." On the other hand, his music is concerned with types of human attitudes which view the ubiquity of technique as a schema of the entire life process: whoever wishes to avoid being crushed by the wheels of the times must react in the same manner as this music does. Today there is no music showing any trace of the power of the historical hour that has remained totally unaffected by the decline of experience—by the substitution, for "life," of a process of economic adjustment dictated by concentrated economic forces of domination. The dying out of subjective time in music seems totally unavoidable in the midst of a humanity which had made itself into a thing—into an object of its own organization. The result is that similar aspects can be observed at the extreme poles of composition. The Expressionistic miniature of the new Viennese School contracts the time dimension by expressing—in Schoenberg's words—"an entire novel through a single gesture." Furthermore, in the most convincing twelve-tone compositions, time plays a role through an integral procedure seemingly without development, because it tolerates nothing outside itself upon which development could experiment. However, there is a significant difference between such a change in time-consciousness in the inner organization of music and the established pseudomorphism of the spatial dimension within musical time—its inhibition through shock and electric blows which disrupt its continuity. In this inner change, on the one hand, music—in the unconscious depth of its struc-

---

serve to uproot the protected past from within the music. Traces thereof form the background both of the mother and the taboo. The course "back to the land of childhood"—as prescribed in the song by Brahms—becomes the cardinal sin of an art which would like to restore the pre-subjective aspect of childhood.

194

ture—lags far behind the historical destiny of time-consciousness. In the pseudomorphism, on the other hand, it establishes
itself as an arbiter of time, causing the listener to forget the
subjective and psychological experience of time in music and to
abandon himself to its spatialized dimension. It proclaims, as
its unique achievement the fact that there is no longer any life—
as though it had achieved the objectification of life. For this
reason, immanent revenge descends upon it. One trick characterizes all of Stravinsky's formal endeavors: the effort of this
music to portray time as in a circus tableau and to present time
complexes as though they were spatial. This trick, however, soon
exhausts itself. He loses his power over the consciousness of
continuousness: continuousness now reveals itself and appears
heteronomously. It discloses Stravinsky's musical intentions as
a lie, unmasking this intention as nothing but boredom. Instead
of working out the tension between music and time in composition, he plays another of his tricks upon this tension. Therefore,
all those forces shrivel in his hands, which otherwise thrive in
music, whenever it absorbs time into itself. The mannerized
impoverishment which asserts itself, as soon as Stravinsky attempts to go beyond his speciality, is encumbered by the spatial
expansion. To the extent that he renounced all possible means
for the production of time-relationships—transition, intensification, the distinction between the field of tension and the field of
release, further of exposition and continuation, and of question
and answer—all artistic musical means fall under this edict, with
the exception of his one artistic trick.[42] A regression now sets in

42. Stravinsky is in many respects the opposite pole of Gustav Mahler,
to whom he is nevertheless related in his thoroughly disjunct compositional procedure. Stravinsky has often opposed the highest ambition of
Mahler's symphonic composition: the concluding section, those moments
in which music—having come to a standstill—must move on. Essentially
he grounds his dictate over the listener (proof of the latter's impotence)
—in the withholding of that which he feels entitled to for the sake of the
element of tension in the models: this right is denied, and tension in itself
—an undefined and irrational effort without a goal—is made the law
of the composition and of its adequate perception as well. There is a
tendency to become enthusiastic about a wicked man if he once does
something respectable; in like manner, such music is praised for its

—justified by the literary-regressive intention—but it becomes his undoing when the absolute musical demand is seriously raised. The weakness of Stravinsky's production during the last twenty-five years—which can be detected even by the most insensitive ear—is not just a matter of the composer having nothing more or new to say. It rather arises out of a chain of events which degrades music to the status of a parasite of painting. That weakness—the non-intrinsic element in the general compositional make-up of Stravinsky—is the price he has had to pay for his restriction to the dance; although this limitation once seemed to him a guarantee of order and objectivity. From the beginning it imposed upon his music an aspect of servitude which required the renunciation of autonomy. True dance—in contrast to mature music—is an art of static time, a turning in a circle, movement without progress. It was in this consciousness that sonata form came to replace dance form: throughout the entire history of modern music—with the exception of Beethoven—minuettes and scherzi have always been a matter of convenience and of secondary importance; this is particularly true when they are compared to serious sonata form and to the adagio. Music for the dance lies on this side of—and not beyond —subjective dynamics; to this extent, it contains an anachronistic element, which in Stravinsky stands in highly peculiar contrast to the literary-modish success of his hostility towards expression. The past is foisted upon the future as a changeling. It is suited to this purpose because of the disciplinary nature of the dance. Stravinsky has restored it again. His accents are just so many acoustic signals to the stage. He has, therewith, infused into dance music—from the viewpoint of its usefulness—a pre-

---

moments of respectability. In rare exceptional cases of cleverness, the music permits conclusion-like sections which, by contrast— precisely by virtue of their rarity—border on ethereal bliss. An example is the intensive final "cantilena" from the "Danse de l'Elue" (from number 184 to number 186), before the last entrance of the rondo theme. But even here, where the violins are permitted to "sing themselves out" for a moment, the same, unchanged rigid ostinato remains in the accompaniment. The concluding section is not intrinsic in nature.

cision which it had totally forfeited beyond the pantomimic-psychologizing or illustrative intentions of the Romantic ballet. A glance at Richard Strauss's *Josefslegende* clarifies the drastic effect of the cooperation between Stravinsky and Diaghilev; something of this effect has adhered to the music, which—even as absolute music—has not forgotten one moment of its dance-ability. All symbolic intermediate instances, however, have been removed from the relationship between dance and music; as a result, that fatal principle gains control which everyday speech designates with expressions such as "dancing to one's tune." The effective relationship for which Stravinsky's music strives is, to be sure, not the identification of the public with psychic impulses which are supposedly expressed in the dance. Stravinsky aspired, rather, for an electrification equal to that of the dancer.

MODES OF LISTENING

Stravinsky—by means of the preceding—proves himself as the executor of a social tendency, of progress to a negative lack of historical relevance to a new order which is hierarchically rigid. His trick—self-preservation through self-annihilation—falls into the behaviorist scheme of the total incorporation of mankind. His music attracts all those who wish to rid themselves of their ego, because it stands in the way of their egoistic interest within the total composition of commanded collectivization; similarly, his music concurs with a spatially regressive mode of listening. On the whole, two such types can be distinguished; they are not determined by nature, but are historical in essence and belong to the predominant syndrome of character at a given time. They are the expressive-dynamic and rhythmic-spatial modes of listening. The former has its origin in singing; it is directed towards the fulfilling domination of time and, in its highest manifestations, transforms the heterogeneous course of time into the force of the musical process. The latter obeys the beat of the drum. It is intent upon the articulation of time through the division into

197

equal measures which time virtually abrogates and spatializes.[43] The two types are separated by force of that social alienation which separates subject and object. Musically, everything subjective is threatened by coincidence; everything which appears as collective objectivity is under the threat of externalization, of the repressive hardness of mere existence. The idea of great music lay in a mutual penetration of both modes of listening and by the categories of composition suited to each. The unity of discipline and freedom was conceived in the sonata. From the dance it received its integral regularity, and the intention regarding the entirety; from the Lied it received that opposing and negative impulse which, out of its own consequences, again produces the entirety. In so doing, the sonata fulfills the form which preserves its identity as a matter of principle—even if not in the sense of a literal beat, or tempo. It does this with such a multiplicity of rhythmic-melodic figures and profiles that the "mathematical" pseudo-spatial time, which is recognized as tendential in its objectivity, coincides with the psychological time of experience in the happy balance of the moment. This conception of a musical subject-object was forcibly extracted from the realistic dissociation of subject and object. Consequently, a paradoxical element was present in the conception from the beginning. Beethoven—closer, from the perspective of such a conception, to Hegel than to Kant—had need of the most extraordinary configurations of the formal spirit to attain so complete a musical synthesis as he did in the *Seventh Symphony*. In his late phase he added a paradoxical unity, permitting the unreconciled character of these two categories to merge openly and eloquently as the highest truth of his music. It might be felt that the history of music after Beethoven—Romantic music as well as that which is actually modern—indicates a decline parallel to that of the bourgeois class; it does this in a more meaningful sense than in mere idealistic phrases regarding beauty. If this is in any way true, then this decline is conditioned

43. Ernst Bloch's distinction between the dialectical and mathematical essence within music approximates the distinction between these two types quite closely.

by the impossibility of resolving the conflict between the defined categories.[44] The two types of musical experience, torn from each other, have today diverged without mediation and must pay with untruth. This untruth is decoratively concealed in the products of artistic music, but is revealed in light music, whose shameless incorrectness disavows what takes place on the higher level under the mask of taste, routine, and surprise. Light music is polarized; the one extreme is "Schmalz"—the region of sweet sentimentality, detached from every objective time organization, and either arbitrary or standard in expression. The other extreme is mechanical—a fiddling and tooting—the ironic imitation of which provided the training for Stravinsky's style. The innovation which he brought to music is not only that of the spatial-mathematical type of music as such, but also the apotheosis thereof—a parody of Beethoven's apotheosis of the dance. The academic illusion of synthesis is scorned without illusion. However, the scorn directed towards the illusion also affects the subjective element in the subject. Stravinsky's work draws the

44. The most important theoretical document on this topic is Wagner's essay on conducting. The subjective expressive ability to react dominates so totally in the spatial-mathematical sense of music that the latter appears only in the Philistine phenomenon of the provincial German metronomical conductor. Wagner demands radical modifications of tempi even in Beethoven, depending upon the varying character of the figures. Consequently, even in the most obvious aspects the paradoxical unity in multiplicity is sacrificed. The abyss between the total architectural scheme and details laden with expression can be bridged only by dramatic force—a theatrical factor which by its innermost nature is alien to music, particularly in the form in which it became the interpretive medium of modern virtuoso conductors. In contrast to this shift of the symphonic time problem to the merely subjective-expressive side, which renounces the musical domination of time and entrusts itself to permanence (totally lacking, as it were, in will), Stravinsky's procedure simply represents a counter-blow, by no means the reassumption of the actual symphonic dialectics of time. The only thing he accomplishes is the severing of the Gordian knot, which opposes the subjective disintegration of time with its objective-geometrical division, but does not establish a constructional relationship between the time dimension and the musical content. In the spatial expansion of music, time disintegrates, by means of stylistic attitude, just as it decomposes into lyric moments in lyric expressive style. (Adorno refers to Wagner's "About Conducting," *Wagner's Prose Works*, trans. W. A. Ellis, London, 1895, Vol. 4, 289–364. —Trans.)

consequence from the dying-out of the expressive-dynamic type of music, to which he is related by natural affinity. He then turns solely to the rhythmic-spatial, playfully adept type, which today sprouts forth everywhere with amateurs and mechanics, as though it were rooted in nature and not in society. Stravinsky sees in this musical type the supreme task. He has to expose himself to its attacks—to its irregular, jolting accents, without being diverted from the order of the ever-constant underlying meter. Thus this music trains him to resist every impulse which might possibly challenge the heterogeneous alienated progression. In so doing it refers to the body as though this were its legal basis; in extreme cases, even the heartbeat is evoked as the basis for authority. However, justification through a supposedly constant or physiological element cancels out that through which music becomes music: its spiritualization consists of its modifying influence. Music is as little bound by any particular allegiance to the constancy of the heart beat as it is to a musical law of nature—as, for example, it is possible to explain only the simpler overtone relationships as harmonies: however, musical consciousness has liberated the physiological-aural perception from such fetters. In his antagonism towards the spiritualization of music, out of which he draws his energies, Stravinsky's rage over a certain lie has played an important role; this lie maintains that music implies an escape from the enchanted realm of the physical, and, furthermore, that it is in itself the ideal. The physical aspect of music, however, is not indicative of a natural state—of an essence pure and free of all ideology—but rather it accords with the retrogression of society. The mere negation of the spirit puts on airs, as though this negation were the realization of its own intentions. This negation is a result of the pressure of a system whose traditionally superior power over everything subject to it can maintain itself only if it is able to break the subject's habit of engaging in whims of thought, and to make of him nothing more than a center of reactions—the monad of conditioned reflexes. Stravinsky's sweetest dream is versatile submissiveness and hysterical obedience—the very pattern of the authoritarian character which is today in formulation on all sides. His music no longer succumbs to any temptation to be otherwise. The previously occurring subjective deviation has been transformed into a mere means of shock, employed to terrify the subject in order that the hold upon him can be made still tighter. In so doing, the aesthetic discipline or order, which actually no longer has any substratum, becomes empty and irresponsible; it remains only as a ritual of capitulation. The claim to authenticity is relegated to an authoritarian manner of procedure. Unwavering parrying establishes itself as an aesthetic principle, good taste, or asceticism, thus degrading expression —the mark of memory in the subject—to the level of kitsch. The negation of the subjectively negative in such an authoritarian attitude—the negation of the spirit itself—asserts itself as a new ideology. This is the deceptive aspect of negation, for it is in reality hostile to every ideology.

THE DECEPTION OF OBJECTIVISM

Negation establishes itself only as an ideology; for the authority of effect is surreptitious: it does not proceed from the specific law of the structure—out of its own logic and correctness—but rather from the gesture which it directs to the listener. The bearing of the composition is *sempre marcato*. Its objectivity is a subjective arrangement, embellished and elevated to the level of super-human *a priori* validity; it is ordained dehumanization as an *ordo*. The illusory appearance thereof is produced by a small number of tested measures of technical demagogy which are continually carried out without concern for the changing nature of the cause. All becoming is eliminated, as though it were the contamination of the object itself. The object is now excluded from any intervening treatment; in this position it pretends to have been liberated from all elaboration and to have achieved self-contained monumentality. Every complex is restricted to a basic material which resembles something photo-

201

graphed from changing perspectives, but essentially untouched in its harmonic-melodic nucleus. The resulting lack of meaningful musical forms lends the entire object an aspect of the intransitory: the omission of dynamics feigns an eternity in which only a few satanic metric tricks relieve the monotony. The objectivism in this case is a façade, because there is nothing to objectify—because, further, this objectivism is therefore nothing but an illusory façade of power and security. It proves itself all the more ineffective because the basic material—statically atrophied and emasculated from the very beginning—dispenses with its own substance, thereby gaining life only within the context of function. Stravinsky's style resists precisely such a context. Instead his music offers, with great aplomb, something totally ephemeral which gives the impression that it is of the essence. The listener is made a fool by means of the authoritarian repetition of something which does not really exist. At first the listener feels that he is confronted by something which is by no means architectural in its structure but totally irregular, and, in its continual transformation, he considers it to be his own image. At the same time, however, the stomping and hammering of it all teaches him something still worse—its immutability. He has to submit. Stravinsky's authenticity is built upon this schema; such authenticity is usurpatory. An arbitrary concept—highly subjective because of its coincidental nature—asserts itself as if it were confirmed and generally obligatory. The order which it embraces is equally questionable because of the principal exchangeability of all its successive elements. The convincing force which it exerts is due, on the one hand, to the self-suppression of the subject, and on the other to the musical language which has been especially contrived for authoritarian effects. This is most obvious in the emphatic, strikingly dictatorial instrumentation which unites brevity and vehemence. This is all as far removed from that musical cosmos which later generations perceive in Bach, as is the conformism—superimposed from above—of an atomized society from the dream image of hermetic culture, based upon a guild economy and an earlier stage of industry.

THE FINAL TRICK

How treacherous that Stravinsky—as soon as he had stated his objective demands in positive terms—had to assemble his armature out of the supposedly pre-subjective phases of music. It would have been preferable if this formal language had primarily extended beyond the incriminated Romantic element therein by virtue of its own gravitational force. In this case, however, he was able to come to his own aid, in that he derived a stimulus from the inconsistency between the "pre-Classic" formulae, and his own state of consciousness and the condition of material. In an ironic game, he then enjoyed the impossibility of restoration which he initiated. The subjective aestheticism of the objective attitude is unmistakable: it is reminiscent of Nietzsche who, in order to prove that he was cured of Wagner, claimed to love in Rossini, Bizet, and the journalistic Offenbach all of those elements which made a mockery of his own pathos and differentiation. Subjectivity was retained through the exclusion of it from the creative process, as, for example, in the somewhat graceful insult to Pergolesi in the *Pulcinella* suite. This has been the major accomplishment of Stravinsky in recent years. The work is, of course, lightly colored by speculation upon those listeners who wish their music to be familiar, but at the same time to be labeled modern. This indicates the willingness inherent in this music to be used as fashionable commercial music—similar to the willingness of surrealism to be used for shop-window decoration. The penchant for conciliation, which becomes ever more pressing, cannot find relief in the face of the contradiction between modernity and pre-Classicism. Stravinsky tries to balance this out in a double manner. On the one hand, the devices of the eighteenth century—to which this new style was restricted in the beginning and which, once taken from their context, are painfully dissonant both in the literal and figurative sense—are blended into the compositional idiom. They by no means protrude as foreign elements; rather the total musical inventory is

203

developed therefrom. They are no longer evident, and with the mediation of their contradiction to the modern element, the musical language is increasingly toned down from work to work. At the same time, however, the musical idiom now no longer limits itself to the quoted conventions of the eighteenth century. The specifically unromantic, pre-subjective nature of time-past, mobilized in any particular case, is no longer decisive; it is only that it is past at all and sufficiently conventional that it could be a conventionalizing factor of subjectivity itself. Indiscriminate sympathy flirts with every hypostatization, but by no means binds itself to the *imago* of undynamic order. Weber, Tchaikov-sky, and the entire rhetoric of ballet of the nineteenth century attain grace before the uncompromising ear; even expression is tolerated, so long as it is no longer true expression, but merely the death-mask thereof. Universal necrophilia is the last per-versity of style; it is hardly still possible to distinguish it from the normalcy in which it finds its affirmation—that sediment, namely, in the conventions of music which is looked upon as its second nature. In the graphic montages of Max Ernst, the parental world of images—red plush, buffets, and balloons—is intended to evoke panic by suddenly appearing as though it were already a matter of history. In like manner, Stravinsky's shock technique assumes a command of that musical world of images of the most recent past. This shock, however, loses its effectiveness with ever-increasing speed; today, for example, only twenty years after its composition, *Le Baiser de la Fée* sounds honestly innocuous in spite of the lovely skirts of the ballerinas and the Swiss tourist costumes out of Andersen's day. At the same time, the increase in quotable musical goods grad-ually bridges the gap between past and present. The idiom, finally developed with such great effort, no longer shocks any-one: it is the very essence of everything approved and certified in the two hundred years of bourgeois music, treated according to the procedure of rhythmic tricks which has meanwhile found approval. As a revenant, healthy common sense is re-established to the right which it had forfeited long ago. The authoritarian character of today is, without exception, conformist; likewise the authoritarian claim of Stravinsky's music is extended totally and completely to conformism. In the final analysis, this music tends to become the style for everyone, because it coincides with the man-in-the-street style in which they have always believed and to which this music automatically directs them again. Its indifference, and its anemia—which becomes evident as soon as the last aggressive impulses are subdued—are the price which it must pay for its recognition of the consensus as the moment of authenticity. Stravinsky, in his later years, reserves schizoid alienation for use as an alternate course. The shrinking process, which causes his earlier achievements—in themselves results of the shrinking process—to disappear, without the pursuit of new discoveries, guarantees easy comprehension of his works. Furthermore, as long as the shock-gesture and the addition of ingredients which are to some degree tasteful still function, he is assured of success, at least in the sphere of good taste. Of course, it is not long before such simplification extinguishes even the interest in domesticated sensation, and those who like the easy life so well make it still easier for themselves and run to the camp of Stravinsky's followers—the modest pranksters or youthful fossils. The formerly rough surface is now sealed and polished. Previously, expression had been cut off from the subject; now even the ominous secret of the sacrifice of the subject is concealed in silence. Those who long for the administration of society through direct domination by force continually acclaim the traditional values which they wish to preserve from ruin. From this point, in like manner, objectivistic music appears as the force of preservation, proclaiming its own recovery. Out of the disintegration of the subject it designs for itself the formula of the aesthetic integration of the world. It recoins in counterfeit the destructive law of society itself—of absolute power, that is— as the constructive law of authenticity. The farewell trick of Stravinsky—who otherwise, in an elegant gesture, renounced everything astonishing—is the enthroning of the self-forgotten negative as the self-conscious positive.

205

NEOCLASSICISM

Stravinsky's entire work has had this maneuver as its goal; in pursuing it, however, it becomes a modestly pompous event in the transition to neo-classicism. It is decisive that according to its purely musical nature, no distinction between infantile and neo-classic works can be discerned. The reproach that Stravinsky—in the manner of a German classicist—had developed from a revolutionary into a reactionary cannot be validated. All compositional elements of the neo-classic phase are not only implicitly contained in what preceded this phase, but in both cases they define the entire compositional inventory. Even the mask-like "as if" of the first compositions of the new style coincides with the old process of writing music about music. There are works of the early nineteen-twenties—such as the *Concertino for String Quartet* and the *Woodwind Octet*—which would be difficult to classify as either infantile or neo-classic. They are particularly successful because they preserve the aggressive fragmentation of infantilism without deforming a model in any obvious way: They neither parody nor celebrate. It would be a simple matter to compare the transition to neo-classicism to that from free atonality to twelve-tone technique, which Schoenberg completed at the very same time: both developments have in common the transformation of highly specifically designed and employed means into, as it were, disqualified, neutral material, severed from the original intention of its appearance. But the analogy is not valid beyond this point. The transformation of the vehicles of atonal expression into the expressive means of twelve-tone came to pass in Schoenberg out of specific compositional force itself. For this reason it has changed decisively the language of music as well as the essence of the individual compositions. In Stravinsky, there is no trace of this. To be sure, his regression to tonality gradually becomes less scrupulous, until the provocatively false is mellowed to the point that it is no more than a spice within the work—as, for example, the chorale contained in *L'Histoire du Soldat*. If there is any essential change, however, it is not the musical, but rather the literary aspect; it involves the claim made by the musical, or, it could almost be said—by its ideology.[45] All of a sudden, music wishes to be taken literally. It is the idolatrously fixed grimace, which is revered as an image of the gods. The authoritarian principle of making-music-about-music is applied in such a way that all possible antiquated musical formulae are vindicated of their binding responsibility, which they have lost historically and which they seem to possess only when they actually no longer possess them. At the same time, the usurpatory element in authority is cynically underscored by means of arbitrary acts which inform the confused listener of the illegitimacy of the claim to authority without relenting from this claim in the slightest degree. Stravinsky's older jokes—which were often somewhat more discrete—ridicule the norm in the same breath in which they proclaim it: this norm is to be obeyed not for the sake of its own justice but merely because of the dictatorial powers which it possesses. This strategy of courteous terror takes

45. This touches upon a condition of affairs which is characteristic of Stravinsky's works as a whole. The individual compositions are not developed in themselves; the works and the various phases of style follow one another without any actual development. All are unified in the rigidity of ritual. The eternal constancy of the individual works corresponds to the surprising change of his periods. Because there is no essential change, the original phenomenon can be shown from disarming perspectives and in countless circumventions. Even those transitions in Stravinsky's career as a composer—dictated by rationalization—are dominated by the law of trickery. "The main thing is the resolution" (Arnold Schoenberg, "Der neue Klassizismus," Introduction to the *Three Satires for Mixed Chorus*). One of the difficulties involved in a theoretical treatment of Stravinsky, and by no means the least, is that the modification of the immutable in the succession of his works forces the observer either to arbitrary antitheses or to mediation without contours of all contrasts, as they are practiced by "understanding" intellectual history. In Schoenberg the phases are far less openly contrasted with each other and it can be said—even in his early works, the songs of *opus* 6, for example—that what later is to break forth with the force of a revolution is already anticipated or pre-thought under a cotyledon. But the revelation of new quality as the self-equation—along with the differentiation from the old—is actually a process. Mediation—the process of becoming—in the dialectical composer contributes to its own substance; this is not accomplished in that which does no more than manipulate this substance.

the following technical course. There are passages in which the traditional language of music, particularly in the pre-classic practice of sequences, seems automatically to demand certain continuations as a matter of course. These continuations are, however, avoided. Instead a surprise—an *imprévu*—is offered, which amuses the listener by cheating him out of what he has been waiting for. The schema prevails, but the continuity of progress which it has promised is not developed. Thus Stravinsky's neo-classicism practices the old custom of joining brokenly disparate models together. It is traditional music combed in the wrong direction. The surprises, however, fade away like little pink clouds; they are nothing but a volatile disturbance of the order within which they remain. They consist only in the dismantling of formulae. Characteristic means—for example, Händel's formulations of suspensions and other tones alien to harmony—are employed independently of their technical purpose, which is that of combining in a manner producing tension without preparation and release; indeed they are employed while being maliciously avoided. It is by no means the least of Stravinsky's paradoxes that his unique New Objectivist, functionalistic procedure involves elements which had their purpose in precise functions of musical continuity which he now separates from these functions, making them independent and allowing them to ossify. Therefore, his earlier neo-classic compositions sound as though they were dangling on strings and many of them —such as the dissolute *Concerto for Piano and Winds*—insult the culturally responsible ear far more fundamentally than did dissonances previously. This they do particularly with consonances which are twisted in their very joints. Compositions of this type—in A minor—are incomprehensible; common sense, which labeled such works atonal chaos, was fond of hurtling this reproach at Stravinsky. The flourishes which he exorcises are not organized into a unity of musical-logical structure which constitutes musical meaning; they present, rather, the inexorable denial of any such meaning. They are "anorganic." Their judiciousness is a phantasm, resulting from the vague familiarity of the materials presented and the reminiscent exultant pomp of it all, the cloak of forced affirmation. The objective incomprehensibility in face of the subjective impression of the traditional sternly admonishes every contradictory question of the listener to silence. Blind obedience, anticipated by authoritarian music, corresponds to the blindness of the authoritarian principle itself. The statement attributed to Hitler, that a man could only die for an idea which he does not understand, could be engraved as an inscription over the gate of the temple of neo-classicism.

EXPERIMENTS IN EXPANSION

The works of Stravinsky's neo-classic phase are of a vacillating niveau throughout. Insofar as it is even possible to speak of development in Stravinsky's later years, it is a mere matter of removing the thorn of absurdity. In contrast to Picasso, from whom the neo-classic stimulus comes, Stravinsky soon no longer felt any need to damage this questionable orderliness. It is only the most steadfast critics who are still in search of traces of the wild Stravinsky. A certain amount of consequence has to be admitted in his carefully planned disappointment: "Let them be bored." It lets slip the secret of a rebellion which from the very first impulse was not concerned with freedom, but with the suppression of the impulse. The pretended positivism of late Stravinsky affirms that his type of negativity—which contradicted the subject and justified every kind of pressure—was in itself positive and stood in alliance with the stronger battalions. At first, to be sure, the turn to the positive—to cohesively absolute music—resulted in the most extreme impoverishment of the musical absolute. From this perspective, compositions such as the *Serenade in A* for piano or the ballet *Apollon Musagète* have never been equalled.[46] On the other hand, this was not Stravinsky's goal. He rather exploited the newly proclaimed quiescence to expand the inner reach of specialistic music and to overtake some of the compositional dimensions

46. Cf. the analysis by H. F. Redlich in *Anbruch* (1929), 41f.

proscribed since *Sacre,* insofar as this was possible within the boundaries which he had set for himself. At times he has tolerated innovative thematic figures; he has pursued modest questions of larger structural form; or he has offered rather complex—even polyphonic—forms. Artists such as he, who thrive on slogans, have always had the tactical advantage that they need only bring forth again, from a period of imprisonment, one single means, which they had once cast aside as hopelessly antiquated, in order to launch it as an avant-garde achievement. Stravinsky's efforts towards a musical structure, which would be richer in itself, are responsible for a few penetrating moments: for example, the first three movements of the *Concerto for Two Pianos*—the second of these is a thoroughly unusual and streamlined piece; or, for example, passages in the *Violin Concerto* or the *Capriccio for Piano and Orchestra,* which is significant and colorful until its energetically banal finale. All of this, however, has been wrung out of the style by abstract intellect and is hardly to be regarded as the product of any neo-classic procedure. To be sure, Stravinsky's monotonously effervescent production gradually designs the most outspoken model of childishly plastic incidental motifs—as the *Violin Concerto* still offers them—overture-like accentuation, and terraced groups of sequences. His composition, however, is so restricted to the material resources of impaired tonality, left behind by his infantile phase, that the possibilities of fully matured formulations are thereby limited. This is particularly conditioned by the diatonic within individual groups, soiled through accidentally "false" notes. It is as though the repression of the compositional process through the technique of tricks resulted everywhere else in appearances of deficiency. In this way the fugue of the *Concerto for Two Pianos* contradicts everything which preceded it; it should also be noted that the fugue itself is much too short and insufficiently developed. Furthermore, the painfully compulsory octaves in the stretto at the conclusion ridicule this master of renunciation as soon as he reaches out for that counterpoint which his cleverness denied itself. Through shocks, his music forfeits its power. Compositions such as the ballet

Jeu de Cartes or the *Duo for Violin and Piano* and, for the most part, everything which he composed in the nineteen-forties, have a dullness characteristic of commercial art, not at all dissimilar to the last works of Ravel. The only aspect of Stravinsky which can be publicly appreciated is his prestige; a number of his secondary works—such as the *Scherzo à la Russe*—which are officious copies of his own youthful works—evoke a spontaneous pleasure. He gives the audience more than its rightful share, and consequently he gives them too little: the cold-hearted flocked to the asocial Stravinsky; where as they are now left cold by the affable Stravinsky. Most difficult to tolerate are the major works of the new genre, in which the collective pretense sets its immediate goal in monumentality—the Latin *Oedipus Rex,* that is, and the *Symphony of Psalms.* The contradiction between the pretension of greatness and grandeur and the embittered and pitiful musical content causes the wit from which he shies away to be reflected upon with seriousness. Among his most recent works, there is one more which makes an impressive entry: the *Symphony in Three Movements,* for orchestra, composed in 1945. It is cleansed of antiquated components, presents contours of cutting sharpness, and applies itself to a lapidary homophony which might well have had Beethoven in mind: he had hardly ever before so openly presented the ideal of authenticity. This orchestral achievement is totally suited to that ideal: it is totally sure of its goal; it is economical; and it is not found wanting in new coloration, as for example in the brittly thematic harp scoring or the combination of piano and trombone in fugato. Nevertheless, he again only suggests to the listener what the composition might have had in mind. The reduction of all thematic material in the work to the most simple primitive motives, which the analysts simply label Beethoven-like, has no influence upon the structure. This represents—just as it did previously—the static juxtaposition of "blocks"—with the addition of a few time-honored displacements. According to the theory, the mere relationship of the parts is to be created by that synthesis which in Beethoven resulted in the dynamics of form. The extreme reduction of

211

motivic models, however, demanded a dynamic treatment of them and their expansion. Through Stravinsky's usual methods, to which the work rigidly clings, the contrived void of its elements becomes insufficiency, the emphatic guarantee of its absence of content; and the inner tension—which had been pre-demonstrated—is not developed. Only the tone is brazenly successful; the course of the work crumbles, and the two outer movements break off, at the point where they could have been arbitrarily continued: they do not undertake the dialectical work, which in this case they promised through the very character of the thesis itself. As soon as something similar recurs, it degenerates monotonously and even the development-like contrapuntal interpolations have no power over the fate of the formal course of the composition. Even the dissonances which have been widely acclaimed as tragic symbols prove upon closer observation to be completely tame: the familiar Bartók effect of the neutral third through the coupling of the major with the minor is exploited. Symphonic pathos is nothing but the obscure countenance of an abstract ballet suite.

SCHOENBERG AND STRAVINSKY

That ideal of authenticity for which Stravinsky's music strives here and in all its phases is, as such, by no means its unique privilege: this, however, is precisely the impression which the style would attempt to give. From an abstract point of view, this ideal guides all great music today and defines—for better or for worse—the concept of such music. Everything depends, however, upon whether this music, by its attitude, advertises this authenticity as something which it has already attained, or whether—with closed eyes, as it were—it surrenders itself to the demands of the entire matter in the hope of mastering it. It is the willingness to do this which defines—in spite of all the exasperating antinomies—the incomparable superiority of Schoenberg over that objectivism which in the meantime has degenerated to everyday jargon. Schoenberg's school obeys without excuses the reality of a perfected nominalism in composition. Schoenberg draws the consequences from the dissolution of all binding forms in music, as this existed in the law of its own development: he affirms the liberation of ever broader levels of musical material and the musical domination of nature which progresses towards the absolute. He does not falsify that which, in the world of sculpture, is called the obliteration of style-developing power into that dawning self-awareness of the bourgeois principle of art. His answer to this is: Discard it, if you would win. He sacrifices the illusion of authenticity, viewing it as incompatible with the state of that consciousness which was driven so far towards individuation by liberal order, to the point that this consciousness negates the order which had advanced it thus far. In the state of such negativity, he does not feign any collective responsibility: such a factor would here-and-now stand in contrast to the subject as an external and repressive responsibility which, in its incompatability with the subject, would be unbinding and irresponsible in terms of its content of truth. He entrusts himself openly to the aesthetic principle of individuation, without concealing his entanglement in the actual decline of traditional society. He does not conceive—as a "philosopher of culture"—the ideal of comprehensive totality, but relies step by step upon that which becomes concrete as a demand in the encounter between the compositional subject which is conscious of itself, and the socially established material. In so doing he preserves with particular objectivity the greater philosophical truth as the open attempt at the reconstruction of responsibility; he does this entirely on his own. The obscure driving force within him is nourished by the certainty that nothing in art is successfully binding except that which can be totally filled by the historical state of consciousness which determines its own substance—by its "experience" in the emphatic sense. This drive is guided by the desperate hope that such a movement of the spirit—always undertaken in a certain obscure blindness—can through the force of its own logic transcend every private concern from which it proceeds. This hope is criticized, because of this private

213

aspect, by those who demonstrate that they are not the equal of such objective logic of the matter. The absolute renunciation of the gesture of authenticity becomes the only indication of the authenticity of the structure. This school, which has been reproached for its intellectualism, is in such a venture naïve compared to the pretentious manipulation of authenticity, as it thrives in Stravinsky and in his total circle. In view of the course of events in the world, this naïveté has many traits of retardation and provincialism: it expects more from the integrity of the work of art than it is able to accomplish in integral society.[47] In so doing, this school endangers almost every one of its own structures, but at the same time it gains, on the other hand, not only a more cohesive and instinctive artistic view, but also a higher objectivity than that objectivism—an objectivity, namely, of the immanent correctness—and, further, of the undisguised appropriateness to the historical condition. It is forced to go above and beyond this to a manifest objectivity which is

47. The provincialism of the Schoenberg school is not to be separated from its contradictory quality, its intransigent radicalism. Wherever there is reason to still hope for an absolute from art, art looks upon every factor, every tone, as absolute and in this way pursues authenticity. Stravinsky is clever with regard to aesthetic seriousness. His consciousness of the transformation of all art into consumer goods is today of relevance for the organization of the elements of his style. The objectivistic emphasis of play as play means—and this is true above and beyond his aesthetic program as well—that the entire matter is not to be taken too seriously; to do so would be awkward, pretentious in a characteristically German manner—to a certain degree it would even be alien to art because of the contamination of art by reality. Taste had always been supported by a certain lack of seriousness; at this point it seems—within the development of a long tradition—that seriousness itself has become tasteless. On the other hand, it is precisely in the denial of seriousness, in the negation of any responsibility in art—including resistance to the preponderance of existence—that seriousness should consist: music is seen as the parable of an attitude which ridicules seriousness, while this attitude itself is actually rooted in terror. In the authenticity of the buffoon or the clown, to be sure, such a realistic disposition is outdone and driven to absurdity by the pride of the "tune-smiths" who behave as though they were expression of the times. These tune-smiths tack their formulae together on pianos prepared in F-sharp major. On the other hand, Stravinsky—to them—is a "long-haired musician," while they are sufficiently unfamiliar with the name of Schoenberg that they guess him to be a hit-tune composer.

sui generis—to twelve-tone constructivism—without total il-lumination by the subject of the animation of the material. The naïveté, or the clinging to the semi-professional ideal of the German "good musician"—who is concerned about nothing beyond the massive inventory of his product—finds in this objectivity, no matter how consistent it might be, its punishment through the transition of the absolute autonomy into something heteronomous, into unresolved self-alienation on the material level—even, therefore, if self-alienation pays its debt to its own spirit of enlightenment, to the spirit of heteronomy, to the sense-less integration of that which has been atomized. It is exactly this which happens willfully in Stravinsky: the epoch forcibly binds the contrasts together. Stravinsky, however, spares himself the tormenting self-animation of the material and treats it as would a producer. For this reason, his language is as close to the language of communication as it is to the language of the practical joke: non-seriousness itself, play—from which the subject remains aloof, abdication to the aesthetic "development of truth," considers itself the guarantee of authenticity and therewith of truth as well. This contradiction destroys his music: the contrived style of objectivity is demanded of the recalcitrant material as forcefully and irresponsibly as *art nouveau* was formulated fifty years ago. (It is the renunciation of *art nouveau* which has nourished all aesthetic objectivity down to the present day.) The will to style replaces style itself and therewith sabotages it. No objectivity of that which the structure wills from within itself is present in objectivism. It establishes itself by eradicating the traces of subjectivity; the hollows are proclaimed as the cells of a true brotherhood. The decay of the subject—which the Schoenberg school bitterly defends itself against—is directly interpreted by Stravinsky's music as that higher form in which the subject is to be preserved. Thus he arrives at the aesthetic transfiguration of the reflective character of present-day man. His neo-classicism fashions im-ages of Oedipus and Persephone, but the employed myth has already become the metaphysics of the universally dependent, who neither want nor need metaphysics. They mock the very

215

principle thereof. Therewith objectivism designates itself as that which it fears and the proclamation of which constitutes its entire content. It defines itself as the vain private concern of the aesthetic subject—as a trick of the isolated individual—who poses as though he were the objective spirit. If this were today of the same essence, then such art would still not be validated by it; for the objective spirit of a society, integrated by its presumed domination over its subjects, has become transparent as false in itself. All of this raises doubts, of course, about the absolute proof of the ideal of authenticity itself. The revolt of Schoenberg's school against the hermetic work of art in the years of Expressionism actually jolted that concept in itself. In so doing, however, the school was unable permanently to break its primacy, for it was caught up in the actual survival of that which it challenged spiritually. The concept includes the basic demand of traditional art: that something should sound as though it had been present since the beginning of time. This means that it retrieves what has existed through the ages—that which as a matter of actuality preserved the power to repress the possible. Aesthetic authenticity is a socially necessary illusion: no work of art can thrive in a society founded upon power, without insisting upon its own power. However, it thus comes into conflict with its own truth, with the administration for a future society, which no longer relies upon power in any way and has no need of it. The echo of the primeval—the recollection of the pre-historical world—upon which any claim to aesthetic authenticity is based, is the trace of perpetuated injustice. This injustice at the same time preserves this authenticity in thought, and is further solely responsible, down to the present day, for its pervasiveness and binding force. Stravinsky's regression to archaism is not totally alien to authenticity, even if authenticity is completely destroyed by it, particularly by means of the immanent disjunction of its structure. When he concocts a mythology, thereby both violating and falsifying myth, he reveals not only the usurpatory nature of the new order proclaimed by his music, but also the negative factor of myth itself. The qualities of myth which fascinate him are its image of eternity, of salvation from death, and that which came into being in time through the fear of death and through barbaric suppression. The falsification of myth documents an elective affinity with authentic myth. Art would perhaps be authentic only when it had totally rid itself of the idea of authenticity— of the concept of being-so-and-not-otherwise.

NOTE

The Philosophy of New Music, now appearing in its third edition, had been out of print since 1953. In making the decision to publish a new edition in 1958 the author was influenced less by a feeling of grateful obligation to those who sought the book in vain than by the less-friendly assertion that the book had done its duty and that there was no longer any particular need for it today. Whenever intellectual formulations are treated simply by relegating them to the past and permitting the simple passage of time to substitute for development the suspicion is justified that such formulations have not really been mastered, but rather that they are being suppressed. The present condition of music might profit from the stigma contained in the *Philosophy of Modern Music.* That part of the book dealing with Schoenberg, written almost twenty years ago, critically anticipates developments in music which manifested themselves only after 1950. The convictions of the author regarding the book are strengthened not only by these developments, but further, subsequently, by the emphatic endorsements by such composers as Gyorgy Ligeti and Franco Evangelisti and theorists such as Heinz-Klaus Metzger.

Since he feels that the fulfillment of the thoughts out of which the book is composed still remains to be accomplished, and since he still endorses its fundamental motives, the author presents the text unchanged from its first publication. He has corrected only printing errors and mistakes which were pointed out to him for the most part by the Italian translator, Giacomo Manzoni. To Manzoni's careful conscientiousness he owes a great deal. Faithfulness to previous concepts is, however, not to be confused with a stubborn clinging to every detail thereof.

219

ie author would like to emphasize even more
he did twenty years ago the fact that one musical
i be substituted for another. He would attempt
ater emphasis that mediation which the animation
material accomplished through the concrete work.
supplementing the text itself with considerations of
he will content himself only to indicate a number of
lications. The following are the most significant:

rnold Schönberg," *Prismen* (Frankfurt, 1955); paper-
ick reprint in *Deutscher Taschenbuch Verlag* (Munich,
963).

"Arnold Schönberg," *Die grossen Deutschen* (Berlin,
1957), Vol. 4.

"Das Altern der Neuen Musik," *Dissonanzen*, Göttingen,
1958. (This volume further contains Adorno's first American essay, "Über den Fetischcharakter in der Musik und
die Regression des Hörens," written in New York in 1938.
—Trans.)

"Die Funktion des Kontrapunkts in der neuen Musik,"
published by the Berlin Academy of Arts in 1937.

Klangfiguren, Frankfurt, 1955.

Quasi una Fantasia, Frankfurt, 1963.

Der getreue Korrepetitor, Frankfurt, 1963.

"Schwierigkeiten," in *Impromptus*, Frankfurt, 1968.

Berg: Der Meister des kleinsten Übergangs, Vienna, 1968.